"Debra Burdick provides invaluable tools that every clinician, teacher, and par
with mental health issues as well as in helping kids and teens through no
Thoughtful, clear, and concise, she shares practical techniques for teaching ch
thoughts, and feelings as the stepping stones to improve attention, emotion regulation, self-esteem, and the
ability to relate to others with kindness and compassion. A much needed guide for our children, our times,
and ourselves."

Patricia L. Gerbarg, MD,
Assistant Clinical Professor in Psychiatry, New York Medical College
Co-author of *The Healing Power of the Breath and Non-Drug Treatments for ADHD*

"Outstanding, thoughtful, and well-researched guide for working with children. These methods are applicable
to the treatment of children under stress who may be struggling with anxiety, depression, ADHD, posttraumatic stress disorder, medical illness, or other conditions. Excellent integration of neuroscience, child
development, and mindfulness, with attention to the nitty-gritty of sound clinical work. Highly recommended
for parents, educators, and healthcare professionals."

Richard P. Brown, MD,
Associate Clinical Professor in Psychiatry, Columbia University Medical College
Co-author of *The Healing Power of the Breath and Non-Drug Treatments for ADHD*

"Debra Burdick provides a very practical and easy-to-use guide for teaching mindfulness techniques and
practices to kids and teens. The skills that are developed through these practices empower children to
improve their focus, mood, and emotional self-regulation while becoming more relaxed and less reactive to
stress. Burdick breaks down the more than 150 tools and techniques she offers into categories based on age,
making it easier to choose the appropriate ones whether you are working with a 5 or a 15 year old. This is
an excellent workbook for clinicians and clients but also useful to parents, educators and yoga teachers who
want to integrate mindfulness practices into their work with children."

Lawrence Edwards, PhD, LMHC, BCN,
Senior Fellow, author of *Awakening Kundalini: The Path To Radical Freedom*

"At last we have an easy to use step-by-step guide for clinicians, parents, teachers and youth practitioners that
provide solutions for kids of all ages to become more grounded, confident and successful. Debra's book needs
to be in every teacher's possession so they can implement these mindfulness techniques in their day to day
lessons and interactions with students.

Debra's style is fun, engaging and relevant to the issues and needs of children of all ages. She gives clear, easy to
follow instructions and activities that will ensure the success of everyone involved. With our fast paced world,
Mindfulness has been left out of the equation in our homes and in our schools. Debra is taking it back to basics
in her brilliantly written book that makes neurobiology fun and easy to understand! I will certainly use this
book with my students and clients."

Julie Kleinhans,
Certified Law of Attraction Coach, Confidence and Youth Empowerment Expert, Mentor for Youth,
Parents and Teachers, Creator of Mind Focus Generation and Host of Successful Kids Revolution

"Debra Burdick's new book, Mindfulness Skills for Kids and Teens is a goldmine of on the spot tools and techniques that every clinician, teacher and parent will want to acquire. She takes you through all ages and stages of development with specific directions on how to use and implement her mindfulness techniques. These techniques coupled with the explanation of neuroscience bring a richness and beauty to this amazing book."

Susan P. Epstein, LCSW, Parent Coach,
author of *55 Creative Approaches for Challenging & Resistant Children & Adolescents,*
and *Over 60 Techniques, Activities & Worksheets for Challenging Children & Adolescents*

This is an amazing, practical addition to the growing resources to help children and adolescents with a range of neurodevelopmental and emotional difficulties develop specific skills to manage stress, tolerate frustration, and gain more awareness of blocks to obtaining what they want in life.

This book is clearly written and will be helpful to children of all ages. It is specific enough to help clinicians and teachers who have limited training in mindfulness integrate these strategies into their work and will be helpful for parents and kids as well. I am very excited to have this resource as difficulties with self-regulation, emotional and behavioral control contribute to clear distress and difficulties for kids as well as their care providers and professionals working to help them.

This resource will empower children and adolescents to learn skills that will serve them for a lifetime, no matter what their struggles are. Thank you for such a pragmatic, clear, and handy manual.

Laurie C. Dietzel, PhD, co-author, *Late, Lost, & Unprepared*

"Debra Burdick's Mindfulness Skills for Kids and Teens provides a wealth of practical life skill building tips and tools for Clinicians who want to incorporate Mindfulness into their practice. This "user-friendly" book offers clinicians a wealth of "hands on," practical step-by-step exercises and strategies, supported by numerous handouts to use with clients. Refreshing in its approach and well organized, this book will provide clinicians, teachers and even parents an excellent resource to impart skills of mindfulness to children and teens. Based on popular scientific and psychological research, distilled in a way that is easy to understand, these tips and activities can also be easily applied to working with adults. I will certainly add this book to my Therapeutic Toolbox."

Judith Belmont, MS, LPC,
author of the *Tips and Tools for the Therapeutic Toolbox series*

"Of all the experienced psychotherapy and neurofeedback practitioners I know, Deb Burdick is the most talented and assiduous at providing the badly needed ancillary materials that all practitioners need. The skills in this book can be used in session or as homework assignments for younger clients and their families. They will insure that the skills acquired in the psychotherapy or neurofeedback session are integrated, assimilated and utilized. Hats off to Deb Burdick for her continued work in this neglected but oh-so-needed area."

Stephen Larsen, PhD, LMHC, BCN
author of *The Healing Power of Neurofeedback, The Fundamentalist Mind,*
The Neurofeedback Solution and Heal the Brain, Awaken the Soul.

MINDFULNESS SKILLS
FOR KIDS & TEENS

A WORKBOOK FOR CLINICIANS & CLIENTS WITH 154 TOOLS, TECHNIQUES, ACTIVITIES & WORKSHEETS

By
Debra E Burdick, LCSWR, BCN
deb@TheBrainLady.com

PESI
Publishing
& Media
www.pesipublishing.com

Copyright © 2014 by Debra E Burdick

Published by
PESI Publishing & Media
PESI, Inc
3839 White Ave
Eau Claire, WI 54703

Cover Design: Amy Rubenzer
Layout Design: Bookmasters
Editing: Marietta Whittlesey

Printed in the United States of America

ISBN: 978-1-937661-57-1

PESI
Publishing
& Media
www.pesipublishing.com

Acknowledgements

Over the past 25 years many people have contributed to the eventual writing of this book. I am forever grateful to the numerous mindfulness experts I encountered along the way who taught me how to develop my own mindfulness practice which originally helped me deal with a chronic illness (thankfully healed) and which continues to enrich my life in so many ways.

I am repeatedly inspired by my kid and teen clients who continue to amaze me as they embrace mindfulness, reduce and sometimes eliminate their symptoms, and who often teach their classmates and parents the skills. And I appreciate my workshop participants and readers of my previous books for their on-going feedback about how they incorporate the skills into their practices.

Many thanks to Linda Jackson, my publisher at PESI for supporting, encouraging, guiding, and refining my work. And thank you to Michael Olson, Meg Mickelson Graf, and Marnie Sullivan for steering me through the process of creating and presenting workshops, some of which have then become books.

My heartfelt thanks to my daughter, Jennifer Kanyock who was 3 when I first started learning about mindfulness and taught me so much about teaching mindfulness skills to a child. And thanks to my sweetheart, Al Zipperle who encourages and inspires me every day as I endeavor to help others.

Table of Contents

Section III
Tools for Teaching Specific Mindfulness Skills

Section IV
Tools for Using Mindfulness
for Specific Disorders

Section V
Tools for Tracking Progress

SECTION I
INTRODUCTION

Chapter 1
Introduction

WHY THIS BOOK IS NEEDED

Mindfulness can direcly improve the lives of kids and teens in significant ways. Some of the benefits suggested by the latest research include:

- Increased emotional regulation
- Increased social skills
- Increased ability to orient attention
- Increased working memory and planning and organization
- Increased self esteem
- Increased sense of calmness, relaxation, and self-acceptance
- Increased quality of sleep
- Decreased test anxiety
- Decreased ADHD behaviors- hyperactivity and impulsivity
- Decreased negative affect/emotions
- Decreased anxiety, decreased depression
- Fewer conduct and anger management problems
  (Burke, 2009)

The Mindfulness Skills for Kids and Teens Workbook is specifically designed to meet the needs of mental health practitioners, teachers, other helping professionals, and parents who want to incorporate mindfulness skills into their work with children and teens. It provides over one hundred and fifty tools, techniques, activities and worksheets that can be used with clients and students to help them experience mindfulness, incorporate it into their daily lives, and reap its proven benefits.

The workbook provides specific tools for:
- Explaining What Mindfulness Is To Your Clients in Their Language
- Increasing Client Use of Mindfulness at Home
- Teaching the Fundamentals of Mindfulness for Kids and Teens
- Teaching a Wide Variety of Kid and Teen Friendly Mindfulness Skills
- Using Mindfulness Skills For Specific Childhood Mental Health Disorders
- Tracking Progress

It explains the background behind each tool, leads you through the step-by-step skill-building process, and then gives you expert guidance on practicing and teaching reflection. It includes tools to explain the neurobiology behind mindfulness in a way kids and teens will understand.

It also includes a full set of handouts containing the text of specific mindfulness skills and meditations, games, play activities, and mindful movement techniques you can use to engage kids and teens in becoming more mindful and self-aware. It also provides prompts for journaling to help kids and teens integrate their learning. The workbook gives you everything you need to incorporate mindfulness into your work with kids and teens in a hands-on, practical way that has been proven to be highly effective.

WHAT'S DIFFERENT ABOUT THIS BOOK?

There are a number of excellent books about mindfulness available today (although 95% of them are written for adults). Most of them provide the theory and research and some examples of mindfulness skills. This *Mindfulness Skills for Kids and Teens Workbook* differs from these other books in that it is written explicitly for kids and teens and starts where the others leave off. It is a comprehensive collection of mindfulness skills, techniques, games and activities specifically designed for kids and teens based on research and clinical practice that are proven to help kids and teens improve their self-awareness, self-regulation skills, mental health, and social connectedness. It consists of step-by-step, easy-to-use tools, techniques, skills, games and activities that you can use in a clinical or educational setting to teach mindfulness to kids and teens and improve treatment outcomes. Parents will also enjoy sharing these skills with their children.

HOW TO USE THIS BOOK

The tools provided in this book are organized to provide you with the background behind each tool, instructions for teaching the mindfulness skill, and guidelines for helping both you and your clients reflect on the result. Step-by-step instructions are provided to help you use the tools with kids or teens. Chapter 2 provides a framework for teaching mindfulness to kids and teens and guidance on involving parents, as well as where to start based on the age, developmental, cognitive, and maturity level of the client.

The tools are organized in a logical progression but are designed to be used independently and in any order that makes sense for each particular child or teen. Tools in Chapter 5 will help you start where the client is and move forward. The tools can be used with individuals as well as groups.

Many of the tools call for clients to answer prompts in their journal. It is highly recommended that clients have a way to keep all of their entries organized either in a simple blank journal or for older kids and teens, on the computer or tablet. For younger kids this might simply be a bound pad of construction paper or a drawing tablet.

For convenience, the tools described in the book will reference their use with "clients." Please translate the word "client" to whatever term you use for the people you work with, such as "patient", "student" or "your child or teen".

Thank you to all the kids and teens who continue to show me again and again how much these mindfulness skills improve their lives.

Please let me know how you use this workbook and how it helps your clients.

SECTION II

TOOLS FOR INTEGRATING MINDFULNESS IN PRACTICE

Chapter 2
Tools for Tailoring Mindfulness for Kids and Teens

Tool 2-1: Involving the Parents

BACKGROUND: One of the key ways teaching mindfulness for kids differs from mindfulness for adults is that kids have parents or guardians who are responsible for the kids and their schedule and activities. Since children are firmly integrated into their family environment, family involvement in treatment can enhance outcomes (Kaslow and Racusin, 1994)

The research on mindfulness in children (Semple, R, Lee, J et al, 2010) generally includes parental involvement to educate them about what mindfulness is, to encourage them to practice mindfulness themselves at home and to enlist them in supporting their kids' practice. The level of parental involvement will vary depending on the setting. Including the parent in some way will give the child support and help the child's practice be more successful.

SKILL BUILDING: Whenever possible involve the parent of the client to teach them what mindfulness is and to encourage them to practice mindfulness and support their child/teen in doing so. Periodic contact will also help define treatment goals and track progress. Use Handout 2-1 as a guideline for the various ways parents can be involved. Many kids and teens who learn mindfulness skills report they wish their parents would practice and some even teach the skills to their parents themselves.

Some families are too chaotic and dysfunctional for the parent to provide the desired support. That's okay. Just work with the child. Many of my clients have learned specific mindfulness skills and used them right away at home and school without any parental involvement. Others will only practice while in session but many gradually start using the skills on their own.

Encourage teens to share what they are learning with their parent in those cases when it is not appropriate for parents to be as involved as it is with younger children.

Follow appropriate ethical practice by getting specific consent from parents so that it is clear that teaching mindfulness to their child doesn't conflict with religious or other belief systems of the parents.

REFLECTION: Is the setting conducive to parental involvement? How responsive was the client's parent to your request that they be involved? Did the client want their parent involved? Was the parent supportive of their child learning mindfulness? Does the parent get in the way of the child's pactice? How can the client benefit from mindfulness even if their parent does not get involved? Is parental involvement not appropriate in this case?

PARENTAL INVOLVEMENT IN KIDS' AND TEENS' MINDFULNESS

In group or one-on-one setting:

- Invite parents to a therapist-conducted mindfulness session at the beginning of treatment

- Give parent Handout 3-1 and explain what mindfulness is

- Use Tools 3-22 and 5-15 to review the benefits you expect their child or teen to gain from practice

- Use Tool 27-1 to ask parents to define treatment goals

- Touch base with parent periodically and use Tool 27-2 to assess child or teen's progress

- Use Tools 5-6 and 5-7 to discuss and overcome obstacles and resistance for both the parent and child or teen

- Encourage home practice for parents

- Update them when new skills are being taught

- Invite parents to a review and dialogue session at the conclusion of the program

Tool 2-2: Consider Age, Developmental, and Cognitive Levels

BACKGROUND: While choosing which mindfulness skills to teach to kids and teens it is important to consider their age, and developmental and cognitive levels. The teaching of mindfulness to children and adolescents needs to be developmentally appropriate (Jha, 2005; Ott, 2002).

It is unclear exactly what stage needs to have been reached before mindfulness practice can begin. A Piagetian framework (Wagner, Rathus, & Miller, 2006; Wall, 2005; Piaget, 1962) suggests it may be necessary for kids to have attained the stage of 'formal operations' where abstract and hypothetical reasoning is possible (i.e. from around age 12). A cognitive behavioral therapy (CBT) perspective (Verduyn, 2000) suggests that clinically useful work is possible within the 'concrete operations' stage (approximately 7–12 years).

Note the ages of subjects in research which has already been published: Ages 7 and 8 (Semple et al., 2005), 9–12 (Semple et al., 2006), 7–9 (Linden, 1973), 9 (Ott, 2002), 11–13 (Wall, 2005) and 14–19 (Miller et al., 2000). Fifteen studies reviewed by Burke include ages 4-18 (Burke, 2009). Susan Kaiser Greenland (2011) states in her blog: "Teaching children mindfulness may begin during pregnancy and proceed by how we are and what mindfulness activities we model for our children" She feels that preschool is a good time to start and successfully teaches mindfulness skills to preschoolers. I have found that 3-year-olds love to learn mindfulness skills when they are taught age-appropriate skills. Even playing Peek-A-Boo with a toddler is actually training mindfulness. Grouping children Pre-K through 2nd grade, 3rd grade through 5th grade, 6th grade through 8th grade, (Hawn Foundation, 2011) and then high school is commonly done to address the differing skill levels of these age groups.

This tool provides guidance on matching the client's age and cognitive and developmental level with appropriate mindfulness skills.

SKILL BUILDING: In choosing appropriate mindfulness skills you must assess and take into account the child's maturity level and cognitive and language skills, how long they can pay attention, and how hard it is for them to sit still. My experience has shown that most of the skills in this book are appropriate for any child age 2 years and up with only slight modifications needed. Handout 2-2 provides a brief summary of skills that children and teens may be able to perform according to their age and developmental level. The skills are listed at the earliest age they might be used and can be used from that age and up. Use this as a general guideline. Try lots of skills with all different ages. Young kids continue to surprise me with what mindfulness skills they can master.

REFLECTION: Think about the age and cognitive and developmental stages of your client. While doing your assessment keep in mind what skills you think they might possess or be able to learn. As you practice mindfulness skills with a variety of ages, what are you discovering about what works and what doesn't work for different clients? Think about how to modify various skills to match the needs of each client.

APPROPRIATE MINDFULNESS SKILLS FOR AGE, DEVELOPMENTAL, AND COGNITIVE LEVEL

Use this handout as a general guideline and modify based on your assessment of your client's skill level. The skills are listed at the youngest age at which they can be tried and can be used from that age and up. Don't be afraid to try various skills with each age group including the youngest clients.

- **Birth to 2**
  - Sensorimotor stage of Piaget's childhood theory of cognitive development
  - Modify behavior by using the senses
  - Facial expression, tone of voice
  - Eye contact, smile

- **Age 2**
  - Object Permanence, magical thinking
  - Peek-A-Boo, hide and find an object
  - Loves to be read to, but likes the pictures most
  - Mindful seeing

- **Age 3**
  - Listens to stories
  - Answer what are you doing? What is this? Where?
  - Use their imagination to pretend and visualize
  - Relaxation breath
  - Mindful listening, touching, motion, smelling skills
  - Blow bubbles, smell flowers

- **Age 4**
  - Identify missing pieces in picture, puzzle, objects
  - Participate in group activities
  - Role play and make believe
  - Belly breathe
  - Mindful tasting
  - Mindful greeting

- **Age 5**
  - Eager to learn
  - Can play cooperatively, take turns, share

- Participates in group play and shared activities
- Imaginary friend
- Drawing
- Lazy River

- **Age 6**
  - Increased span of attention
  - Time sense improves
  - Love puzzles
  - Still can't see the world from another's point of view
  - Increased fear of the dark, animals, noises
  - Mindfulness of Physical Body

- **1st grade to early adolescence**
  - Concrete thinking becomes abstract thinking
  - Competence: industry vs inferiority
  - Increased attention span
  - Loving-kindness or friendly wishes
  - Changing the channel
  - "I'm feeling" game
  - Mindfulness of thoughts – tweens
  - Mindfulness of intention
  - Mindfulness of tasks

- **Age 12-20**
  - Identity vs Role Confusion —> Formal Operations
  - Who am I?
  - How do I fit in?
  - Where am I going in life?
  - Magical thinking is gone
  - Mindfulness of emotions
  - Mindfulness of intuition

Tool 2-3: How to Adapt Adult Mindfulness Skills for Kids

BACKGROUND: Teaching mindfulness skills to kids is not dramatically different from teaching them to adults. Mindfulness exercises that are used with adults can be adapted to fit different ages and abilities. This must take into account the fact that children's thinking is more concrete; therefore, activities should be clear, concrete, and descriptive in their instructions. Children are also imaginative and are often able to use their creativity and imagination much more than adults. Since kids' work is their play it is important to present the basic skills of mindfulness in the form of games and play activities, especially for younger kids. And since kids are integrated into their family it is recommended that parents be involved as often as possible. See Tools 2-1 and 5-14 for more detail.

SKILL BUILDING: Refer to Handout 2-3 for guidance on how to adapt common mindfulness skills for kids. Kids typically need to start with much shorter time durations for each skill and build up gradually. This is especially true for kids who have a hard time sitting still or focusing, such as those with ADHD or anxiety. Make sure your client understands your language and teach them the words you will be using. For example, teach them what "exhale" and "inhale" mean by demonstrating or use expressions like "breathe in like smelling a flower" or "breathe out like blowing a bubble."

Turn the mindfulness exercises into games and make them fun. Kids love to play and to try new things. Start with bringing their attention to the external environment and their immediate surroundings with skills such as Mindfulness of Breath, Surroundings, Mindful Listening, Seeing, Tasting, Touching, and Motion. Then Introduce skills of Mindfulness of Physical Body, and Tasks. Then add Mindfulness of Intention, Relationships, Intuition and Compassion. Vary this according to your client's age and developmental and cognitive level.

REFLECTION: Reflect on how you can introduce mindfulness skills to your client in their language, with play, humor, and fun. Pay close attention to how your client responds during various mindfulness exercises and activities and modify the length as needed to match their abilities. Expect that with practice your client will be able to tolerate gradually increasing the time. Notice how quickly your client learns and improves their skills.

GUIDELINES FOR ADAPTING ADULT MINDFULNESS SKILLS FOR KIDS

- Shorten duration - Start with 30 seconds and gradually increase time

- Keep it SIMPLE

- Use language kids understand

- Demonstrate each skill, do it with them, fine-tune their practice

- Use repetition

- Use Play, activities and movement skills

- Have FUN

- Use humor

- Improvise as you see fit

- Use a gradual process

- Teach inner awareness, outer awareness, self-reflection and compassion

- Use 3-step progression

    1. Begin with the more concrete attention to the external environment

    2. Then move to the experience of the body

    3. Finally, introduce attention to the mind and meditation exercises

- Progression of Mindfulness Skills

    1. Awareness of Surroundings

    2. Awareness of Breath

    3. Awareness of Sensory

    4. Awareness of Mind

    5. Awareness of Others

    6. Awareness of Everything

Tool 2-4: How to Make Mindfulness Skills Relevant for Teens

BACKGROUND: Mindfulness is particularly helpful for teens as the transition to adolescence presents developmental challenges in physical, social, intellectual and psychological arenas. Adolescent brains are still under construction, and are laying down neural pathways related to emotion management that can shape the course of adulthood. Teens typically experience intense emotions and in fact some mental Illness begins in adolescence. (Kessler et al, 2007) Mindfulness research suggests that mindfulness practice changes the brain in positive ways and helps improve and stabilize mood, strengthens emotional regulation and bolsters self-esteem so vulnerable during adolescence. See Tools 3-21 for relevant research.

In general, teens need more explanation than adults about the relevance of mindfulness practice to their lives. They may find it hard to see the connection between sitting still with their eyes closed and their daily life.

SKILL BUILDING: In order for teens to embrace mindfulness practice you will need to help them to 'buy in' to the whole thing by helping them understand and experience the benefits that mindfulness will bring to their daily lives. Gather as much information as possible about their life so you can show them how mindfulness can help them. Use the guidelines on Handout 2-4 to make mindfulness skills more relevant to teen clients. Most teens engage quickly when they learn that mindfulness skills might help them get better grades or get into a good college (improved concentration); or might help them create a healthy relationship with someone they have their eye on.

Be prepared to see some teen clients rolling their eyes, looking around the room, and having a hard time getting into any particular mindfulness exercise – just being a teen. Help them reflect on and process what the experience was like for them and gently address their resistance. (See Tool 5-7) But do not be surprised if some teen clients get right into it. Teaching mindfulness to groups of teens can be very powerful in helping the more resistant teen to let go and engage in the process as they observe their peers enjoying the process.

Be advised that research suggests that young teens may be uncomfortable paying attention to themselves. They may experience heightened anxiety while practicing mindfulness as they focus on their inner selves. If the thoughts and sensations they are observing are related to worries and fears, they may feel increased anxiety by recognizing them (Kabat-Zinn, 1990). They have trouble letting go and fear that letting go will increase anxiety. Be prepared to help teens who experience this to process their feelings and learn to self-soothe and calm their anxiety.

REFLECTION: Find out and think about what your teen client is currently experiencing in his or her life. Consider which tasks of adolescence the client is presently facing. Use this information to help you adapt mindfulness skills to be more relevant to each particular client.

HOW TO MAKE MINDFULNESS SKILLS RELEVANT FOR TEENS

- Use examples from their life of when they need to be mindful

    ✓ Realizing that they are exhausted or need the bathroom

    ✓ Having no idea what the teacher just said

    ✓ Barely remembering what they just ate

    ✓ Being able to focus on their schoolwork/homework

    ✓ Being totally present on a date

    ✓ Mindful 'texting'

    ✓ Safe driving

    ✓ Building friendships

    ✓ Choosing a college

    ✓ Choosing a love relationship

    ✓ Choosing a career

- Compare mindfulness practice to practice in sports, dance, music

- Use relevant (teen friendly) music in mindfulness listening skills

- Help them integrate mindfulness practice into their daily life: walking, eating, brushing teeth, listening to music, studying, dating, texting

- Vary exercises to avoid boredom

- Use walking, dancing and movement mindfulness skills

- Keep mindfulness exercises short, < 10 minutes and increase gradually

Tool 2-5: Involve the Whole Child: Body, Mind, Heart

BACKGROUND: Mindfulness provides a great opportunity to involve the whole child including their body, their mind and their heart. Susan Kaiser Greenland suggests that mindfulness is the 'new ABCs': Attention, Balance, and Compassion. "By practicing mindfulness kids learn life skills that help them soothe and calm themselves, bring awareness to their inner and outer experience, and bring a reflective quality to their actions and relationships" (Kaiser Greenland, 2010, p.12) This tool sets the framework for doing so with child and teen clients using a variety of tools throughout this workbook.

SKILL BUILDING: Using mindfulness for the whole child is a great way to help clients improve attention, balance and compassion and for developing the life skills everyone needs. Teaching clients a variety of types of skills from this workbook will help clients achieve this. This involves teaching clients mindfulness skills that increase their inner awareness of their body, mind and heart.

For teaching awareness of body, use Tools in Chapter 6, Mindfulness of Breath, and Chapter 16, Mindfulness of Physical Body.

Awareness of mind Involves the client's intellect and emotions. These are included in Chapter 14, Mindfulness of Thoughts, Chapter 15, Mindfulness of Emotions and Chapter 21, Mindfulness of Intuition.

Awareness of the heart increases and expresses compassion for self and others. These skills are found in Chapter 17, Mindfulness of Relationships, and Chapter 19, Mindfulness of Compassion.

REFLECTION: As you introduce and practice this array of skills with your clients over time, reflect on how this specific collection of skills addresses the whole person. What do you notice about how mindfulness increases the client's ability to pay attention, to live in emotional balance and self-regulation, and to experience and express compassion towards themselves and others? How important do you think it is for mindfulness practices to incorporate skills for all aspects of the whole client?

Tool 2-6: Format for Mindfulness Sessions

BACKGROUND: The format used for introducing and practicing mindfulness skills is crucial to success with kids and teens. Kids love to play. They love to use their imaginations in creative play. They love to test their skills. Kids and teens would much rather be doing something fun than boring. The last thing we want to do is force kids and teens to practice mindfulness or to make it boring or even intolerable. If we do, they may end up feeling like mindfulness is a form of punishment, almost like a time out. This tool describes a format that has been used successfully in several children's mindfulness programs including the Inner Child (Kaiser Greenland, 2010) and MindUp (Hawn Foundation, 2011).

SKILL BUILDING: Handout 2-6 provides the basic structure for mindfulness sessions for kids and teens. The format should address the needs and developmental and cognitive levels of the client. Since the work of childhood is play, include an element of play in the mindfulness practice sessions. Have some fun. Laugh. Help the client enjoy themselves. This might be done before settling down to a quieter meditation. Or the mindfulness skill itself may be in the form of a game such as Mindful Touching (Chapter 12), Mindful Smelling (Chapter 11), Mindful Listening (Chapter 8), Mindful Seeing (Chapter 9), Simon Says, etc.

If the mindfulness skill is done quietly while sitting still then play one of the mindfulness type games before hand. Then settle the client down by focusing on the breath and begin one of the quiet skills. Tell them you will keep your eyes open so they feel safe to close their eyes.

After completing the mindfulness skill ask the client to share what it was like for them to do that skill. This is an essential part of the process of increasing the ability to become more aware. Ask them to reflect on what came up for them. Ask them to give you feedback about their experience. They may share verbally, in writing, or by drawing a picture. Encourage them to share freely without judgment. There is no right or wrong here.

Be aware that some kids and teens will experience some painful or scary thoughts and feelings during some types of inner focused mindfulness skills. Be prepared to process these feelings with them if you are a therapist or refer them to a therapist if you are not equipped to help them process what came up for them.

The last component of many children's mindfulness programs is to apply what they are learning in the form of an activity, project or community service. If the skill is teaching them about the neurobiology of the brain, then they might draw a brain. Perhaps they could draw a picture of something that came up during the mindfulness skill. They might write a poem about their experience or write a journal entry. If you are doing a Mindful Smelling skill, perhaps you could pop some popcorn together being mindful of the delicious aroma of the popped corn. For loving kindness, compassion, or friendly wishes they might practice some acts of kindness during the week and share their feelings about it. Or they might plan and participate in a community service project or raise money for a worthy cause.

REFLECTION: Use what you hear during the sharing to assess progress and give feedback to shape mindfulness practice by reinforcing, encouraging, and giving tips that will increase their skills. Be mindful to avoid judgment of their practice. Help your client connect practice with increased mindfulness in their life. Help them move from "I was distracted" to "I noticed I was distracted" which is the process of "awareness of awareness" so central to mindfulness.

MINDFULNESS SESSION FORMAT FOR KIDS

- **Play**
  - ✓ Have fun
  - ✓ Activity or game related to mindfulness
    - Go outside and smell the flowers
    - Blow some bubbles
    - Play Simon Says
  - ✓ Play a mindfulness game
- **Mindfulness Practice**
  - ✓ Mindfulness skill
  - ✓ Mindfulness game
  - ✓ Meditation
- **Share**
  - ✓ Reflect on what came up for them during the mindfulness skill
  - ✓ Talk about the experience
  - ✓ Express feelings
- **Activity**
  - ✓ Apply what they learned
  - ✓ Do an activity related to topic of skill
    - Draw
      - Example: A picture of their brain when angry
    - Build
      - Example: Add glitter to a water bottle to use as a mindfulness tool
    - Cook
      - Example: Make some popcorn or cider or cookies to practice mindful smelling
  - ✓ Draw or write in journal
  - ✓ Practice giving loving kindness or friendly wishes
  - ✓ Perform acts of kindness
  - ✓ Plan and participate in a community service project

Chapter 3
Tools for Explaining
What Mindfulness Is

DEFINING MINDFULNESS AND EXPLAINING TO KIDS AND TEENS

Tool 3-1: Define Mindfulness

BACKGROUND: Most kids and teens have no real concept of what mindfulness is or how it could help them. Their parents may not know much about it either. Therefore, it is important to use a simple, basic definition to introduce the concept. As clients use more of the tools in this workbook, they will develop their own personal understanding of what mindfulness means to them and will be able to explain it to you and others.

Caution: Some teens are totally put off by the word "meditation," picturing a process of sitting completely still with no thoughts for 20 or 30 minutes. This is a totally overwhelming and unbearable concept for many, particularly if they have ADHD or experience anxiety. Most of the mindfulness tools included here teach the process of gradually becoming better at dismissing distracting thoughts and gaining the ability to "meditate." But start small, where the client is, so you don't turn them off to the process. Most of the mindfulness skills in this workbook do not require sitting still for long.

This tool provides several definitions of mindfulness including Jon Kabat-Zinn's (Kabat-Zinn, 2003), Susan Kaiser Greenland's (Kaiser Greenland, 2006), and Amy Saltzman's (Saltzman, A., 2011) as well as my own simple version that I use with kids.

SKILL BUILDING: Start by asking your client what they think mindfulness is. Review the three definitions in Handout 3-1 and choose the one that fits your client best. Then use the chosen version to explain what mindfulness is. Break down whichever one you choose and go over each component of the definition. For example with Kabat-Zinn's, start with "paying attention to something." This can be anything you choose to pay attention to. It often begins with paying attention to the breath but it could also be paying attention to your surroundings, driving, eating, washing the dishes, your thoughts or emotions, taking a shower, your physical body, or even your parent, teacher or friend. Then go over "in a particular way" and discuss what that means, such as focusing your attention, closing your eyes and going within, looking at something, listening, tasting, smelling, or touching. Next, discuss "on purpose," which simply means that you set the intention and decide to pay attention to this specific "something." "In the present moment" means right now, while dismissing thoughts of the past or future that arise in the present. "Non-judgmentally" means without comparing, judging, or be criticizing yourself or what arises while paying attention.

REFLECTION: Initiate a discussion with your client about their reaction to hearing this definition. Ask them to think of examples of how they might do each part of the definition. For example, ask them to choose something to pay attention to. Ask them how they will focus on it (visual, auditory, tactile senses, etc.). Discuss how once they've set the intention to focus on something, they can then focus "on purpose." Ask how they would stay in the present moment. Discuss judgment and how commonly we all do it, and what it feels like not to judge. Give them examples of being judgmental. Ask them to write their own definition of mindfulness in words that resonate with them.

"Paying attention to
something,
in a particular way,
on purpose,
in the present moment,
non-judgmentally"
(Kabat-Zinn, 2003)

———

"Being aware of what's happening
as it's happening"
(Kaiser-Greenland, 2006)

———

"Paying attention to your life, here and now,
with kindness and curiosity"
(Saltzman, A, 2011)

———

"Paying attention
to what's going on
right here,
right now
inside of us
or outside of us."
(Debra Burdick, 2013)

Tool 3-2: Busy versus Calm Mind

BACKGROUND: With more than 60,000 thoughts a day (and the emotions they evoke) whirling through the mind, it is easy to understand how the mind can get cluttered, overwhelmed, and unfocused. A calm, clear mind can be easily overwhelmed by the constant flow of thoughts, feelings, and sensations. This exercise illustrates the concept of mindfulness as clarity of mind, clearing away the clutter, settling down, quieting, calming. Thich Nhat Hanh described this process using a glass of cloudy apple juice. (Thich Nhat Hanh, 2011) It provides a great way to visualize mindfulness. This tool is great for kids and teens who often experience intense feelings of anger, anxiety, fear, sadness, stress and overwhelm. It gives them a way to turn down the volume on their anger, worry, stress, etc.

SKILL BUILDING: Explain that this exercise will give clients a way to imagine and visualize their mind calming down. Do the Busy Versus Calm Mind exercise described in Handout 3-2. Play with this exercise. Invite kids to pour the baking soda or glitter, to stir, or to hold a toy beside the bowl.

REFLECTION: Ask the client how they felt as they watched the baking soda swirling around and making the water cloudy. Ask them what they noticed as they watched the water clear. Were they able to calm their mind as the water cleared? Did they feel calmer in their body? Could they relate to the comparison of cloudy versus clear water to a cloudy versus clear mind? Ask them to tell you about a time when their brain was cloudy. Was it angry, scared, wired, or stressed? What do they think a happy peaceful brain looks like? When was their brain clear?

BUSY VERSUS CALM MIND

Place water in a clear glass bowl.

Ask the client to look through the bowl to the other side of the room. Hold a small toy beside the bowl and ask if they can see it.

Then sprinkle some baking soda or glitter into the water, stir, and watch the water get cloudy and the objects around the bowl disappear.

Ask them if they can see through the bowl now. Can they see the toy?

Explain that this is what happens in their mind when they are worried, angry, distracted, stressed out, or revved up and their thoughts and feelings are whirling around.

Stop stirring. Guide them to keep watching the water in the bowl to see what happens as the baking soda or glitter settles to the bottom.

Tell them that's what mindful breathing does for their mind. It clears and calms their mind, settles their thoughts and feelings, and helps them to feel more relaxed and better able to concentrate.

Then tell them to wiggle their body to get their mind revved up again while stirring the water or adding more baking soda or glitter.

Show them how cloudy the water is again—like their mind when it's busy—and watch it settle as they sit quietly breathing and watching. Ask them to raise their hand when they can see through the water again.

Tell them to breathe slowly as they watch the water clear. Explain that by breathing slowly and steadily their thoughts and feelings settle and their minds become calm and clear.

Inspired by apple juice story (Thich Nhat Hanh, 2011)

Tool 3-3: Making a Mindfulness Glitter Bottle

BACKGROUND: Another way to explain mindfulness is with a snow globe or glitter ball. Just shake the globe or ball and follow the same process described in Tool 3-2. A 7 year old client taught me that a simple water bottle with a teaspoon of glitter will work well, too. This tool expands on Tool 3-2 to provide a hands-on activity kids can do to make their own "mindfulness glitter bottle".

SKILL BUILDING: Do the activity on Handout 3-3 with your client.

REFLECTION: Help your client reflect on what happened when they shook the bottle and then when they were still. Ask them: were you able to see through the bottle? What happened when you shook it? What did you feel like when you couldn't see through the bottle? What happened when you stayed still? How did you feel when the glitter sank to the bottom of the bottle? When did you use the mindfulness glitter bottle at home? Did it help you calm down and feel better?

MAKING A MINDFULNESS GLITTER BOTTLE

Materials:

- Clear water bottle full of water with cover and label removed. (The smoother the sides of the bottle, the easier it is to see through the bottle.)
- Glitter in various colors
- ¼ teaspoon measure

Process:

Give the client the water bottle. Ask them to look through the bottle. What can they see? Can they see their hand that is holding the bottle? Can they see through the bottle?

Provide glitter and a small spoon to put some glitter inside the bottle. Guide them in taking the cap off the bottle, putting some glitter in the bottle, and placing the cap back on tightly. Try using 1 tsp of glitter.

Ask them to shake the bottle and watch what happens as the glitter disperses in the water. Ask them to look through the bottle. What can they see now?

Ask them to shake the bottle and imagine that their mind is revved up, wired, angry, worried, or busy. Then tell them to hold the bottle completely still and watch what happens inside the bottle.

Explain that as they become quiet and still in their mind, their busy or angry or worried thoughts calm and clear just like the glitter settles to the bottom and top of the bottle.

Now ask them to hold the bottle and jump up and down and twirl around and watch what happens in the bottle. Then encourage them to stop and stand completely still as they again watch what happens in the bottle.

Explain that as they calm their body, their mind quiets and thoughts settle just like the glitter in the bottle. They feel peaceful and clear.

Encourage them to use their glitter bottle to help them calm anger or worry.

Now ask them to watch the glitter settle until the water is clear again. Encourage them to breathe slowly and calmly while they watch.

Let them take their glitter bottle home and encourage them to hold it, shake it, and then still themselves and watch the glitter settle whenever they feel upset, angry, afraid, or too revved up.

Note: Another option is to use baking soda instead of glitter for this activity. Please caution children not to open the glitter bottle nor drink it. Gorilla glue can be used to glue the cap back on for safety.

Tool 3-4: Let's Clap to the Beat to Illustrate Mindfulness

BACKGROUND: Mindfulness can be thought of like a rest in music. The rest in music is a place where the music stops for a brief moment, in time with the overall rhythm of the song. It is an interval of silence. The rest is just as important to the song as the sounds. It informs the music like mindfulness informs life. Mindfulness can be thought of as a rest from the busy activity of the mind. It puts a brief pause in the chatter. It improves mental clarity. This tool provides a way for kids and teens to use their bodies to understand this concept.

SKILL BUILDING: Explain that a rest in music is a brief interval of silence where the music or song stops for a moment. Mindfulness is like the rest in music when we take a quick break from activity and busy thinking.

- ✓ Ask the client to clap four times in a row with an even beat and count one, two, three, four, as they clap. Clap with them – clap, clap, clap, clap, repeat.

- ✓ Now ask them to clap two times, hold one beat, and clap on beat four—clap, clap, hold, clap, repeat.

- ✓ Play with it. Change the pattern—clap, rest, clap, clap, repeat.

- ✓ Hold two beats instead of one—clap, rest, rest, clap.

- ✓ Change the beat to one, two, three. – clap, clap, clap.

- ✓ Then change the pattern such as – clap, rest, clap, repeat.

- ✓ Do it with a favorite song the client knows.

REFLECTION: Help your client reflect on what this exercise was like for them. How did it feel different when there was no rest? What if they had to just keep clapping without stopping? Would they get tired? Would their hands hurt? Would they lose their place? That's what happens in life if we don't take time out for mindfulness. With practice was it easier to clap the beat? Explain that mindfulness get easier with practice, too.

CORE TOOLS

Tool 3-5: Set Intention

BACKGROUND: Setting intention is a basic step in any practice. Intention is the goal you wish to achieve from an action. It is your directed attention. In mindfulness, intention refers to what you are choosing to pay attention to. Your intention might be to pay attention to your breath. It might be to pay attention to the task at hand or to your surroundings. Being mindful involves bringing your attention back to your intention over and over again. This tool explains how to help kids and teens with the process of setting intention at the beginning of mindfulness practice.

SKILL BUILDING: Kids and teens often struggle with paying attention and staying on task. At the beginning of each mindfulness skill help your client decide what their intention is for that particular skill. Setting the intention will help them identify what to bring their attention back to over and over again throughout the practice. The intention may be to focus on breath, a task, surroundings, sound, taste, emotions, etc.

- Explain to clients what an intention is and discuss intentions they have set.
- Explain that by choosing what to pay attention to and returning their attention to it over and over, they are training their brains in specific ways that will help them throughout their lives.
- Help them take a moment to identify their intention at the beginning of every mindfulness practice whether formal or not. For example, if you lead them in a Core Practice (Tool 6-8) help them set their intention to focus their attention on their breath.
- Remind them to:
  - Keep awareness of their intention present in mind.
  - Notice as soon as they become aware of a thought, feeling, or distraction that their intention is to focus on their breath, and shift their attention back to their breath.
  - Check in periodically to ensure their thoughts, words, and actions remain consistent with their intention.
  - Do this over and over during the entire Core Practice mindfulness practice.
- Apply this process to every mindfulness practice

REFLECTION: Help clients reflect on what it was like for them to set an intention. Ask them: How hard or easy was it to set your intention? Did you find your mind wandering from your intention? How did you bring it back to your intention? What did you notice when you listened to the Core Practice tool? How can you apply this process of setting intention to your daily life?

Tool 3-6: Use Mindfulness Bells

BACKGROUND: Mindfulness bells are often used to start or stop a mindfulness practice. There are a variety of styles available but the basic idea is that when the bell is rung the sound continues for 10 of more seconds. This tool describes a number of ways to incorporate mindfulness/meditation bells into practice with kids and teens.

SKILL BUILDING: Mindfulness bells can be used in a number of ways with kids and teens. The traditional use is to start and stop a mindfulness practice or meditation. The bell gets the attention of the listener and quickly becomes associated with becoming still and quieting the mind. Then at the end of the practice it can signify time to transition from a quiet state back to the day.

Another use is as a mindful listening skill. See Tool 8-1 for how to do this.

Ringing the mindfulness bells is a sure way to get everyone's attention right away. Therefore, they can be used to get kids and teens to pay attention to what you are saying or what you want them to do next or to quiet the room.

The mindfulness bells can also be used by kids or teens (as well as therapists and teachers), when they feel overwhelmed or stressed and need some quiet. Explain that they may ring them if they want the group to settle down a bit or if the room is getting too noisy. This gives them a sense of control over their environment as they become mindful of how they are being affected by it.

Teach young kids how to ring the bells and instruct them to only ring them once each time. Some young clients have love ringing them so much that they ring them over and over and drive everyone a bit crazy.

REFLECTION: Was the client able to pay attention to the sound of the bell until it stopped? How does ringing the bell change the energy in the room? Ask the client how they feel when they hear the bell ring. Did the bell help them quiet their mind? Did the client find the bell soothing, or maybe annoying?

Tool 3-7: Cultivate a Witnessing Awareness

BACKGROUND: Being "aware of awareness" is a new concept for most kids and teens. The idea is to notice what's arising as it is arising. This includes awareness of thoughts, feelings, body sensations, and physical surroundings. It involves paying attention to what is happening in this moment and acknowledging and dismissing distractions. The goal is to remain aware without trying to change anything. Observe and accept what you observe. Awareness is the first step in eventually being able to change unwanted patterns. With practice, kids and teens can get very good at becoming more "aware of awareness". They can move from "I am hungry" to "I noticed I am hungry". This tool gives a simple process for improving this skill.

SKILL BUILDING: Guide clients in the following process.
- Stop. Pause for a moment.
- Notice what's arising as it's arising.
- Pay attention to thoughts, feelings, body sensations, surroundings.
- Just be aware without trying to change anything.
- As distractions occur, remember your intention and bring your attention back to what's arising.
- Continue for 10 seconds, increasing gradually to 5 minutes depending on the client's age and ability.

REFLECTION: Help clients reflect on (and share) what their experience was like when doing this mindfulness exercise. Ask them: What did you notice? Did you notice any sounds or smells? Did you notice any body sensations anywhere on your body? What thoughts arose? Were you aware of any feelings? What distracted you? How did you refocus on being a witness to your awareness? With kids and teens you may have to give them some ideas of what might have come up or share what came up for you the first couple of times they do this until they get the idea. Even some young kids are amazingly good at this skill.

Tool 3-8: Regulate Attention – Pay Attention

BACKGROUND: Kids and teens today live in a very distracting and distracted world. They may easily get overwhelmed and overloaded with too many things competing for their attention. Being able to regulate attention improves concentration, memory, and overall mental clarity. This tool provides the basic steps involved in improving the ability to regulate attention and to pay attention on purpose.

SKILL BUILDING: Lead clients in the following meditation after helping them decide what they intend to pay attention to. For some clients it can be helpful to provide something specific for them to pay attention to such as music, a brightly colored piece of artwork, or something they can hold in their hands. Be creative.

- Set your intention to pay attention.
- Select something to pay attention to. This might be your breath, or the feeling of your hands as you rub them together, or any object in your surroundings or outside in nature such as the leaves on a tree.
- Now just notice everything you can about the object of your attention.
- Notice if you are being distracted by a thought, feeling, body sensation, or something in your environment.
- Acknowledge the distraction and dismiss it without judging.
- Just let it go.
- Return your focus to the intended object of your attention.
- Notice the details of whatever you have chosen to focus on.
- Notice how it looks, how it feels, how it smells.
- Continue this process in silence for 1 minute (30 seconds for young kids).

As you practice this, gradually increase the time by 1 minute each time until you are doing it for 5 minutes or up to 15 minutes for older kids and teens. Set a soothing alarm on your smartphone to time this.

REFLECTION: Help your client reflect, explore and share what they experienced. Ask them: Did your mind wander as you did this exercise? What did you do when you noticed you were distracted? What did you notice about whatever you were paying attention to? Did you notice anything new about it? Were you aware of any inner thoughts or conversation making comments on the process? Help them understand that it is normal to have a running commentary and give them examples such as: "oh, I never noticed that before", or, "I hope this is over soon. I can't sit still any longer."

Tool 3-9: Strengthen Self-Regulation—Use a Word or Color as Body–Mind Signal

BACKGROUND: Practicing mindfulness increases the brain's ability to regulate itself. Neuronal pathways are created and strengthened by the repeated practice of calming the mind and paying attention to something on purpose. Mindfulness can decrease the emotional hijacking that occurs often below the level of awareness. The brains of kids and teens are constantly developing in a process that pares down neuronal pathways that are not needed and develops and strengthens pathways that are used regularly. This tool describes a technique kids and teens can use to improve their ability to stay focused on what they've chosen to pay attention to.

SKILL BUILDING: Explain that repeating a word often helps one stay focused. Ask clients to choose a word to use to help them stay focused. Tell clients: For example you might repeat "homework, homework" when doing your homework to remind yourself to be mindful and pay attention to doing your homework while doing your homework, and nothing else. Or you might silently repeat "breathing, breathing" during a breathing meditation or when you need a brief break. You might use the words "mindful, mindful" to remind yourself to stay in the present and be aware of whatever task or practice you are doing at the moment. You could repeat "calming, calming" when you start to get angry, or "kindness, kindness" to remind yourself to be kind to a classmate who annoys you.

Some people find that picturing a color of their choosing helps them to stay focused better than using a word. Help clients choose a color that is significant or pleasing to them. Ask them to name their favorite color. For example, they might picture the color blue whenever they feel stressed to remind themselves to breathe so they can stay calm and lower their stress response. Or they might picture yellow to remind themselves to be mindful while performing a task such as reading or doing chores. Help kids and teens experiment with different colors until they find the best one(s) for them. Do an art project where they draw a pretty design using their chosen color. Encourage them to hang it someplace to remind them to be mindful.

REFLECTION: Explore what works best with clients by asking: What words did you try this week? Which one(s) work best for you? Would you rather use a color or a word? What color did you try? How/when did you use this skill during the past week? How might you have used it? Did you notice any improvement in your ability to stay calm or to pay attention?

Tool 3-10: Journal About Your Understanding of What Mindfulness Is

BACKGROUND: Journaling can be an effective way for kids and teens to process and integrate their experiences while learning mindfulness. Some will love to journal. Others will not. Ask them to write about what they think mindfulness is, or to draw a picture that represents something about their experience with a basic mindfulness skill such as awareness of breathing. If they don't want to journal, you might still ask them the following prompts and process their verbal responses.

SKILL BUILDING: Use this tool after the client has some introduction to what mindfulness is and again several more times as clients gain experience and skill with mindfulness. This will show them how their understanding about mindfulness changes. This can be assigned as homework but is more likely to get done if completed during the session.

No matter whether your client is a mindfulness beginner or an experienced mindfulness practitioner, journaling can help them process and integrate how mindfulness is affecting their life. Instruct clients to answer the journal prompts on Handout 3-10. If they are too young to write the answers offer to write what they dictate or encourage them to draw a picture about what they think mindfulness is. This is a great time to involve the parent as the scribe if appropriate.

If you are tech savvy you might set up a closed group on Facebook for teens to share their mindfulness experiences and answer the prompts as a less formal way to journal.

REFLECTION: Ask your client if they would feel comfortable sharing what they wrote or drew in their journal. Explore their answers. Help them clarify their intention and understanding about mindfulness practice. Discuss the process from wherever they are starting mindfulness practice.

JOURNAL ABOUT YOUR UNDERSTANDING OF WHAT MINDFULNESS IS

Journal Prompts:

- What do you think mindfulness is?

- How does your new understanding about mindfulness differ from what you thought it was?

- Why have you decided to learn about mindfulness?

- Thus far, what have you noticed about yourself while practicing mindfulness skills?

- How have you started to be more mindful during your day?

- What do you hope to change or improve by being more mindful?

- What is your intention for mindfulness practice?

- Write about the mindfulness skills you learned thus far.

- Which mindfulness skills do you like the best so far?

- How do you feel about being more mindful?

Picture Prompts

- Draw a picture of you being mindful.

- Draw a picture of you not being mindful.

- Draw a picture of the colors of mindfulness.

- Draw a picture of your life when you are being mindful.

THE NEUROBIOLOGY OF MINDFULNESS - IN KIDS LANGUAGE

Tool 3-11: What Is Neuroplasticity and Why Do We Care?

BACKGROUND: Neuroplasticity is the ability of the brain to change itself. MRI studies, SPECT scan studies, and EEG studies confirm the ability of mindfulness practice to change brain structure as well as brain functioning. (See Tool 3-21 for research) According to Hebb's axiom, neurons that fire together wire together (Hebb, 2009), and dendrites increase in size and efficiency when something is repeated over and over. So, like a path worn in the grass or sand from lots of foot traffic, the neuronal pathway gets stronger and stronger with repetition. Mindfulness practice is an effective way to create more healthy "pathways" in the brain.

SKILL BUILDING: Explain that the brain's ability to change itself is called neuroplasticity. Write 'neuroplasticity' on the board or a paper and ask them to say it with you. Have a discussion about change such as learning to ride a bicycle or to sing a song. Explore how these activities get easier and easier the more you do them. Relate this to how the brain changes and gets better and better at doing something the more it is repeated.

Use the two exercises (Paths in the Grass or Sand and Paper Folding) in Handout 3-11a and b to illustrate how neuronal pathways are "worn" into the brain. Ask them how they learned to tie their shoes or write their name. Relate these skills to how the brain learns how to do things and gets better with practice. Discuss how this may be helpful, such as when we learn something new like how to read, or harmful if the brain gets stuck in a negative pattern such as anxiety or depression. Use the handout to explore how doing something a different way starts to change the pathway, which can be very helpful when shifting out of negative mood states or anxious tendencies.

REFLECTION: Help clients explore how the process of neuroplasticity may be helping them or keeping them stuck by asking: What positive or negative things do you do repeatedly that may have worn a "pathway" in your brain? Do you notice yourself responding automatically to things without stopping to think and choosing a response? Are there any pathways you would like to reinforce or eliminate? Does fear or anxiety play a role in your life? In what ways do you feel stuck?

NEUROPLASTICITY – LIKE PATHS IN THE GRASS OR SAND

Outside on the grass.

If possible take clients outside onto a lawn or field of grass or a sandy beach.

Bring their attention to the grass/sand and how it looks.

Then ask them to walk a straight line across the grass/sand. Do it with them.

Now look at the grass/sand and see if they can see where they walked.

Walk back and forth several times until they can see where the grass/sand is beginning to get matted down.

Ask them if they have ever seen a path worn in the grass right down to the dirt. Show them one if possible.

Ask them what happens if no one walks on the path anymore.

Explain that this is like the process of neuroplasticity in the brain. According to Hebb's axiom, neurons that fire together wire together (Hebb, 2009), and dendrites increase in size and efficiency when something is repeated over and over. So, like the path worn in the grass or sand, the neuronal pathway gets stronger and stronger with repetition and weaker and weaker with disuse. Mindfulness practice can help rewire the brain and is an effective way to create more healthy "pathways" in the brain.

Indoors.

Lead clients through the following visualization:

Close your eyes and picture a lawn of green grass.

Now imagine that someone walks across the grass diagonally from one corner of the lawn to the opposite corner.

Notice how the grass changes. Perhaps the grass is a bit matted down where they walked.

Now imagine lots of people walking across the grass following the same path.

After a while, notice that some of the grass is dying where so many footsteps have fallen.

Imagine that this process continues until there is a path worn in the lawn where there is no longer any grass—just a dirt path worn smooth from all the foot traffic.

This is like the process of neuroplasticity in the brain. According to Hebb's axiom, neurons that fire together wire together (Hebb, 2009), and dendrites increase in size and efficiency when something is repeated over and over. So, like the path worn in the grass, the neuronal pathway gets stronger and stronger with repetition. Mindfulness practice is an effective way to create more healthy "pathways" in the brain.

Now imagine the lawn with the path across it. Notice what happens to it over time when no one walks on it anymore. The grass slowly starts to grow where the path was until at some point there is no longer a path at all.

Mindfulness practice can help rewire the brain so it no longer automatically responds with anxiety, or anger, or fear, or feeling stressed. Mindfulness helps to decrease the negative pathways in the brain.

PAPER FOLDING EXERCISE

Give clients a piece of heavy paper.

Ask them to fold the paper in half, then fold it again, and then again. Do it with them. Guide them to press down on the fold to sharpen it. Encourage them to notice how difficult or easy it is to fold the paper each time.

Have them unfold it and fold it again where it was already folded.

Ask them if refolding is faster and easier than folding the paper in the first place.

Relate this to moving information along a well-traveled path of neurons.

Discuss whether it is easier for your brain to think something new or the same thought.

Ask them if it is easier to learn something new or do something you have done before.

Tool 3-12: The Prefrontal Cortex (PFC) – Let's Conduct

BACKGROUND: The prefrontal cortex (PFC) can be thought of as the conductor of the brain as it orchestrates thoughts and actions according to internal goals. It links the cortex, limbic areas, and brainstem and carries out executive functions. One study showed that mindful breathing practice increased PFC activation, which may reflect stronger processing of distracting events and emotions, respectively (Hölzel et al., 2007b). This tool explains where the PFC is located and what it does.

SKILL BUILDING: Explain that the prefrontal cortex is located in the frontal lobe of the brain. Show clients where the PFC is located by placing your hand on your forehead. Ask clients to point to their PFC. Ask them to repeat "prefrontal cortex" a few times and then tell them they can call it the PFC.

Explain that the PFC acts like a conductor, controlling the activities of the rest of the brain. It is involved in paying attention, planning, organizing, personality expression, decision making, and moderating social behavior. The executive functions are performed in the PFC. Use Handout 3-12-1 to explain the functions of the PFC and the graphics, activity, and exercise on Handout 3-12-2 to compare it to the functions of a conductor of an orchestra.

REFLECTION: Review the location and function of the PFC. Explore some examples of difficulties that occur if the PFC isn't working optimally such as ADHD, depression, stress response, being overwhelmed, disorganization, poor planning, depressed mood, and poor mood regulation. Relate these to any issues your client may be experiencing. Ask clients what their PFC does for them and how they know whether it's working well or not.

THE PREFRONTAL CORTEX (PFC)

The following executive functions are performed by the PFC:

- Planning

- Organizing time, activity and space

- Regulating Attention

- Decision Making

- Moderating Behavior

- Personality Expression

- Motivation

- Mood Regulation

THE PREFRONTAL CORTEX (PFC) = CONDUCTOR

Conductor

Girl touching PFC

PFC directs brain activities like a conductor directs an orchestra

Activity

Let's pretend we are conducting an orchestra. (Do it with them.) Use your imagination and your conductor baton to bring in the violins; quiet the flutes; make the trumpets louder; and now speed up the drums.

Now pretend we are the PFC in our brain. Use you imaginary conductor baton to tell your brain to concentrate a little more over there; calm down a bit over there; speed up; slow down; turn down that worry; spiff up how it plans and organizes; and turn up happiness.

Exercise

- What does a conductor do in an orchestra?
- Imagine that your PFC is the conductor of your brain. List the ways it "conducts" the activities of your brain, particularly the executive functions such as paying attention, planning, organizing, making decisions, mood regulation, motivation, and time management.
- List things you have trouble doing that are controlled by the PFC.
- List things you do well that are controlled by the PFC.
- Is there anything your PFC has trouble doing, for example concentrating?
- Practice strengthening PFC processing by practicing mindfulness skills.
- What might happen if the PFC is offline and not working well?

Tool 3-13: The Amygdala—Security Guard

BACKGROUND: The amygdala consists of two almond-shaped brain structures that, along with the hippocampus, are part of the limbic system. The amygdala plays a key role in the processing of emotions and is central to survival, arousal, and autonomic responses. It is associated with fear responses, hormonal secretions, and emotional (implicit) memory. It is commonly called the fear center and essentially performs as the security guard in our brain, designed to keep us safe. A 2010 study (Hotzel, Lazar, et al., 2010) shows that reductions in stress (which mindfulness enables) can actually decrease the grey matter density of the amygdala.

SKILL BUILDING: Explain to clients that the amygdala acts like the security guard, panic button, smoke detector, watch dog, or fear center of the brain. Mindfulness calms the activity of the amygdala and increases a feeling of calm and clarity. Ask clients what a security guard does or what a smoke detector does. Use Handout 3-13-1 and 3-13-2 to explore how the amygdala works to keep clients safe and how to calm an over-activated amygdala.

REFLECTION: Help your client explain what the amygdala is, where it is and what its function is. Show them the graphic representation of where it is in the brain. Help them explore when their amygdala might have been doing its job. Discuss how to use mindfulness tools, such as awareness of breath and relaxation breathing, to calm the amygdala.

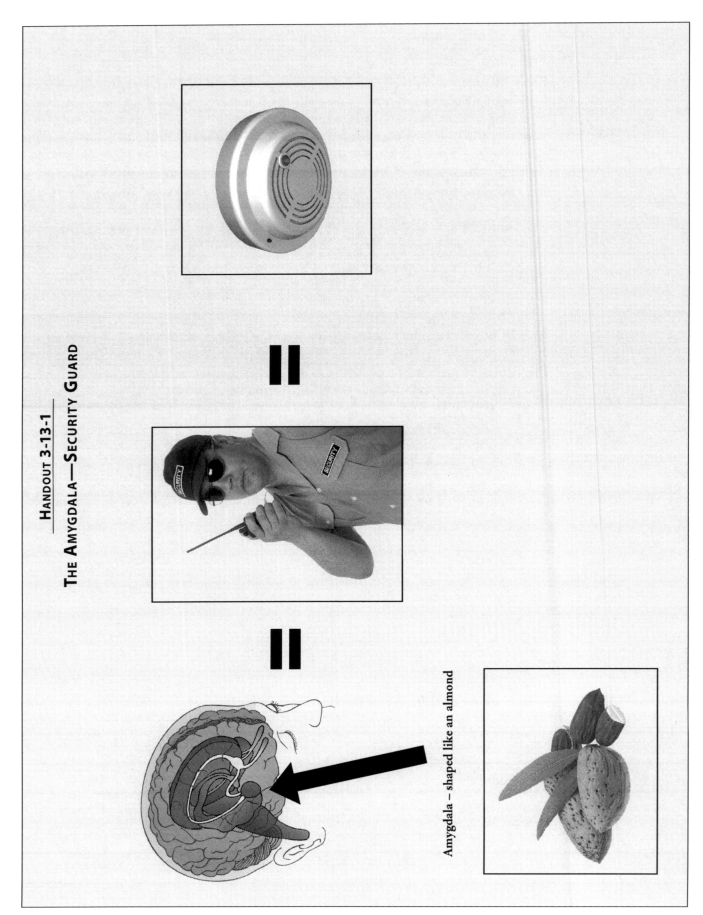

The Amygdala—Security Guard

Amygdala – shaped like an almond

THE AMYGDALA—SECURITY GUARD

Exercise

- What does the amygdala do for you?

  _____

  _____

  _____

- Draw a picture of where the amygdala is in your head

- What might happen if you didn't have the amygdala?

  _____

  _____

  _____

- List 2 or 3 times when you think your amygdala kept you safe.

  _____

  _____

  _____

- Were there any times you were actually safe but your amygdala thought you were in danger?

  _____

  _____

  _____

- Use the Mindfulness of Breath tools (Chapter 6) to calm your amygdala.

Tool 3-14: Pass the marble

BACKGROUND: When the amygdala gets activated by danger, fear, or anger, the information flow in the brain between the amygdala and the PFC is impaired. Information destined for the prefrontal cortex gets derailed, and the PFC function is often impaired. This tool helps kids and teens understand what happens in their brain when their amygdala gets activated when they are afraid, worried, or angry. It shows how the PFC doesn't get the message it was supposed to and therefore can't do its job. Tool 25-2 provides another way to illustrate this concept for anger.

SKILL BUILDING: Explain to clients that when they are in danger, afraid, worried, or angry, their amygdala tries to keep them safe. When it gets turned on, messages that were supposed to be sent to the PFC don't always make it there. Therefore, when this happens, the things that the PFC is supposed to do don't work well such a paying attention, planning, organizing or just plain thinking clearly. Do the activity on Handout 3-14 to help clients understand this concept.

REFLECTION: Help clients reflect on what happens when they are in danger, are afraid, worried, or angry. Explore what happened to the message meant for the PFC when the amygdala was activated. Ask them if there has been a time when this has happened to them.

PASS THE MARBLE

- Use a small object such as a marble or coin and ask clients to pretend it is a message headed for the PFC. Ask them to pass the marble to each other in line or to you if not with a group.

- Place a bowl or cup at the end of the line to symbolize the PFC where the marble (message) is headed.

- Tell the last child in line to place the object in the bowl or cup = the PFC.

- Talk about what happened to the message. Did the PFC get the message? Will it be able to do its job?

- Do it again but this time have one of the kids pretend they are afraid or upset and have that child take the object out of the line and put the object on the floor instead of in the cup

- Talk about what happened to the 'message'. Was the PFC able to do its job?

Tool 3-15: The Insula – What's Happening Here?

BACKGROUND: The right anterior insula is involved in (among other things) interoception—the sensing of body states such as the state of the gut, the heart, and pain. Studies show that mindfulness changes the structure of the insula—specifically, the right anterior insula (Hölzel et al., 2007a). Greater right anterior insular gray matter volume correlates with increased accuracy in the subjective sense of the body and with negative emotional experience as well as with increased sustained attention. Knowing that mindfulness actually changes brain structure in positive ways helps older kids and teens understand the benefits and improves the chances they will practice mindfulness.

SKILL BUILDING: Use Handout 3-15 to introduce the insula, where it is in the brain (one on each side), and what it does for us. Explain that practicing mindfulness changes the actual structure of the insula, specifically the right insula which makes it work even better. Use Tool 3-16 to help clients practice taking their pulse which is one of the things the insula senses.

REFLECTION: Review with clients, what the insula does. Give specific examples they can relate to such as sensing when they have to use the bathroom, or increasing their heart rate and blood pressure when they exercise.

WHAT THE INSULA DOES

The insula is involved in:

- Interoception (sensing body states such as the state of the gut, heart, pain, etc.)
- Helping you know when you have to go to the bathroom
- Sensations of warmth or coldness on skin
- Body movement
- Self-awareness
- Vocalization and music
- Emotional awareness
- Risk, uncertainty, and anticipation
- Feelings of disgust
- Visual and auditory awareness of movement
- Time perception
- Attention
- Perceptual decision making
- Cognitive control and performance monitoring
- Blood pressure and heart beat regulation

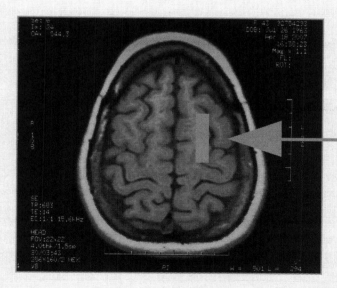

Right Anterior Insula

Tool 3-16: Take Your Pulse

BACKGROUND: Taking your pulse is a great way to illustrate one of the functions of the insula which is sensing body states such as heart beat and blood pressure. This tool helps kids and teens understand the function of the insula and teaches them a key core mindfulness skill they can use to calm down worry, anger, and stress.

SKILL BUILDING: Explain to clients that one important job of the insula is to sense their body such as when they have to go to the bathroom and when their heart beats. Explain what the pulse is and teach clients how to take their pulse using the guidelines on Handout 3-16. It is usually easier for kids and teens to locate and feel their pulse if it is beating faster and many won't find/feel it until it beats faster and harder. If they don't feel it while sitting still, have them run in place for 30 seconds or so and most will say, "oh, I feel it now". Even 3-4 year olds can usually feel their pulse with a little help after they run or jump up and down.

Explain that our pulse gets faster when we exercise or get angry, frightened or stressed. Encourage them to take their pulse during the day and notice when it is fast or slow. If they are angry or upset they can take their pulse and use the breathing techniques in Chapter 6 to calm down and help themselves feel better.

REFLECTION: Help clients reflect on what it was like to take their pulse. Was this a new experience for them? Did they have trouble finding it? Did it speed up and beat harder when they jogged in place? Were they able to slow it back down when they breathed slowly in and out? When might be a good time for them to take their pulse during the day? How could taking their pulse when they are upset help them calm down?

TAKING YOUR PULSE

- Interoception is one important job of the insula and includes the awareness of body states including the heartbeat. A simple way to understand this concept is to take your pulse.

- When our heart beats, we can feel it pumping blood. The way and rate at which the heart pumps blood is our pulse.

- There are two places where we can feel our pulse. First, we can take our first two fingers and place them on our wrist on the palm side of our arm. (Demonstrate this.) If you put your fingers there very gently and don't press down, you may feel as if something is lightly tapping on your fingers. Move your fingers around a little and sit quietly until you can feel it.

- The second place is on our neck. Take your first two fingers and place them on the front of your neck below your jaw and above your chest. Gently place them there and move them around until you feel the pulse.

- Let's make it easier to feel your pulse. Stand up. Now run in place.

- Now put your finger lightly on the side of your neck. Can you feel your pulse now? Can you count the beats?

- When you are angry, scared, revved up, stressed, or you have been exercising, your heart beats faster and it makes it easier to feel your pulse.

- Now sit back down. Breathe in slowly through your nose and gently blow out like you are blowing a huge bubble.

- Breathe in and out slowly again.

- Now take your pulse again. Can you feel it? Is it slower? Is it harder to feel?

- Now that you know how to take your pulse, you can tell if you need to calm down by taking it. You know how to calm down by paying attention to your breathing and taking a slow, deep belly breath and blowing it out slowly. Notice how your pulse slows as you become calm.

Tool 3-17: Journal About Your Security Guard and Your Conductor

BACKGROUND: Journaling is an effective way for kids and teens to process and integrate what they are learning. This tool provides prompts to encourage them to think about what their amygdala and prefrontal cortex do for them and what would happen if these weren't working properly.

SKILL BUILDING: Review with clients what jobs their amygdala and prefrontal cortex have. Use the journal prompts provided on Handout 3-17 to help them explore what these brain structures do and what would happen if they weren't doing their jobs. For young children who cannot write, be prepared to write down for them what they dictate to you. Encourage clients to draw pictures or use words whichever they prefer.

REFLECTION: Review the client's answers to the journal prompts and use their answers as a springboard for discussing the job of the amygdala and the prefrontal cortex.

JOURNAL ABOUT YOUR SECURITY GUARD AND YOUR CONDUCTOR

Journal Prompts:

- What job does your prefrontal cortex do?

- Why do we call the prefrontal cortex the "conductor"?

- List some times when your "conductor" was conducting.

- What happens when your "conductor" takes a break?

  Can't pay attention

  Can't make good decisions

  Impulsivity

  No motivation

  Poor choices

  Bad mood

  Losing things

- What happens to your "conductor" when your "security guard" warns DANGER?

- What job does your amygdala do?

- Why do we call the amygdala the "security guard"?

- List some times when your "security guard" was on duty.

- Name a time when your amygdala kept you safe.

- What would happen if you were in danger but your "security guard" was off duty?

Picture Prompts

- Draw a picture of your prefrontal cortex.

- Draw a picture of your "conductor".

- Draw a picture of your "conductor" helping you pay attention.

- Draw a picture of your amygdala.

- Draw a picture of your "security guard."

- Draw a picture of your "security guard" keeping you safe.

TOOLS FOR EASY WAYS TO ENVISION BRAIN ANATOMY

Tool 3-18: Hand Model of the Brain

BACKGROUND: Using a hand model of the brain can help kids and teens visualize and understand the structure and function of the brain. There are two helpful options for using the hands as a model for brain structure: a two-fisted model and a model described by Dan Siegel in his book *Mindsight* (Siegel, 2010).

SKILL BUILDING: Use Handouts 3-18-1 and 3-18-2 containing hand models for understanding the brain to give clients a "handy" way to conceptualize the areas of the brain. Show them the different areas of the brain using each model using their own hands.

REFLECTION: Ask the client to practice describing the basic structure of the brain by using each of the hand models. You might suggest they use Siegel's hand model of the brain to illustrate what happens when they get upset, angry, afraid, or stressed by having them raise their fingers to simulate "flipping their lid." Then have them lower their fingers to simulate the prefrontal cortex regaining control of their limbic system and emotions.

SIEGEL'S HAND MODEL OF THE BRAIN

PreFrontal Cortex

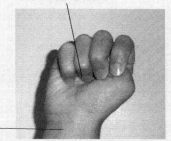 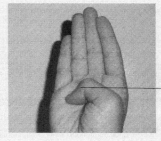

Limbic System

Brain Stem

- Hold up each hand with the thumb in the middle of the palm and the fingers curled over the top of the thumb.

- The face is in the front of the knuckles and the back of the head is toward the back of the hand.

- The wrist represents the spinal cord and the base of the hand the brain stem.

- The thumb represents the location of the limbic system where the amydgala is located.

- The ends of the fingers (from the fingernails to first knuckle) represent the prefrontal cortex.

- The second knuckle represents the cerebral cortex.

- The third knuckle represents the parietal lobes where sensory integration occurs.

- The fingers curled over the thumb illustrate how the prefrontal cortex communicates with most of the brain and particularly helps to control the limbic system. Siegel explains that when we are angry or stressed, the prefrontal cortex loses control of the limbic system, which he illustrates by raising the fingers up straight. He calls this "flipping your lid."

TWO-FISTED MODEL OF THE BRAIN

This brain model uses two closed fists facing each other with thumbs facing you.

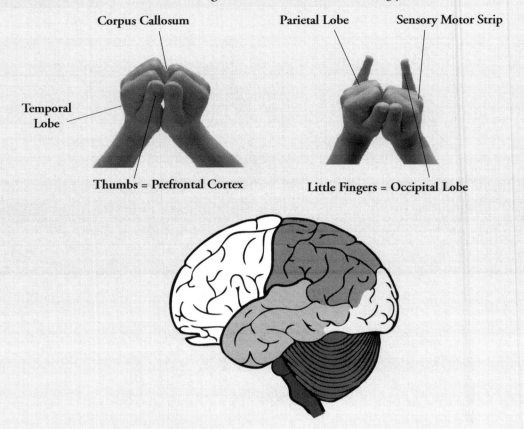

- Make each hand into a fist. Hold the fists next to each other with fingernails touching and the thumbs facing you. The thumbs represent the frontal lobe of the brain. This is where the "conductor" for your brain is located, the area where wise decisions are made. This is also associated with paying attention, reasoning, planning, emotions, and problem solving.

- Lift the little fingers up. These represent the occipital lobe where visual processing takes place.

- Where the knuckles touch represents the corpus callosum, the large nerve fiber connecting the right and left sides of the brain, which allows information to be transferred between the lobes.

- The top of the ring fingers represents the parietal lobes of the brain where sensory processing occurs—touch, sound—and where body perception occurs.

- From one side to the other between the middle and ring fingers represents the sensory motor strip, which divides the front motor cortex from the back sensory cortex.

- Move the hands up beside your head and cup your ears. The knuckles are the outside of the brain model and correspond to the temporal lobes where the amygdala and hippocampus reside. The temporal lobes process auditory information, memory, emotional responses, and visual perception.

Tool 3-19: Neurons—Hand-to-Elbow Model

BACKGROUND: Information in the brain (in the form of electrochemical signals) flows across neurons from the dendrites along the axon out to nerve endings, and across the synapse to the next dendrite. This tool gives kids and teens a basic, concrete way to understand how information flows across the neurons and from neuron to neuron.

SKILL BUILDING:

- Review Handout 3-19 with your client. Explain the flow of information from the dendrites (hand) along the axon (arm) out the nerve ending (elbow) across the synapse (gap) to the next dendrite (hand). Ask the client to use their hand and arm to show the different parts of the neuron.

- Ask clients to pass a coin to each other (or to you, if they are alone) as described in the handout. Ask them what happens as they pass it over and over again.

- Ask them what increases when something is practiced.

REFLECTION: This tool provides a great way to understand the flow of information at the neuronal level of the brain in a way kids and teens can understand. Discuss the fact that the flow gets faster and more efficient the more it happens—as they probably noticed when they did the exercise—with practice. Ask them for examples of when they learned something by practicing it.

THE HAND/ARM MODEL OF A NEURON

How Messages Flow Through Neurons

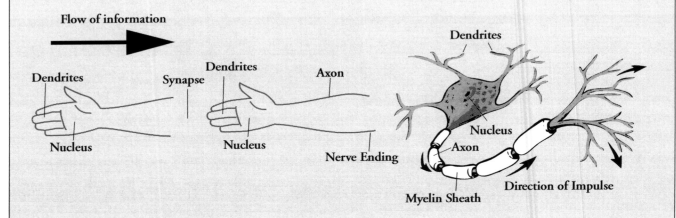

- Nerve cells, or neurons, carry messages through electrochemical impulses or signals. As neurons fire, the number and size of dendrites increase.
- Dendrites are branched projections of a neuron that conduct electrochemical information received from other neural cells to the cell body from which the dendrites project.
- Axons are long projections from a neuron that conduct electrical impulses away from the cell body to the nerve endings.
- Nerve endings transmit information to other neurons across the synapse.
- The synapse permits a neuron to pass an electrical or chemical signal to another cell.

Exercise – The flow of information across a neuron

- Pretend your left hand has dendrites, which receive messages.
- Your body is the cell body.
- Your right arm is the axon.
- Your right hand represents nerve endings.
- Pretend a coin (rock, pencil, eraser) is the message.
- Place the coin in your left hand, and then pass it to your right hand.

Exercise – The flow of information between neurons

- If in a group, stand in line. If there are only two people, pass back and forth as below.
- Pass the "message" to the next person across the gap between your hands (the synapse) as above.
- Does this get easier and faster with practice?
- How is that like the brain?

Tool 3-20: Draw a Picture of Your Brain in Your Journal

BACKGROUND: Now that clients have learned about the prefrontal cortex, the amygdala, and the insula, it is time to put all the pieces together where they go in the brain.

SKILL BUILDING: Use Handout 3-20 to show clients the names and locations of some of the basic brain structures. Then ask them to draw a picture of their brain and label the basic brain structures. Ask them to list what the different brain structures do. Encourage them to reference the previous handouts on brain structure as needed.

REFLECTION: Review the functions of the brain structures relevant to mindfulness. Review the client's picture. Answer their questions and clarify the location and function of the brain structures.

DRAW A PICTURE OF YOUR BRAIN IN YOUR JOURNAL

Draw a line between the structure and the function below.

Structures	Functions
Prefrontal Cortex	Security Guard
Amygdala	Sensory Integration
Insula	Visual Processing
Parietal Lobes	Conductor
Occipital Lobes	Auditory Processing
Temporal Lobes	Interoception

Draw a line from the name of the structure in the list above to its location on this brain.

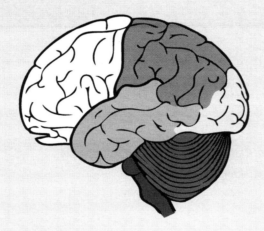

Draw a picture of your brain in your journal. Include the structures listed above.

TOOLS FOR EXPLAINING THE RESEARCH

Tool 3-21: Explain Mindfulness Research to Parents and to Kids and Teens

BACKGROUND: There is a small but significant amount of research on the benefits of mindfulness for kids and teens. Teens are more likely to ask "what's in it for me" than younger children but it is important to help kids, teens and their parents understand why mindfulness is worth learning and practicing. This tool provides a quick summary of the research, which gives mindfulness more credibility and helps clients and their parents understand why they should incorporate it into their lives.

SKILL BUILDING: Review research Handout 3-21 to give yourself a solid base of information about how mindfulness might benefit your client. Review the research with parents. Share the benefits with clients as appropriate to their age and developmental level. Ask the older child or teen client to make a list of the benefits that mindfulness research proves might help them.

REFLECTION: At this point some clients or their parents may still be struggling to understand the benefits of mindfulness and "what's in it for me/my child?" This tool shows them the broad range of benefits of mindfulness. Help clients and parents begin to relate how benefits gained from mindfulness practice apply to their child's life and the issues they are dealing with. Ask them how they would feel if the problems for which they are seeking treatment were resolved.

SUMMARY OF MINDFULNESS RESEARCH FOR KIDS AND TEENS

Benefits Suggested By Research

- Increased emotional regulation
- Increased social skills
- Increased ability to orient attention
- Increased working memory and planning and organization
- Increased self esteem
- Increased sense of calmness, relaxation, and self-acceptance.

- Increased quality of sleep
- Decreased test anxiety
- Decreased ADHD behaviors- hyperactivity and impulsivity
- Decreased negative affect/emotions
- Decreased anxiety, decreased depression
- Fewer conduct and anger management problems (Burke, 2009)

Sample of Mindfulness Research

- A feasibility study titled "Mindfulness meditation training in adults and adolescents with ADHD" published in the *Journal of Attention Disorders* found that meditation led to **improvements in self-reported ADHD symptoms and test performance on tasks measuring attention and cognitive inhibition. Improvements in anxiety and depressive symptoms** so common in people with ADHD were also observed (Zylowska, et al., 2008).

- A randomized clinical trial titled "Mindfulness-based stress reduction for the treatment of adolescent psychiatric outpatients" published in *Social Cognitive and Affective Neuroscience*, included eight weekly 2-hour classes training in the following formal mindfulness practices: body scan meditation, sitting meditation, and Hatha yoga. **Significant improvements were noted in state and trait anxiety; perceived stress; self-esteem; somatic complaints; obsessive – compulsive behaviors; interpersonal sensitivity; and depressive symptoms.** (Hotzel, et al., 2007)

- A randomized trial of mindfulness-based cognitive therapy for children: Promoting mindful attention to enhance social-emotional resiliency in children, published in *The Journal of Child and Family Studies*. Results showed **improved attention, behavior and anxiety.** (Semple, et al, 2010).

- The effects of a mindfulness-based education program on pre- and early adolescents' well-being and social and emotional competence published in *Mindfulness*. Study found **improvements in self-reported optimism, positive affect, and externalizing behavior, and improvements for self-concept, with more positive benefits for preadolescents than early adolescents.** (Schonert-Reich, 2010).

- The effectiveness of mindfulness training for children with ADHD and mindful parenting for their parents published in *The Journal of Child and Family Studies*. There was a **significant reduction of parent-rated ADHD behavior** of themselves and their child and a significant **increase of mindful awareness**. (van de Oord, et al., 2012).

- Mindfulness-based approaches with children and adolescents: A preliminary review of current research in an emergent field published in *The Journal of Child and Family Studies*. **This article reviews 15 studies with kids and teens ages 4 – 18.** (Burke, 2009)

- Mindfulness training for elementary school students: The attention academy, published in *The Journal of Applied School Psychology. This study* showed **significant differences on three attentional measures** between students who did and did not participate in mindfulness practice training. (Napoli, 2005)

- School based Inner Kids program: "Effects of mindful awareness practices on executive functions in elementary school children" published in *Journal of Applied School Psychology* found **improved behavioral regulation, metacognition, and overall global executive control.** (Flook, et al., 2010).

Tool 3-22: Connect Mindfulness Research with Benefits for Client's Condition

BACKGROUND: Despite the fact that many mindfulness practitioners resist setting an intention for any specific result from practicing mindfulness, I have found that helping the client connect the benefit with the practice makes them much more likely to incorporate mindfulness into their lives. Best practice for clinicians also guides us to define treatment goals and track progress which this tool assists in doing.

Kids tend to accept and participate in mindfulness more readily than some teens who need more understanding of "what's in it for me" for them to "buy into it". See Tool 5-13 for help with this issue. Use this tool to help older kids, teens and parents understand how the scientific research suggests that practicing mindfulness might help their specific condition.

SKILL BUILDING: With the client and parent, look through the Summary of Mindfulness Research in Handout 3-21 and find some that pertain to the condition(s) the client is dealing with. Help them understand how mindfulness practice might be beneficial for them. Ask them if they would be willing to learn some mindfulness exercises like those done in the studies if it would decrease their symptoms. This helps them make a commitment to giving this a try. Use language appropriate to the age of the child. Simplify this step for very young children by using words like "relax our bodies", "calm our busy brains", "smile more", "help us worry less or be less afraid", "feel happier".

REFLECTION: Explore client and parent understanding of how mindfulness may be helpful to them. Answer questions. Give examples from research and from your practice. This is a good time to write treatment goals with the older child or with the parent. List the specific symptoms they want to improve that mindfulness might positively impact. See Tools 27-1 and 27-2 for guidance on defining treatment goals and tracking progress. This sets up the process for monitoring progress and helps ensure accountability during the therapeutic process.

Tool 3-23: Journal About Why Mindfulness Helps People with Your Condition

BACKGROUND: Journaling about what the client would like to change that mindfulness could help with will clarify their understanding of what benefits they might experience from mindfulness.

SKILL BUILDING: Ask clients to respond to the journal prompts on Handout 3-23. Younger kids may draw or dictate their answers for you to write. This can also be done with the parent helping the child.

REFLECTION: Review the client's journal entries with them. Help them connect their condition with the mindfulness research and neurobiology that pertains to their condition in age appropriate language. Provide suggestions about how mindfulness might help them. Give them some examples from your practice or your reading about others who have the same condition and who have been helped with mindfulness. Address any resistance or obstacles that they present (Tool 5-7).

JOURNAL ABOUT WHY MINDFULNESS HELPS PEOPLE WITH YOUR CONDITION

Journal Prompts:

- List the conditions you need help with, such as depression, anxiety, concentration, hyperactivity, anger, well-being, sleep, stress, self-confidence, getting along with other kids, etc.

- What research show that mindfulness helpts your condition?

- List the parts of the brain that mindfulness affects that may help with your condition.

- Do you know anyone who practices mindfulness and, if yes, how does being mindful help them?

- What would keep you from using mindfulness?

- Do you believe mindfulness can help you?

- How would you feel if mindfulness improved the symptoms of your condition?

- How would you feel if you could concentrate better at school?

- How would you feel if your teacher didn't yell at you for being out of your seat?

- How would you feel if you liked yourself better?

- How would you feel if you could stop worrying?

- How would you feel if you felt confident enough to ask someone on a date?

- How would you feel if you could get your homework done faster?

- How would you feel if you could fall asleep faster at night?

- Use questions related to why the client is in treatment.

Picture Prompts

- Draw a picture that shows the change you want.

- Draw a picture of what will be different for you if you practice mindfulness.

Chapter 4
Tools to Increase Client Use of Mindfulness at Home

Tool 4-1: How to Find a Comfortable Position

BACKGROUND: When practicing a sitting mindfulness meditation, the client will be maintaining their physical position for anywhere from a few minutes to 20 minutes. Therefore it is important to help them find a position they can comfortably maintain for the duration of their practice. Discomfort will distract them from their meditation. Positions range from a basic sitting position in a chair to the Full Lotus position. Some kids and teens may find it impossible to sit for any length of time and in this case a walking or movement meditation may be most suitable. This tool introduces the client to several possible positions that work best for kids and teens and helps them select the one(s) that work best for them. The position of the hands is also included in this tool. Note that many of the skills included in this workbook do not require the client to sit still.

SKILL BUILDING: Review Handouts 4-1-1 and 4-1-2 with the client, show them how to do each position, watch them do it, and make suggestions to help them get comfortable. Kids are usually most comfortable sitting cross legged on the floor or lying on their back with arms and legs uncrossed. Teens may like to sit on a cushion or meditation stool when sitting cross legged. Active kids and teens may prefer a walking or movement option. Ask them to try each position while practicing various mindfulness skills. Help them select the position that works best for them.

CASE EXAMPLE:
An extremely active 4 year-old learned what we called the 'meditation pose', which was to touch his middle fingers to his thumbs (see Healing Mudra on Handout 4-1-2) with his hands palms up on his thighs. Any time he started getting rambunctious I would cue him with 'meditation pose' and he would laugh and pop right into position, calm down instantly, and sit quietly. He thought it was really fun and it was visibly calming his body. The more we practiced this the longer he was able to hold the position and keep his body still.

REFLECTION: Assist the client in finding the position(s) that works best for them. Observe them and notice in which position they are the stillest. After they try each position, ask them what they noticed about their body. Was it comfortable? Were they able to relax? Was it hard to stay in that position? Did they have trouble staying still? Did they have the urge to change positions? Also ask them what they noticed about their mindfulness in each position. Were they distracted by body sensations? Were they able to stay focused on their intended mindfulness target such as breath? Did their hand position change anything about their practice? How did the walking meditation impact their mindfulness?

POSITIONS FOR MINDFULNESS MEDITATION PRACTICE

Sitting in a Chair

Sit in a chair with feet flat on the floor, back straight, and palms turned upward resting lightly on your lap or with hands resting on your belly. You may lean back against the back of the chair for support as long as you keep your back straight.

Lying Down

Lie flat on your back with arms and legs uncrossed, arms lying by your side with palms up or with hands resting lightly on your belly. You may place a pillow under your head and perhaps under your knees for comfort.

Sitting with Crossed Legs

Sit with legs crossed, palms face up on your knees. You may sit on a small pillow or meditation stool for comfort.

Full Lotus Position

The Lotus Position is the ultimate meditation pose. It requires flexibility in the hips and knees and can take years of practice to attain. Sit with both knees folded with each foot placed up on the thighs and palms placed upward on the thighs. Do not worry if you cannot do this. Just use the cross-legged position instead. But if you can, go for it. Kids are often flexible enough to use this position.

Walking

Walk with arms swinging freely at your sides, body upright, eyes looking ahead, hands unclenched, and shoulders relaxed.

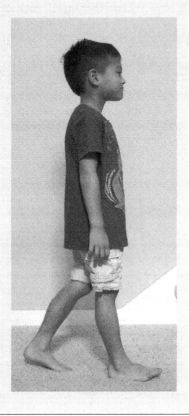

HAND POSITIONS

Touch thumb and forefinger in a circle

Chin or Pran Mudra: Join the thumb and forefinger on each of both hands as a zero. Extend the rest of the fingers, with the middle finger touching the non-folded part of the forefinger. Place the hands palms-up on the thighs while sitting.

Touch thumb and middle finger together in a circle

Healing Mudra: Join thumb and middle finger to form a circle. Extend the rest of the fingers. Place the hands palms-up on the thighs while sitting.

Tool 4-2: How to Find a Time That Works and Schedule It

BACKGROUND: Most people find that the best way to ensure they incorporate mindfulness into their daily life is to set aside a specific time each day to practice. "Fitting it in" rarely works for most people. This applies to formal sitting mindfulness meditation as well as mindfulness practices that can be integrated into daily activities. Since kids are rarely in charge of their schedule enlist their parents to remind them to practice. Most teens will need help either from a parent reminder or by helping them to schedule practice in their planner. There is no one best time to practice. Some people prefer first thing in the morning before the daily demands start as a way to set up for a great day. Others prefer the end of the day as a way to "unwind" before sleep. Many mindfulness skills can be incorporated into the day's activities. The goal of this tool is to help clients deliberately choose a time and commit to making it work for them.

SKILL BUILDING:

Mindfulness Practice During Daily Activities

One goal of teaching mindfulness skills to kids and teens is to teach them skills they can use whenever they need them through the day to calm anxiety, lower stress levels, calm down anger or hyperactivity, or concentrate better. Explain to your client that many of the mindfulness tools in this workbook are designed to be incorporated while doing the activities of the day. For example, the Awareness of Surroundings (Tools 7-1 and 7-2) can be used at any time but is particularly helpful upon arrival in a new environment and after transitions such as when they get to school or change classes. You will be teaching this skill to your client later on. But for now tell them to stop, breathe, and notice their surroundings periodically throughout their day. Use Handout 4-2 to help them choose when they will practice this tool.

The Mindfulness of Tasks Tools (Chapter 18) are specifically designed to be practiced while doing a task. This task might be doing homework, eating, doing chores, taking a shower, using the restroom, brushing teeth, doing a school project, texting friends, using the computer or any commonly performed task at home or in school. Help your client use the handout to pick two tasks during which they will intend to be mindful using the Mindfulness of Tasks tool. These can be scheduled throughout their day.

Formal Sitting Mindfulness Meditations

Kids typically need parental guidance to set aside time for doing the more formal sitting mindfulness skills. Older teens might be able to schedule time for practice. Ask your client, or their parent, to think about their current daily schedule. Encourage parents to do these skills with their kids. You might need to suggest they use a planner and schedule the time. Help them find a time that they could set aside 10 to 15 minutes at the same time every day. For some people this might be first thing in the morning before they start their morning routine. For others this might be after school or before or after dinner. Teens may find that taking a break for themselves during their lunchtime or a study hall works well. Another favorite time is at night just before going to bed when the household is settled in for the night. Ask them to choose a time and fill it in on Handout 4-2.

It may be that the only time kids practice these more formal skills is in session or in a group setting. Giving them a CD or mp3 containing guided mindfulness skills can also increase the chance that they will practice. Visit www.TheBrainLady.com for some great options.

REFLECTION: Help your client deliberately think about when they will incorporate mindfulness into their day and commit to doing it then. This will greatly increase the chances that they will actually practice it. At each session, ask them when they practiced and help them fine-tune the best time for them. Many clients will raise objections, stating that they simply don't have time. Use Tool 5-7a to help them overcome this objection.

SCHEDULING TIME TO PRACTICE MINDFULNESS

Mindfulness Practice During Daily Activities

- Many of the mindfulness tools are designed to be incorporated as you go through the activities of your day. For example, Mindfulness of Surroundings (Tools 7-1 and 7-2) can be used at any time but is particularly helpful when you:
  - arrive in a new environment
  - get to school or work for older teens
  - change classes
  - get home from school
  - climb in the car
  - walk into the house
  - go into a store
  - go anyplace else during the day
  - feel stressed or overwhelmed
  - I intend to be mindful of my surroundings in these two places:
    1.) _____ 2.) _____

- The Mindfulness of Tasks Mindfulness Skill (Chapter 18) is specifically designed to be practiced while you are doing a task. This task might be:
  - doing homework
  - doing schoolwork during class
  - eating
  - doing a chore
  - playing a game
  - working on the computer
  - brushing your teeth
  - taking a shower or using the restroom
  - driving for older teens – keeps them safer
  - exercising
  - any task you commonly perform
  - I intend to be mindful while doing these two tasks every day:
    1.) _____ 2.) _____

Formal Sitting Mindfulness Meditations

- Think about your current daily schedule. Ask parents to participate.

- Find a time to set aside 5 to 15 minutes at the same time every day.
  - first thing in the morning before you start your morning routine
  - during lunchtime
  - during study hall
  - during a rest time at school or home
  - after school
  - before or after dinner
  - before homework
  - at night just before going to bed when the household is settled in for the night
  - I intend to practice my formal sitting mindfulness at: _____ o'clock each day.

Tool 4-3: How to Find a Place for Core Practice

BACKGROUND: Setting aside a specific location for regularly scheduled core sitting meditation practice helps the client associate that place with mindfulness, which helps them relax into the meditation more quickly. Carefully choosing a place can ensure both comfort and fewer distractions. Generally, this will make it easier to practice. While it is certainly acceptable to practice anywhere and for some clients this works great, setting up a suitable space is very important for most clients. Encourage parents to help with this.

SKILL BUILDING: Use Handout 4-3 to help your client and their parent make a list of potential practice locations. Help them identify and eliminate potential sources of distraction such as phones, TVs, computers, street noise, family demands, and uncomfortable temperature. Assist them in setting up a space that is calming, soothing, and pleasing to them.

REFLECTION: Now that your client (with the assistance of their parent) has gone through the process of choosing and setting up a space, ask them how it is working out for them. Help them fine-tune it, if necessary. If they have resisted doing this step and are not having success with their practice, encourage them to complete this step to see for themselves how it changes their practice.

FIND A PLACE FOR CORE MINDFULNESS PRACTICE

- List the elements of a suitable place. This might include:
  - quiet
  - comfortable temperature
  - soothing lighting
  - calming décor
  - pictures that are soothing
  - free of distractions such as phones, TV, computer, family demands, noise
  - easily accessible
  - convenient
  - inside
  - outside in a natural setting
  - candles or incense for older teens (avoid if allergic)
  - Make a list of possible locations for your practice.

- Examples
  - Dining room chair
  - Lying on a rug
  - Sitting on the floor (may use cushion)
  - Lying on the couch
  - Sitting on the bottom step of the stairs
  - Sitting at a desk
  - In the bathtub
  - In a parked car
  - In bed right before sleep or before you get up in the AM
  - On a bus or train (use headphones to avoid noise distraction)
  - Chaise lounge outside
  - Outside on the deck, porch or patio
  - On a blanket on the grass or beach
  - In a state or national park
  - On the beach
- Make a list of possible locations for your practice. List the pros and cons of each place
  - Location   Pros   Cons

Tool 4-4: How to Incorporate Mindfulness into Daily Activities

BACKGROUND: Mindfulness practice will never be effective if clients don't actually do it. Although kids and teens often become quite skilled at being mindful, they may still need to be reminded to practice. Depending on the child's age, maturity level, and cognitive level, parental involvement may be necessary. Many kids and teens feel so good when they practice mindfulness that they will practice on their own. Many of my clients have spontaneously taught a friend or parent the skills they have learned.

This workbook provides many mindfulness tools that can be incorporated directly into the daily life of kids and teens. Some others are considered formal sitting meditations. Many others are mindfulness tools that the client can use as they do tasks throughout the day. One significant goal of mindfulness is to increase "awareness of awareness" on a moment-to-moment basis throughout the day. The more formal sitting mindfulness meditation skills train this "awareness of awareness" skill. This tool helps kids and teen apply this skill actively throughout the day using tools such as Mindfulness of Breath (Chapter 6), Mindfulness of Surroundings (Tools 7-1 and 7-2), Mindfulness of Tasks (Tools 18-1 and 18-2), Mindful Motion (Chapter 13) and Mindfulness of Intention (Tools 20-1 and 20-2).

SKILL BUILDING: For some non-supportive or chaotic family situations, the practice the client does with you in session may be the only time they practice. Accept this. They will still benefit from mindfulness even with less frequent practice. And they may incorporate mindfulness automatically into their day.

Encourage the client to incorporate mindfulness practice into their daily life.

- Help them establish a **time and place** for regular sitting practice.
- As you teach your client the specific mindfulness tools, help them **choose styles** that work best for them.
- Show them how to **practice mindfulness outside of sitting meditations.**
    - Mindfulness of Breath (Chapter 6)
    - Present Moment Awareness (Chapter 7)
    - Mindfulness of Tasks (Chapter 18)
    - Mindfulness of Intention (Chapter 20)
    - Mindfulness of Motion (Chapter 13)
- **Start small** and gradually increase little by little.
- **Help them commit** to the practice.
- Explain how and why to **give practice priority**.
- Teach them or their parent how to **monitor progress** (Chapter 27).

REFLECTION: Discuss the importance of incorporating mindfulness into everyday life. Ask the client when they used both sitting and active mindfulness. Ask them when they might have used it but didn't. Explore their commitment to using mindfulness. Discuss what they expect to get out of it. Explore the importance of giving it priority. Did they teach anyone else what they were doing?

Tool 4-5: Parental Involvement

BACKGROUND: Depending on age, maturity level, and cognitive functioning, many kids and teens will need the support and encouragement of their parent to incorporate mindfulness practice into their daily lives. Therefore, it is important to make every effort to involve the parent whenever possible. See Tool 2-1 for more general guidance on overall parental involvement.

SKILL BUILDING: Assess the ability of the client to self-motivate and practice mindfulness on their own. This varies dramatically from child to child and teen to teen. Certainly, younger kids and kids and teens with cognitive, emotional and behavioral challenges need more parental involvement. Encourage parents to attend some parent guidance sessions and teach them some basic mindfulness skills. Review how mindfulness may help their child and how helpful it is to practice at home. Explore how they can help their child or teen increase home practice. Encourage parents to practice with their child. Doing so will double or triple the positive effect on the family.

In some cases parent involvement is not possible. In that case explore the possibility of another person in the child or teen's life who could provide the support and encouragement to practice such as a teacher, coach, or other professionals working with the family. If no one can be identified for this role, trust that the mindfulness practice the child or teen does with you will still help them enormously.

REFLECTION: Does the child or teen need parental support? Is the parent willing and able to participate? If not, what other resources exist for this child, teen, and family? How might you provide the guidance needed when the parent cannot be involved?

Tool 4-6: Journaling About Your Plans to Use Mindfulness

BACKGROUND: As with any new practice it is important to clarify and understand personal expectations and commitment. This journaling tool will help kids and teens explore their personal motivation and commitment to this work.

SKILL BUILDING: Ask your client to review the journal prompts in Handout 4-6 and to respond to as many as they can. Explain that starting any new practice requires commitment, time, and energy and that these journal prompts will help them clarify their commitment and intention. For younger clients, write their answers for them or encourage them to draw pictures.

REFLECTION: Review client answers to the journal prompts with them. Discuss their answers and their commitment to learning and practicing mindfulness. Address any obstacles or resistance using Tool 5-7. Encourage them and praise their efforts.

JOURNALING ABOUT YOUR PLANS TO USE MINDFULNESS

Journal Prompts:

- Why do you want to learn and use mindfulness skills?

- What do you want mindfulness practice to help you with?

- When have you been mindful this week?

- Where and when will you practice sitting mindfulness meditation?

- What questions do you have about doing this practice?

- Does anything about learning mindfulness worry you?

- What physical positions work best for you?

- How much time are you willing to commit to mindfulness practice?

- How important is this practice to you?

- What would you be willing to give up doing in order to make time to practice?

- What would you rather be doing?

- Are you surprised that there is more to mindfulness than sitting meditations?

- What are you most looking forward to about this practice?

Picture Prompts

- Draw a picture of yourself being mindful.

- Draw a place where you can be mindful.

Chapter 5
Tools for Teaching Mindfulness Basics

EXPLAINING THE BASIC PROCESS OF MINDFULNESS

Tool 5-1: Notice, Accept, Dismiss, Return

BACKGROUND: The basic process of mindfulness involves setting an intention about what to pay attention to (Tool 3-5) and returning your attention to this when you notice that your mind has wandered. This tool provides two ways to explain this process.

SKILL BUILDING: Explain to clients that it is normal for thoughts to wander. Engage them in a discussion about what distracts them and when they notice they aren't paying attention to what they are supposed to pay attention to. Discuss how this happens in school, while doing homework, when they are bored or anxious, while talking with people and when there are distractions around them vying for their attention. Ask them how they get back on task. This is the basic process that kids and teens with ADHD struggle with all day every day. Hence it is a great tool for them to practice to improve their ability to pay attention.

Mindfulness is not about having no thoughts. Rather it is about noticing when you are not paying attention to what you've chosen to pay attention to, accepting without judgment that your mind has wandered, dismissing whatever thought, feeling, physical sensation or external event has distracted you, and then returning your attention to what you are supposed to be paying attention to.

Review Handout 5-1 with clients for two easy ways to learn this process.

REFLECTION: Explore with your client how they are doing with this process. How does it feel to know that being mindful does not mean they have an empty mind? Are they able to notice thoughts as they arise? What emotions or physical sensations have they noticed during practice? What distracts them? When were they distracted? How are they returning their attention to their target of attention? When did they use this process? Is it getting easier with practice?

BASIC PROCESS OF MINDFULNESS

Explain the basic process of mindfulness:

1. **Decide** what to pay attention to

2. **Notice** when they aren't paying attention to it

3. **Accept** without judgment that they have been distracted

4. **Dismiss** whatever has distracted them

5. **Return** their attention to what they are supposed to be paying attention to

Another easy way to remember this process is with the acronym **SOLAR**: Stop. Observe the thought without judgment. Let the thought go without engaging in it. And Return your attention to your chosen target. Ask the client to repeat this process using different rhythms and clap hands to keep the beat. For younger children add motions to this: Stop – raise their hand in a stop motion; Observe – put their hands above their eyes and look around; Let it go – pretend they are holding a butterfly in their hand and they open their hand and let it go; And – make a plus sign with their fingers; Return – walk ahead two steps, turn around and return.

1. Stop

2. Observe

3. Let It Go

4. And

5. Return

DOING THE EXERCISES WITH YOUR CLIENT

Tool 5-2: Find an Opening to Introduce Concept in Session

BACKGROUND: Mindfulness practice is a whole new concept to most kids and teens. Knowing when and how to introduce mindfulness skills to the client in session so that they embrace them can be tricky. This tool provides guidance on how to comfortably and appropriately introduce mindfulness concepts.

SKILL BUILDING: First and foremost you need to practice mindfulness yourself before teaching it to your clients. Your own practice as well as familiarity with the mindfulness research will ensure that you recognize when issues that could benefit from mindfulness practice present themselves in session. Let clients know how mindfulness practice has helped you or other clients with issues like theirs.

With individual clients, simply integrate mindfulness skills into your work with them. Look for an opening to present itself during a session where you can suggest that mindfulness skills might help the client with a particular condition. With kids you might not even need to explain that what you are teaching them is a mindfulness skill but often, doing so will help them understand it better. For example, if a client is experiencing anxiety, tell them you would like to show them a way to help them lower and gain control over their anxiety and then teach them basic relaxation breathing (Tool 6-4) , to belly breathe (Tool 6-5), or to change the channel (Tool 14-4). Or lead them in a progressive relaxation meditation or recommend they listen to a meditation CD. If they have trouble concentrating, teach them the SOLAR concept to train themselves to stay on task (Tool 5-1). If they are hyperactive use the skills for helping ADHD in Chapter 23. Mindfulness will help clients with most issues so you will find plenty of opportunities to introduce it. Review Section IV for ideas on how to use mindfulness to treat specific disorders.

Depending on the client, you may tell them you think they could benefit from learning mindfulness skills, or you might just teach them individual skills without necessarily calling it mindfulness or meditation. The word "meditation" often puts people off as they picture sitting still for long periods and feel they could never do that. They may not realize that they can incorporate mindfulness right into their day as they walk, do school work, or do their chores.

Obviously it's easier to introduce mindfulness if you are facilitating a "mindfulness or meditation" group as the clients already know the focus of the group. Other types of groups also benefit from mindfulness. Talk to the group participants about incorporating mindfulness skills into the group session. Group therapy and Social skills groups are excellent places to teach mindfulness.

REFLECTION: How did your client react when you introduced mindfulness? Did they object? If so, review the section on how to overcome obstacles and resistance (Tools 5-6 through 5-8). What did they like about it? How was it helpful? Are they willing to learn more skills? Will they agree to practice at home or only in the session? Were you able to explain the benefits?

Tool 5-3: Assign Mindfulness Tool Practice

BACKGROUND: In order to achieve the most benefit from mindfulness, the skills must be practiced and incorporated into daily life. This tool reviews the process for encouraging clients to practice them at home.

SKILL BUILDING: Explain that in order to work best mindfulness skills need to be practiced and incorporated into the client's daily routine. After teaching any specific skill in session, encourage the client to practice it at home, at school or work (for teens). Ask them when they think they might do it and help them find time if they don't know. Discuss what might get in the way and options for overcoming obstacles (Tool 5-7). Help them brainstorm about when and where they can practice the skill. For example, if you are teaching Mindfulness of Surroundings (Tools 7-1 and 7-2), suggest they might stop, breathe, and notice their surroundings every day when they first arrive at school, or when they change classes or get home from school. Or if you are teaching Mindfulness of Tasks (Tools 18-1 and 18-2), pick a specific task during which they will practice mindfulness. This might be as simple as while brushing their teeth or making their bed or while doing homework. Choose something they do every day.

For kids and some teens it is necessary to explain to their parent the skill that's being assigned. This way, the parent can remind the client, encourage them and help them refine the skill.

One of my 9-year-old clients had trouble learning the relaxation and belly breaths. His mother was instrumental in reminding him to practice when he was not already feeling upset and then to use the skill when he needed to. She really helped him learn and practice the skill outside of the session until he used it on his own to calm himself. He even noticed that a classmate was having trouble and taught him how to breathe.

REFLECTION: Did the client understand how to do the skill? Were they willing to practice at home? Were you able to help them find a time and place for practice? How did you feel assigning them "homework"? Think about how you will feel if they don't follow through. How might they feel if they don't practice? Was their parent supportive? Can you provide them with enough practice time in session?

PROCESS WHAT HAPPENS WITH YOUR CLIENT

Tool 5-4: What Happened During and After Practice?

BACKGROUND: After assigning a specific skill for home practice, it is important to explore what happened when the client tried it. This helps them overcome obstacles and ensures they will find skills that work best for them. It will help their practice become more effective as you help them fine-tune it. It also provides opportunities for helping them explore their feelings and for helping them therapeutically. This tool provides guidance on how to help the client process their experience.

SKILL BUILDING: Review the skill that was assigned. Ask the client: "So, were you able to practice the skill?" If they were, then ask them: "When did you do it? What happened when you did it? How did it go? Did you feel like you were able to do it like we discussed or did you do it differently? How did you feel? Were you comfortable doing it? Did anything negative happen? What got in your way? How did it help? Do you have any questions about it? How can you adjust it to work better?"

Sadly, many clients will say, "No, I forgot to do it," or "I didn't have time," or any number of other excuses. That's okay. Use the Tool 5-7, to handle this situation. Most young kids won't be able to answer these questions. Ask the parent how things went when their child practiced. Find out if the parent was supportive.

REFLECTION: Help your client examine their overall experience doing the practice. Answer questions. Did they do it effectively? Help them fine-tune their practice depending on how it went. Suggest other skills that might work better for them.

Tool 5-5: What to Do if Client Didn't Practice?

BACKGROUND: Unfortunately, many clients will not follow through on their practice. They will say, "I forgot to do it," or "I didn't have time," or any number of other excuses. Their parent might not have assisted them. That's okay. This tool helps you handle the situation when the client didn't practice.

SKILL BUILDING: If the client did not practice the assigned skill, say, "That's okay. When might you have practiced the skill?" Then help them identify a time they might have done it. Explore why they didn't practice and what got in their way. If they forgot, ask them what they could do this week to remember. If they raised other objections, see Tools 5-7 for how to handle common objections. Be sure to do the assigned skill with them in session. Find out if the parent is encouraging and reminding them to practice.

Keep in mind that many kids and teens won't practice and that you will need to accept this fact without being critical or judgmental. In this case, simply reinforce the skills every time you meet with them and go back to previous skills when issues come up in session where they could have used the skill. For example, if you taught a child to 'change the channel' when they feel anxious and several weeks later they are experiencing a lot of anxiety, do the skill in the session and gently remind them to use it whenever they feel anxious. Remember that you are teaching skills and learning theory suggests that new skills need to be reviewed at least four times for them to be learned.

REFLECTION: Ask your client what prevented them from practicing. Explore how they are feeling about trying this skill. Explore their objections. Address their fears or concerns. Remind them of the benefits. Help them identify when they might have practiced and also when they were being mindful without realizing it. Explore parental involvement.

HOW TO IDENTIFY AND OVERCOME OBSTACLES AND RESISTANCE

Tool 5-6: How to Recognize Common Obstacles

BACKGROUND: As with learning any new skill, clients may experience resistance and encounter obstacles that prevent them from practicing. That's okay. This tool helps you be prepared for this to happen and helps you recognize it when it does.

SKILL BUILDING:

Some of the common obstacles include:

- I forgot.
- I didn't have time.
- It's too hard.
- I can't stay focused, so why bother?
- I don't know how to do it right.
- This doesn't work for me.
- I fell asleep.
- Mindfulness is for holy men.
- I feel silly doing this.
- It's boring.
- I don't see how this could possibly help me.
- My parent doesn't want me to do this.
- My parent was too busy to help me.

REFLECTION: Be prepared to hear about many obstacles that get in the way of the client's being able to practice. Sort of like "the dog ate my homework" excuse. The next step is to process these excuses with the client and/or their parent to help them resolve them. See Tool

5-7 for ideas on how to address each of these. Remember to encourage the client for what they did do and refrain from being critical or judgmental.

Tool 5-7 Address Objections with Client

BACKGROUND: Many clients will have trouble following through with mindfulness practice. This is especially true for teens and for kids whose parents are not involved. That's okay. This tool provides guidance on how to handle some common objections.

SKILL BUILDING:

a. I didn't have time - overscheduled.   It can be very difficult to practice reflection when schedules are too full. And yet, the stress created by rushing around can be lowered using mindfulness skills. Kids and teens are extremely busy these days. It is not unusual for clients to have after school activities, church activities, family commitments and sports. And, at first, teens may feel that mindfulness is a waste of time and they should use the time to get their homework done. Remind them that it doesn't take any time at all to practice being mindful while brushing teeth or taking a shower or driving. It just takes a small commitment to doing it and something to remind them to do it. Yes, the sitting meditations do take time, anywhere from a few minutes to 15 or 20 minutes. In order for the client to be willing to set aside the time, help them or their parent really understand what the likely benefits will be. Involving the parents in this step can ensure that they give this practice priority and help kids find time to be mindful.

b. I forgot.   Although many kids and teens will quickly incorporate mindfulness skills into their day, it is not unusual for them to forget to practice mindfulness as the busyness of life takes over. Review the benefits of mindfulness and help the client (and parent) make a commitment to practicing. Help them find a way to remind themselves to be mindful. Perhaps they can put a sticky note on the bathroom mirror or on their backpack or steering wheel for older teens. Help them set aside time on a regular basis and put it in their smartphone with an alarm to remind them.

c. I can't stay focused, so why bother?   Explain that it is perfectly normal for thoughts to wander. The goal is to notice those thoughts, dismiss them, and bring attention back to the mindfulness practice. Over and over again. This can be particularly difficult for a client with ADHD or anxiety. Reassure them that it gets easier with practice but even skilled mindfulness practitioners must still do this.

d. I don't know how to do it right, so it won't help.   Discuss how they are doing it and why they don't think it is right. Explain that there is no one "right" way to practice mindfulness. Help them find the ways that work best for them and that they feel confident doing.

e. This doesn't work for me.   Older kids and teens often say, "I've tried this before and it doesn't work for me." This is the opening for you to ask them what they have tried before and what happened when they did it. There are so many different ways to practice mindfulness it is highly unlikely that there aren't some that work for each client. The only mindfulness technique many clients have heard of is formal sitting meditation. They may have attempted to sit still for 20 minutes without thinking about anything and found this intolerable—especially if they are hyperactive or have trouble concentrating. That's okay. Explain about the other options and find some that suit the client. Start small and work up. With practice, wandering thoughts will refocus.

f. I fell asleep.   Some kids and teens fall asleep when they meditate. Many are exhausted, sleep-deprived, and running on empty, so it's no surprise that if they sit quietly for a few minutes and start to relax, they fall asleep. There are several ways to approach this. First, address why they are so tired and help them find ways to reduce their fatigue. This might include everything from helping them improve their sleep hygiene to encouraging them to take a nap. Teens tend to stay up way too late doing homework. Studies show they need 9 hours and 15 minutes of sleep. Rarely do teens get that much. Sleep can be negatively affected by ADHD, sleep, depression and anxiety and vice versa. Explore what is happening for this particular client.

The second way to approach this is to tell them that it's okay to sleep; that if they are that tired, then sleep is probably what they need most. For some, this takes the pressure off and, as they address their sleep deficit, they gradually become more able to stay awake.

The third approach is to help them make a commitment to staying awake while they meditate. Help them make this a priority. Perhaps they could do a walking or movement meditation instead of a sitting meditation so they don't fall asleep. Maybe they could choose a position that doesn't support sleeping such as kneeling or sitting on a chair with no back. Perhaps they can choose a time to meditate when they are not so tired.

g. It's for holy men and saints.   It's true that mindfulness meditation has its roots in Eastern traditions and Buddhism. But Jon Kabat-Zinn brought the skills and practice of mindfulness into the mainstream over 20 years ago. The mindfulness skills taught here are not based in religion and are practiced by those of any or no faith. They can be used in a religious context, but the approach we use for clients is non-secular. This might be a great time to explore why holy men and saints were mindful and how the client might get some of the same benefits they did.

h. I feel embarrassed doing this.   Many kids and teens feel self-conscious sitting, closing their eyes, and doing the mindfulness practice. Explore what feels embarrassing about it and options for making them feel more comfortable. One option is to do it with them in session. Another is to help them find a private place to practice so they avoid embarrassment or judgment. Sometimes it helps to simply let them know that you won't be staring at them.

i. It's boring.   Many clients report that they feel bored when they first try to meditate. That's okay. Explore options for making their practice less boring. This might include trying a different mindfulness skill or finding an interesting focus for their attention. Shorten the length of the practice. Teach them some mindfulness skills that they find more fun. It may also include helping them tolerate the boredom by shortening the time to a tolerable length and gradually increasing it as their tolerance improves. Moving or walking meditations tend to be more tolerable for clients with ADHD or for those who feel bored or anxious just sitting still.

j. I don't see how this could possibly help me.   Review the benefits proven by the research that apply to this client using age appropriate language. Explain how mindfulness works and how it helps their condition. Ask them to trust the process and give it a try before rejecting it out of hand. If they cannot do so, this may not yet be the time to incorporate mindfulness into their life. Everyone is on their own journey. As helpers we can only give people options. It is up to them to decide what they will do. Most kids tend to embrace these practices as they feel so good when they do them.

k. I don't like doing this.   It's okay if a client doesn't like practicing mindfulness. Ask them what they don't like about it to allow you to explore ways to modify what they are doing or teach them different mindfulness skills. Keep in mind that research suggests that young teens may become quite anxious turning their awareness inward if the thoughts and sensations they are observing are related to worries and fear as they may feel increased anxiety by recognizing them (Kabat-Zinn, 1990) Clients with a history or trauma or PTSD may find it too uncomfortable to go within at first. More outwardly focused skills may be helpful for them. This may be a good time to explore their fears and worries in the appropriate setting.

l. It's not cool. If you work with teens you have certainly experienced their reluctance to try something they think is weird or that peers will criticize. You may notice them not engaging in the skill you are teaching, rolling their eyes, and looking around the room. That's okay. If the setting is conducive you might ask them what it's like for them to do these skills and why it seems difficult. In groups, some teens will readily engage and this seems to give the okay for more reluctant teens to participate.

m. I'm hungry (but I might not know it). It's difficult for kids and teens to concentrate and quiet their mind when their stomach is growling. Ask them when they last ate and what they had. Many kids and teens don't eat healthy foods or eat regularly enough. Encourage teens to get a snack before practice. Encourage parents to make sure their kids get a snack. If necessary, plan to provide a small, healthy snack as part of the session, before practice or as a mindful tasting exercise.

n. Lack of parental support. Many of my clients have learned mindfulness skills without their parent's support. But clients whose parents can remind them to be mindful and encourage them to practice are more likely to practice. See Involving the Parents Tools 2-1 and 5-14.

REFLECTION: Explore the objections raised or presented by your client to help them overcome them. Be prepared to ask a lot of questions in order to figure this out. Discuss options for making a commitment to practice. When assigning a new skill, explore how they will overcome their objections and practice the skill this time.

Tool 5-8: Journal About Your Objections and How to Overcome Them

BACKGROUND: Journaling about their experiences with learning new mindfulness skills will help clients address their objections and raise their awareness about the process (which in itself is a mindfulness exercise). This tool provides prompts that guide clients through this self-awareness process.

SKILL BUILDING: Use Handout 5-8 as a guideline for kids and teens to write or draw about things that get in their way of practicing mindfulness. Ask them to write, draw, or verbally answer the prompts. Explain the definition of an objection and give them some common examples. This tool can be used at the beginning of teaching kids and teens mindfulness skills and also after any new skill is introduced.

REFLECTION: Review the answers with clients. What did they learn about themselves through answering the prompts? What got in the way of being mindful? What objections do they still have? How are they overcoming these objections?

JOURNAL ABOUT YOUR OBJECTIONS AND HOW TO OVERCOME THEM

Journal Prompts:

- What objections do (or did) you have about doing this mindfulness practice?

- Are these objections connected to anything else such as ADHD, anxiety, depression, trauma, or previous experience with practice?

- What are you doing to handle and overcome your objections?

- Do you feel you can overcome them?

- Can you practice mindfulness despite your objections?

- Are there any objections that are "show stoppers" that will prevent you from practicing mindfulness?

- Have you noticed these objections in other areas of your life?

- List three benefits you expect from mindfulness practice.

Picture Prompts

- Draw a picture of yourself having trouble being mindful.

- Draw a picture of yourself easily being mindful.

- Draw a picture of what gets in your way of being mindful.

TOOLS FOR GETTING CLIENTS TO BUY INTO USING MINDFULNESS

Tool 5-9: What Do They Know About It?

BACKGROUND: When introducing mindfulness to any client, it is important to understand what they think it is and what they already know about it. This process helps you know where to start to teach mindfulness skills to this client. This tool describes the process as well as pitfalls to be aware of.

SKILL BUILDING: When introducing mindfulness to clients, first ask them if they know what mindfulness is. Ask them if they have practiced mindfulness before and if so exactly what they did. Explore how what they did before compares with the mindfulness skills you want to teach them. Be wary when they tell you they've done it before and it doesn't work for them or that they already know all about it. Go deeper to explore exactly what they did and why it did or didn't work for them. This will help you discover how what they've tried may differ from what you are teaching. It will also give you more information about what might work best for this particular client, what their objections may be, and where to begin.

One eight-year-old boy told me he knew how to breathe to calm his anger, but that it never worked. When I asked him to show me how he did this, he took a huge, rapid in-breath that would effectively activate instead of calm him. By asking him to show me what he knew, I learned that I needed to start with helping him refine his breathing technique.

REFLECTION: Ask clients what mindfulness skills they have practiced before and how they felt about them. Did these skills help them? Use the information you gain from this tool to know where to start with this client and to know what objections clients may have.

Tool 5-10: Show Them How They Are Already Being Mindful

BACKGROUND: Most kids and teens are mindful already in some part of their day, whether they realize it or not. Helping them to notice and identify times when they are being mindful helps them to embrace the process and aids in increasing their self-awareness. It also provides more information about where they are in the process of incorporating mindfulness. This tool explains how to help clients identify when they are being mindful.

SKILL BUILDING: Use the tools in Chapter 3 to explain to kids and teens what being mindful is. Tell clients that mindfulness is being fully present, paying attention to what they are doing or to something in particular.

Ask the client to think about their day and identify when they were being mindful. What did they pay attention to? Give them some suggestions about when they might have been. Were they fully present and mindful when they were talking to their friend? Did their mindfulness increase when they tripped or spilled something? Were they mindful when they tasted the food they were eating? What were they thinking about when they chose what to wear today? Were they mindful when they took a shower, rode or drove to school or work, smelled the fresh-cut grass, listened to their favorite song on the radio, answered the phone, looked at text messages, played their favorite video game, watched TV or played with their pet?

If they can't think of any time they were mindful, ask them what they did today and go over it with them. Help them find at least one time when they were probably being mindful. Let them know they are being mindful right now while they are doing this exercise.

REFLECTION: Everyone is mindful sometimes. Explain what being mindful is and help your client identify times when they were being mindful. Help them understand mindfulness and discuss what caused them to be mindful. Discuss why being mindful is helpful and important.

Tool 5-11: How to Start Small and Where the Client Is

BACKGROUND: As always, in any helping profession, we must start where the client is. Use Tool 5-9 to determine where the client is. This tool uses the information gleaned from Tool 5-9 to decide what mindfulness skills to start with. Be wary of overwhelming kids and teens by introducing mindfulness skills that are too difficult for them but do not be surprised by how easily they learn.

SKILL BUILDING: When choosing mindfulness skills for kids and teens you must always consider their age, and development and cognitive level. Take into consideration the issues the client is dealing with in choosing the specific skills that may be most helpful to them such as ADHD, anxiety, depression, etc. (Tool 5-12). No matter what you have determined that the client already knows about mindfulness, it is helpful to review their knowledge and make sure it is accurate (Tool 5-9). After doing so, you can decide what mindfulness skills to teach first. Since breathing and awareness of breath are such staples of mindfulness, this is often a great place to start. Don't expect a young child or mindfulness newbie to start right in with a 15- or 20- minute sitting meditation, especially if they have trouble sitting still, as might those with ADHD or anxiety. For some, 30 seconds may be a good place to start.

No matter what their mindfulness experience consists of all kids and teens can learn and will benefit from the Mindfulness of Breath skills (Chapter 6). These skills are presented in order of increasing difficulty so start at the beginning and go through them all. Breath awareness skills tend to be non-threatening to kids and teens and readily learned. The Basic Relaxation Breath (Tool 6-4) is found throughout many of the mindfulness skills. When they have mastered basic breath mindfulness the Core Practice (Tool 6-8) might be used ending with a brief period of silence and gradually increasing it as the client practices and gains more skill. Depending on their previous experience and what else you know about them, you might start with an Mindfulness of Surroundings exercise (Tools 7-1 through 7-4), which is easy to do, only takes a few minutes, can be done anywhere, is usually very relaxing, demonstrates mindfulness, and is generally non-threatening to the client. See Tool 5-12 for more guidance on skill selection.

Remember to make learning mindfulness fun. Kids' work is play. There are dozens of mindfulness skills presented throughout this workbook that are fun for both kids and teens. Mix it up and play some of the games and do the activities, all of which teach mindfulness.

Introduce the Core Practice (Tool 6-8) and use it as a staple for repeated practice for most sessions. Start with a very short practice and increase the time as clients get better at it.

Teens can benefit from all the skills in this book including the more advanced sitting meditation. For teens who are more experienced, you might review the basics and start with a Mindfulness of Thoughts or Emotions (Chapters 14 and 15). Keep in mind that young teens often feel increased anxiety when they focus on their thoughts and feelings.

REFLECTION: Gather as much information as possible about what this client needs help with, their age, developmental and cognitive levels and what their experience level is with mindfulness. Use this knowledge to decide which mindfulness skills to start with. A good progression might be the Mindfulness of Breath skills (Chapter 6), Present Moment Awareness (Chapter 7), Mindful Listening (Chapter 8) and so forth through the various skills included here. This progression will vary depending on the needs and experience of the client. Mix in fun activities and games provided throughout this workbook.

Tool 5-12: Choose the Best Mindfulness Tool(s) for the Client

BACKGROUND: Each client will embrace different mindfulness skills that suit them the best. Some will prefer a guided meditation. Others will succeed in doing a sitting meditation on their own. Some will incorporate mindfulness throughout their day while others may prefer a more formal sitting practice. Some will be partial to sitting still while others may prefer a walking or movement meditation. This tool explains how to help clients choose mindfulness skills that they enjoy and from which they receive the most benefit.

SKILL BUILDING: This first step in this tool is to get to know your client. Find out about their previous experience with mindfulness, how they might benefit from the practice, and what issues they are dealing with. For example, if a client has the symptoms of poor concentration and hyperactivity associated with ADHD, then begin with briefer meditations and those that include movement. Clients with ADHD may be put off if you start by asking them to sit still for more than a minute or two as sitting still is exactly what they may be having difficulty doing. Doing so may cause them to reject the whole practice of mindfulness. If they start with a 30-second silent period and master that, then they can gradually increase the period by 30 seconds until at some point they can sit for 5 or 10 minutes. Belly breathing (Tool 6-4) and Mindful Movement (Chapter 13), Mindful Touching (Chapter 12), Mindful Seeing (Chapter 9), Mindful Listening (Chapter 8) or an Mindfulness of Tasks (Chapter 18) practice may be just right for most young kids or a child or teen with ADHD.

If the client is highly anxious, a long meditation of inner reflection may initially be too anxiety-provoking for them. Teach them breathing techniques to help them learn to calm their physiology as well as more active mindfulness skills such as Present Moment Awareness (Chapter 7) and Mindfulness of Tasks (Chapter 18). As they become more comfortable, add in brief Mindfulness of Physical Body (Chapter 16) and eventually Mindfulness of Thoughts (Chapter 14) and Mindfulness of Emotions (Chapter 15) skills. Pepper in more active skills and games provided in Chapters 8-14.

Observe your client as they practice the skills. This plus keeping an open dialogue with your client about what their experience is like as they do each mindfulness skill will provide you with the information you need to modify skill choices or fine-tune existing choices. If a client doesn't like a particular mindfulness skill for whatever reason, don't give up. Ask them why they don't like it, make sure they are doing it in such a way that it should benefit them, modify it, or choose a different skill. Remember, kids like to play so keep it fun.

REFLECTION: Learn as much as possible about your client and their needs. Select and review mindfulness skills you think will help them. Teach them a variety of mindfulness skills and observe how they work for them. Be flexible and be prepared to modify choices, and add more appropriate skills as needed.

Tool 5-13: Teens: What's in it for me?

BACKGROUND: If you work with teens you know they can be very selective about what they participate in. Teens generally need more explanation of why they should incorporate mindfulness into their day. This tool helps you answer what every teen will want to know: "What's in it for me?"

SKILL BUILDING: Teens need more explanation of relevance to their lives. They may have a hard time seeing the connection between sitting still with their eyes shut and their daily life. Therefore, you may need to help them "buy into" learning mindfulness skills by showing them specific ways it is relevant to their life. Relate the benefits of mindfulness to what they need help with.

Use examples from their own life. Explain that increasing daily mindfulness will help them realize when they are exhausted and should rest. Being mindful can even help them notice that they need to go to the bathroom. Ask them if they ever realize they have no idea what the teacher just said, or what they just ate, or what their homework is.

Ask them if they ever have trouble concentrating and if so, discuss how mindfulness has been shown to increase concentration and how that might help them get better grades and get into a good college. Explore how being mindful in relationships may help teens create a better relationship with a girlfriend or boyfriend. Discuss how mindfulness might help them feel happy, more confident and less anxious. Explore their stressors and stress level and relate how mindfulness lowers the stress response.

To explore why mindfulness needs to be practiced you might ask them who their favorite singer or sports team is. Then explore how they think that singer or team got to be so great. Discuss the sports and activities they are involved in. If they take dance or music classes, explore how they learn and get more skilled. Explain that being mindful will get easier and more automatic with practice.

REFLECTION: Ask the teen how they think mindfulness might specifically help them. Help them explore and understand how they can incorporate it into their day. Watch their body language while doing skills to see if they are engaged or tuned out, looking around the room. If they are not engaged, ask them what would help them invest in mindfulness practice. Be accepting and non-judgmental. Teens often feel criticized. Encourage them to practice and be sure to praise them for when they are being mindful.

Tool 5-14: Getting Parental Support

BACKGROUND: As discussed in Tool 2-1, parental support can help the child or teen be more successful with mindfulness practice. Therefore, this tool explores options for helping parents "buy in" to the idea.

SKILL BUILDING: To help parents be more willing and able to be involved, help them understand why you want to teach mindfulness to their child or teen. Review with them the mindfulness research relevant to their child's issues. Explain that their child or teen will be more successful with learning and practicing mindfulness with their involvement and ask them if they are willing to be supportive. Explore what they can do to encourage their child or teen to practice. Use Tool 5-7 to help them overcome obstacles and resistance to supporting their child or teen's practice.

Address any negative preconceived notions they may have about mindfulness. Explore and resolve any concerns they might have that mindfulness might be against their religious beliefs. Follow appropriate ethical practice by getting specific consent from parents so that it is clear that teaching mindfulness to their child doesn't conflict with religious or other belief systems of the parents.

See Tool 2-1 for more ways to involve the parents.

REFLECTION: Is the parent able and willing to participate? Did they agree to be involved? What are they willing to do? Are their actions proving they are supporting their child or teen's practice? Do they understand the benefits of mindfulness practice for their child? Are they undermining their child or teen's practice? Are they practicing themselves?

TOOLS FOR RELATING EFFECTIVENESS OF SPECIFIC TOOLS TO THEIR CONDITION

Tool 5-15: Relate Benefits to the Client's Condition

BACKGROUND: Younger kids are often amazingly willing to try mindfulness skills when you present them as fun activities, games, and short meditations. These kids may not need much explanation of the benefits of mindfulness but may be able to share what they like about it or how it makes them feel. Older kids and teens usually are more curious about why they should learn and practice mindfulness. And parents often need help making the connection between mindfulness techniques and their child or teen's symptoms.

SKILL BUILDING: Learn as much as possible about your client and the issues/conditions they present with. Very young kids will not be able to understand research. Therefore, for younger kids simply teach them some basic skills and help them notice how they feel before and after. Older kids and definitely teens may need to know why they should practice mindfulness. Depending on maturity and cognitive level explain how mindfulness practice might improve their conditions and tell them about specific studies that have shown an improvement in conditions like theirs. See Tools 3-21 and 3-22 for more information about the studies. In general, children's mindfulness studies have shown improvements in:

- social skills
- emotional regulation
- ability to orient attention
- working memory and planning and organization
- self esteem
- calmness, relaxation, and self-acceptance.
- quality of sleep
- test anxiety

- concentration
- ADHD behaviors-hyperactivity and impulsivity
- negative affect/emotions
- anxiety
- depression
- conduct and anger management problems

With time you will accrue many examples from your own practice of kids and teens whose conditions improved with mindfulness practice, which you can share with current clients (of course, protecting confidentiality). If appropriate with a specific client, you might also share your personal story of how mindfulness has helped you. You are practicing yourself, right?

REFLECTION: After explaining the benefits to your client, make sure they understand why mindfulness practice might help them. Ask them to explain in their own words what benefits they expect. Answer any questions they may have. As they learn mindfulness skills, continue to ask them what benefits they feel they are gaining from mindfulness.

Tool 5-16: Journal About What Mindfulness Can Help You With

BACKGROUND: Clients will become more invested in starting a mindfulness practice if they can relate the potential benefits to their own personal issues or conditions. This tool provides journal prompts to help clients reflect on what mindfulness might help them with and what benefits they expect.

SKILL BUILDING: Ask clients to reply to the journal prompts in Handout 5-16. Explain that doing so will help them clarify what they've learned about how mindfulness practice might help them with their issues/conditions. It will also help them define what benefits they hope to gain from their practice.

REFLECTION: Review your client's answers to the journal prompts. Use this process as a springboard for discussion about the benefits of mindfulness. Connect the benefits to your client's particular issues/conditions. Ask older kids and teens if they feel comfortable making a commitment to mindfulness practice in order to help with a specific condition or even simply to gain an improved sense of well-being.

JOURNAL ABOUT BENEFITS YOU EXPECT FROM MINDFULNESS

Journal Prompts:

- What benefits do studies show can be achieved through mindfulness practice?

- List "what's in it for you."

- Do any of these benefits relate to issues or conditions you experience?

- What surprised you most about the research?

- What personal issues/conditions would you like to improve?

- How might mindfulness practice be helpful to you?

- Are you skeptical about the benefits?

- Do you think mindfulness practice will help you?

- Are you willing and able to make a commitment to incorporating mindfulness practice into your life on a regular basis?

- What reservations do you have about practicing mindfulness?

- If mindfulness practice could help you with just one thing, what would you want that to be?

- Would you be willing to practice mindfulness if it simply increased your sense of well-being?

- What emotion arises when you consider how mindfulness practice might help you?

Picture Prompts

- Draw a picture of yourself before and after being mindful

- Draw a picture of your life if you_____

  (fill in the blank for specific issue such as: were happier, worried less, could sit still longer, didn't get yelled at, could concentrate, etc.)

- Draw a picture of something you wish for.

*Select prompts from the list and add your own as appropriate for the age and cognitive level of the child or teen

SECTION III

TOOLS FOR TEACHING SPECIFIC MINDFULNESS SKILLS

Chapter 6
Mindfulness of Breath

Tool 6-1: Do You Know How to Breathe?

BACKGROUND: A fundamental, age-old focus of attention in mindfulness is the breath. Being mindful of breath is a basic, proven technique for practicing mindfulness. Why? Breathing is portable and we can focus on it anywhere, anytime. Although we breathe automatically, far beneath conscious thought, we can deliberately hold our breath, or breathe slowly or quickly if we choose. This tool provides a fun way to introduce the concept of focusing on breath to kids and teens.

SKILL BUILDING: Use Handout 6-1 as a guide to engage in a discussion about breath and breathing with your clients. Ask the questions on the handout and then discuss their answers. Make it fun and help them think about and then play with different ways of breathing. Demonstrate the different ways to breathe and then watch them do it and do it with them.

REFLECTION: Use the Handout 6-1 as a resource to process what it was like for your client to think about and then try different ways to breathe. Ask your clients if they ever thought about their breath before. Discuss what happened to their breathing when they paid attention to it. Explore what it felt like to them to pretend they were blowing up a balloon in their belly. Ask what they noticed about their breathing as they paid attention to it.

DO YOU KNOW HOW TO BREATHE?

How many of you know (or do you) know how to breathe?

How did you learn?

Was it like learning to walk?

Do you have to think about breathing?

Can you hold your breath?

Can you breathe fast?

Can you breathe slowly?

Can you blow hard?

Can you blow softly?

Can you breathe in quickly?

Can you breathe out slowly?

Can you breathe in through your nose?

Can you breathe in through your mouth?

Can you breathe out through your mouth?

How do you blow a bubble?

What happens if you blow too fast?

How do you get the biggest bubble?

How do you blow out a candle?

How do you smell a flower? Fast or slow? Do you use your nose or mouth?

How do you smell popcorn?

Put your hand on your belly and pretend there is a balloon in your belly.

Take a breath in through your nose to the count of 4 and fill that balloon in your belly with air.

Blow out gently through your mouth to the count of 8 like blowing a huge bubble and empty out your belly balloon.

Do it again.

What does that feel like?

Can you feel your belly balloon get bigger?

Did you run out of air or have some left over?

What did you notice when you were breathing?

Tool 6-2: How to Breathe In: Smell the flowers

BACKGROUND: In order for kids and teens to be able to practice being mindful of breath, slow down their breathing and pay attention to the feeling of the breath they must be able to inhale at will. Teens will be able to do this easily. Younger kids often need to learn how to breathe in consciously. This tool provides a number of activities that help younger kids learn to take an in-breath through their nose. Kids as young as 3 can do this activity.

SKILL BUILDING: Use the two methods described on Handout 6-2 to help kids understand how to breathe in through their nose and mouth. Be playful with them and make it a game. Observe them and make sure they are breathing in through their nose when they say they are. Help them notice the difference between breathing in through their nose and their mouth.

REFLECTION: Were they able to breathe in on command? Ask them if they could slow down their in-breath. Discuss what was different about the smell of the flowers when they breathed through their nose versus their mouth. Find out if they had trouble breathing in. Did they have a stuffy nose and couldn't breathe in easily? For kids older than 6 or 7 ask them what it was like to breathe in and what they noticed about what it felt like to do so.

HOW TO BREATHE IN: SMELL THE FLOWERS

The intention of this tool is to teach young kids how to breathe in on command, preferably through their nose.

1. Get a small bouquet of fragrant flowers (or walk to a garden) and ask the client to smell the flowers.

Tell them to show you how to smell the flowers.

Ask them what the flowers smell like.

Ask them if they like the way the flowers smell.

Do they know anything else that smells like these flowers?

Observe them and see if they are actually smelling them with their nose or if they are breathing in through their mouth.

Demonstrate how you smell flowers by breathing in through your nose. Breathe in and out through your nose a few times and ask them to try it.

Put your hand over your mouth so you can't breathe through your mouth and ask them if they can put their hand over their mouth like you.

Ask them to smell the flowers with their hand over their mouth.

Be playful with them. Do it with them.

Ask them to breathe in quickly, then slowly, then with their mouth, then nose.

Watch them do it.

Ask them to listen to see if they make funny noises when they breathe in through their nose, or through their mouth.

Ask them to try and see if they can smell the flowers when they breathe in through their mouth instead of their nose.

2. Put something fragrant in a paper cup and ask the client to smell it and tell you what it smells like. Use the process described in #1.

    Good smells to use:

    ✓ Wintergreen Life Savers

    ✓ Chai Tea Bag

    ✓ Oranges

    ✓ Coffee Grounds

Tool 6-3: How to Breathe Out: Blow a bubble, balloon, candle, pinwheel, Kleenex

BACKGROUND: Being able to deliberately inhale and exhale are basic activities of mindfulness of breath. Teens have this ability but younger children may need to be taught how to breathe in and out on command. This tool provides a variety of activities that help younger kids focus on breathing out.

SKILL BUILDING: Use the games and activities in Handout 6-3 to teach kids to breathe out, preferably through their mouth, at will.

REFLECTION: Was the client able to master breathing out through their mouth? Were they able to slow down their breath, purse their lips, or control it? Did they have fun blowing bubbles? Were they able to slow down how fast they blew and get bigger bubbles? Ask them which is easier, blowing a bubble or blowing up a balloon.

HOW TO BREATHE OUT

Blow Bubbles (3 years +)

Use a jar of soapy water and a bubble wand and ask the client to play with it and blow a bubble. This will help them get the hang of blowing out through their mouth as they quickly discover that's what works to blow up the bubble. Ask them to see what happens when they blow really hard. See if they can blow a really big bubble by blowing very gently. Ask them to show you what happens when they blow fast, slow. Do they blow one big bubble or lots of little ones?

Blow on a Kleenex (2 years +)

Give a tissue to the client and ask them to hold it in front of them and blow on it. Ask them to make it dance by blowing on it. Ask them what happens to the tissue when they blow really hard, or really soft. Can they raise it up by blowing on it for a long while? What happens when they stop blowing? Ask them to blow on the tissue on the count of three or every time you clap your hands.

Blow on a Pinwheel (3 years +)

Use a pinwheel toy and ask the client to blow on it and make it spin. Ask them what happens when they blow really hard or just softly. How long does it spin after they stop blowing? Ask them to blow on it each time you clap your hands.

Blow Up Balloons (8 years +)

Ask the client to blow up a small balloon. This provides a way to contrast gentle versus forceful breaths. Ask them how hard they have to blow to get it going, then how hard after it is partially blown up. Let them play with it and let the air out quickly as it flies around the room. Ask them to pay attention to the balloon as it fills and relate this to their belly when they breathe.

Blow Out Candles (11 years +)

Most kids learn to blow out the candles on their birthday cake pretty young. But for safety reasons, limit the use of this activity to older kids and teens. Light a candle and ask them to blow it out. Light it again and ask them to blow gently to make the flame dance. How hard can they blow before it blows out?

Do these activities with your client and make them fun.

Tool 6-4: Basic Relaxation Breathing

BACKGROUND: By changing our breathing pattern we indirectly change our physiology. When we breathe in, or inhale, we activate our sympathetic nervous system, which activates our physiology as well as our stress response. This is often called the fight or flight response. When we activate our sympathetic nervous system, our heart rate increases, pupils dilate, blood vessels constrict, sweat increases, and the digestive system slows down. We become more alert and overall tension increases.

When we breathe out, or exhale, we activate our parasympathetic nervous system. The parasympathetic nervous system is responsible for the "rest and digest" activities that occur when the body is at rest. Therefore, when we exhale, our heart rate slows down, intestinal and glandular activity increases, and we generally feel more relaxed.

The practice of focusing on breathing leads to reflective rather than reactive responses. It gives kids control over their responses so they respond rather than react.

SKILL BUILDING: Explain that inhaling or breathing in revs us up and exhaling or breathing out calms us down. Use Handout 6-4 to explain the relaxation breathing technique. Demonstrate the technique, and do it with clients. If they tell you they already know how to breathe this way ask them to show you how they do it. This is important because often kids have been taught to take a few deep breaths to calm down and they tend to take a huge, rapid in-breath which effectively activates the stress response instead of deactivating it. Thus far, every child that showed me they already knew how to breathe to calm down did this. Observe them periodically as it can take some weeks for kids to learn this. Teaching their parent how to do it will help the parent de-stress and also get them involved in reminding the child or teen to use the skill and help them do it effectively.

REFLECTION: This breathing technique very quickly calms the physiology of the body and brain. Once kids and teens get the hang of doing this skill properly most feel calmer and less anxious within two to three breaths. This is a great place to start most mindfulness exercises and is the basis for the core practice. By practicing this breathing technique, the client will effectively lower their stress response and anxiety, and improve their physical, emotional, and cognitive health. Caution clients to inhale slowly while counting to four instead of taking a rapid inhale, which may increase the stress response instead of calming it down.

BASIC RELAXATION BREATHING

A breathing technique that is very helpful in deactivating the stress response, and can really help kids and teens calm down anger and anxiety, consists of breathing in through the nose to the count of four and breathing out through the mouth to the count of eight. Thus, we activate the parasympathetic nervous system twice as long as the sympathetic nervous system with a net result of calming our physiology and stress response.

Teach them this simple technique and encourage them to use it during their day as often as they think of it, particularly if they are angry, stressed out, worried, or upset. It is an excellent way to increase their ability to self-regulate.

"Breathe in through your nose to the count of four and out through your mouth to the count of eight. When you breathe out, purse your lips and blow gently like you are blowing a bubble. This will help you slow down the exhale. Don't worry if your nose is stuffy, just breathe in and out through your mouth instead.

Inhale through your nose: 1-2-3-4.

Exhale through your mouth with lips pursed, blowing gently, like blowing a bubble: 1-2-3-4-5-6-7-8."

Repeat 3–4 times.

Be sure to observe them when they are learning this to make sure they are breathing in slowly and then breathing out twice as slowly. Often, kids will inhale very rapidly to get a big breath. This is counterproductive and may activate the stress response instead of deactivating it.

Tool 6-5: How to Belly Breathe

BACKGROUND: Deep breathing, or diaphragmatic breathing, is often referred to as "belly breathing". It involves inhaling and filling the lungs in such a way as to expand the stomach, not the chest. In belly breathing the lungs expand downward, allowing much more air to be inhaled than during a chest breath. A chest breath is the same as anxious breathing while a belly breath is considered to be relaxation breathing. It provides much more oxygen to the body and helps to lower the stress response.

SKILL BUILDING: Use Handout 6-5 to teach clients how to belly breathe. Demonstrate it and do it with them. See Tool 6-6 for how to know if they are getting a belly breath. It may be helpful for the client to lie on their back to get the feel of a belly breath (see Tool 6-9). Have them practice at least several times a day. It can be combined with the Basic Relaxation Breathing Tool 6-4. All ages understand the idea of blowing up an imaginary balloon in their belly when they breathe in and letting the air out when they breathe out.

REFLECTION: Belly breathing can be totally new to many clients. Some may have learned it if they took yoga or singing classes, but most have not. Ask them if they were able to blow up the balloon in their belly. What did it feel like to fill their belly with air? Were they able to feel their belly move? Did their chest move? What did the air feel like as it went in and out of them?

HOW TO BELLY BREATHE

1. Place one hand on your belly above your belly button and one hand on your upper chest.

2. Relax your belly.

3. Breathe in through your nose and fill your lungs.

4. Allow your lungs to fill downward and make the bottom hand move.

5. Pretend you have a balloon in your belly and blow it up with your breath.

6. Avoid shallow chest breathing or raising your shoulders.

7. Breathe out slowly like you are blowing a bubble and empty out the balloon. Feel the belly move.

Tool 6-6: Three Ways to Tell if You Are Belly Breathing

BACKGROUND: Belly breathing has been shown to be an important part of decreasing the stress response. It increases the oxygen intake and generally increases awareness of breathing, which is a basic concept in mindfulness.

SKILL BUILDING: Use Handout 6-6 to teach clients how to know if they are getting a belly breath. Explain and demonstrate these three techniques and watch clients try each of them in session. Encourage them to practice several times a day between sessions until they can readily tell they are belly breathing.

REFLECTION: Learning to belly breathe takes practice for most clients. These three easy ways to tell if you are getting a belly breath help clients gain mastery over this technique very quickly. Explain and demonstrate the three techniques, do them with clients, and then follow up at subsequent sessions by asking them to show you how they are doing with them.

THREE WAYS TO TELL IF YOU ARE BELLY BREATHING

There are three easy ways to tell if you are belly breathing or chest breathing.

1. Place one hand on your belly above your belly button and one hand on your upper chest. Just breathe as you usually breathe and notice which hand moves more. If the bottom hand moves more, great, that's a belly breath. If the top hand moves more, that's a chest breath, which is the same as anxious breathing.

   Deliberately move your stomach in and out just below your rib cage and above your belly button to get the feel of a belly breath. Notice your bottom hand moving.

   Now breathe normally and notice which hand moves more.

   - Bottom hand moves more = belly breath—great
   - Top hand moves more—chest breath = same as anxious breathing

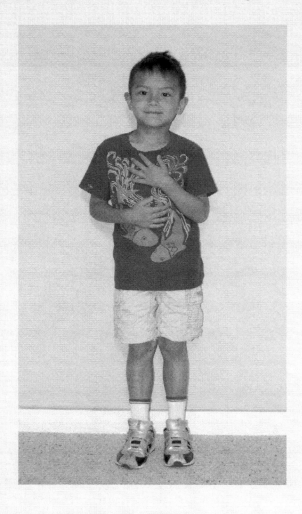

2. **Intentionally take a chest breath and blow on your hand.** Notice the temperature of the air as it flows across your fingers. Now, intentionally take a belly breath and blow on your hand. Again, notice the temperature of the air as it flows across your fingers. You will notice that the air feels warmer when it comes from a belly breath.

- Chest breath → colder air
- Belly breath → warmer air

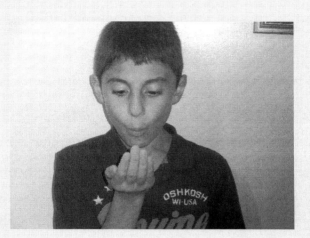

3. **Lie down on your back.** Place an object on your belly such as a small stuffed animal if you are a child or a book or a smartphone if you are a teen. Now make the object go up and down as you breathe; rock the stuffed animal or smartphone.

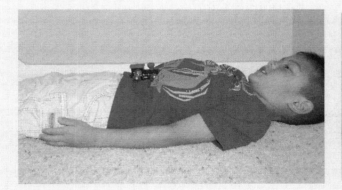

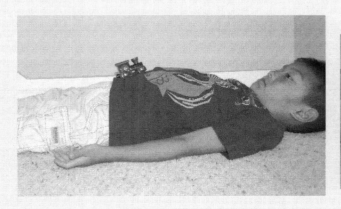

Tool 6-7: Breathing Fast and Slow

BACKGROUND: Breathing is a fundamental focus of attention in mindfulness. This tool helps kids and teens have fun playing with their breath. The goal of this tool is to help kids and teens focus on their breath and learn to pay attention to how their body feels when they breathe. It is a kids' version of a classic awareness of breath skill.

SKILL BUILDING: Use Handout 6-7 to guide clients in playing with their breath. Tell them you are going to have some fun paying attention to breathing. Demonstrate each step and do it with them. Put your hand on your belly and ask them to do the same so they begin to notice if their belly is moving when they breathe.

REFLECTION: Ask clients if they were able to breathe fast and then slow. How did breathing slowly feel different from breathing quickly? Did they feel more relaxed when they breathed fast or slow? What happened to their heart rate when they breathed fast versus slow? Did they have trouble paying attention to their breath? If they got distracted how did they bring their attention back to their breath? Did they feel like they couldn't breathe? Did they breathe more breaths when they breathed quickly or slowly? Ask them, "What do you think your brain looked like when you breathed fast or slow?"

BREATHING FAST AND SLOW

Let's have some fun and play with how we breathe.

First take your time and take a long slow breath in and a long breath out. How long can you make your breath? Pay attention to your long breath in. Then pay attention to your long breath out. Do it again. How does it feel? Where do you feel it in your body? Does your breath feel warm, cold, smooth, soft, or squishy? Do you feel the breath in your mind, in your throat, in your head, in your chest, or perhaps in your belly?

How fast can you breathe?

Take a fast breath in and then a quick breath out. Keep doing it. Do you make noise when you breathe? Check in with your body to see how it feels. What part of your body is moving? How fast is your heart beating?

Now breathe normally.

Check in to see how your body feels. Has it changed from before you started breathing quickly? Do you feel the same or different? Where is it the same? Where is it different? Do you feel it in your mind or your body? Where in your body—your heart, your head, stomach, neck, shoulders?

Now, slow down and take a long breath in and out.

 Take your time. Just pay attention to each part of your breath as you breathe in and then when you breathe out. Do you feel different now? Has anything changed in your body now that you are breathing so slowly? Does your mind feel calmer? How fast is your heart beating?

Now just breathe normally.

Pay attention to when the breath starts, when it ends, and the space between the breaths. Sit in the space between the breaths for a moment. Notice how you feel as you take another breath. Allow your breath to flow in and out easily.

Tool 6-8 Core Practice

BACKGROUND: At the heart of mindfulness is the Core Practice. Core Practice is a way to tell our minds to relax and focus and to calm down the "monkey brain." It can be used several times a day, almost like pushing the reset button. It is the perfect way for kids and teens to remind themselves to be mindful. They can use it to take a quick time-out to calm anger or fear, to think before they act, and to make better choices.

SKILL BUILDING: Use Handout 6-8 to teach clients the basics of Core Practice. The structure of this tool is to Stop, Listen, Breathe, Reflect. Doing this when they are upset, angry, afraid, or impulsive can allow kids and teens the space in time to make a better choice than they might otherwise. Modify the length of the silent period to suit the needs of the client and lengthen it as they practice and gain mastery. This might range from 10 seconds for a beginner or hyperactive or anxious client, on up to 15 minutes for a more advanced client.

Normalize their experience—it is normal for the mind to wander. Recommend they practice this several times a day. They might use a short version of the practice (5 or 10 seconds) if they are starting to feel angry or upset or impatient to allow themselves to calm down, stay in control, and make good choices. They might incorporate it into their day to center or ground themselves during transitions or before settling down to start an activity.

Discuss how the Core Practice helps no matter what they are doing. Relate it to making choices when they are being creative, in choosing what to draw or write about, or preparing to take a photo of their lively kitten, or perhaps responding to a bully.

REFLECTION: Teach the client to reflect on the core practice process. Ask them: what was the practice like for you? How did you feel as you breathed? What did you notice about your breathing? How did you stay focused on breathing? What did you do when your mind wandered? Did you feel different after you were finished? What do you think was happening in your brain while you did this? When could you use this during your day? What might it help you with? How could you use this to make better choices?

CORE PRACTICE

STOP → LISTEN → BREATHE

Stop what you are doing.

Close your eyes.

Be still and listen.

Notice how you feel inside.

Pay attention to your breathing.

Breathe slowly in through your nose and out through your mouth.

Imagine the air slowly filling your lungs and belly and then flowing out again.

If you notice that you are thinking about other things, that's ok. Just accept it, and then bring your attention back to your breath.

Notice your belly moving as you take slow belly breaths.

Ask yourself what am I feeling?

Keep paying attention to your breath.

Continue for a minute in silence (Note: shorten or lengthen as needed).

Open your eyes and return to the room.

Tool 6-9: Belly Breathing Core Practice with a Stuffed Animal or Smartphone

BACKGROUND: At the heart of mindfulness is the Core Practice as described in Tool 6-8. This tool provides another great way for kids and teens to get the benefit of the core practice combined with a fun way to get the hang of the belly breath.

SKILL BUILDING: Use Handout 6-9 to teach clients another version of the Core Practice. A fun way to help kids and teens get the feeling of the belly breath is to have them lie on their back with arms and legs uncrossed while they do this skill or many of the other skills. Place a stuffed animal on their belly and ask them to 'give the stuffed animal a ride'. For teens who are way too cool to use a stuffed animal, suggest they place their smartphone (silenced) or tablet on their belly and give it a ride up and down.

Modify the length of the silent period near the end to suit the needs of the client and lengthen it as they practice and gain mastery. This might range from 10 seconds for a beginner or hyperactive or anxious client, on up to 15 minutes for a more advanced client.

REFLECTION: Teach the client to reflect on the process of breathing. Ask them: How did you feel as you breathed in and out? Did you feel the air going in and out? Did you notice if it was warm or cold? Could you rock the stuffed animal (smartphone)? What did it feel like to pay attention to breathing? Did your mind wander? How did you stay focused on breathing?

CORE PRACTICE BREATHING MEDITATION WITH A STUFFED ANIMAL OR SMARTPHONE

Find yourself a comfortable position lying flat on your back with your arms and legs uncrossed after placing a small stuffed animal on your belly. (For teens, use their smartphone (sound turned off), tablet, or book if they are too cool for a stuffed animal.)

Close your eyes if you like or just look gently up at the ceiling.

Check in to see how your mind and body feel

Now pay attention to your breathing

Take a nice deep belly breath in through your nose and, while you do this, let the air fill your belly and raise the stuffed animal (smartphone)

Now blow gently out through your mouth and lower the stuffed animal (smartphone)

Now breathe in and out and give the stuffed animal a ride up and down (smartphone)

Take a nice deep belly breath in through your nose to the count of four and then blow out gently through your mouth to the count of eight

Now just breathe normally

Notice your breath but don't change it

Notice how your belly moves the stuffed animal (smartphone)

Relax your shoulders

Picture the air coming into your body and then going back out again

Notice how the air feels as it comes into your nose and down into your lungs

Then notice how it feels when the air comes back up into your mouth and out across your lips

If you start to think about other things, that's ok, just bring your attention back to your breath

Feel your belly rising and falling

Can you feel the stuffed animal (smartphone)?

Just keep paying attention to how it feels as you breathe

Now check in with how your mind and body feel

Keep paying attention to your breath for a few moments

Silence (vary the length as appropriate)

When you are ready, open your eyes

Bring your attention back to the room

Take another slow, deep belly breath with your eyes open

Tool 6-10: Counting Sets of Four Breaths

BACKGROUND: Counting sets of four breaths is a simple mindfulness practice that kids and teens love to do. Even young clients who can count to four have enjoyed seeing how many sets of breaths they can count. The tool teaches mindfulness, focus, present moment awareness, and letting go of distractions. This practice can be quite calming as well as fun.

SKILL BUILDING: Use Handout 6-10 to teach the client how to do this mindfulness skill. Do it with them until they get the hang of it. Discuss the benefit of practicing this skill. Explain that this is a fun, playful way to see how long they can focus on counting breaths before they notice they have stopped counting. With practice they will be able to stay focused longer and count more sets. Make it a game with your clients to see who stays focused on counting sets of four breaths the longest.

Kids often have fun doing this and they like to make a game out of seeing how many sets they count before forgetting to count, sometimes competing with a friend or you. It can be done while walking, waiting in line, waiting for the bus or even as a way to calm down a busy brain to fall asleep at night.

REFLECTION: Ask clients to reflect on what happened for them while doing this. Were they able to stay focused? How many sets were they able to count to? Are they able to count more sets now that they have been practicing? When did they practice this during the week? Ask them what they think their brain was doing while they did this.

COUNTING SETS OF FOUR BREATHS

Close your eyes and take a deep belly breath in through your nose to the count of four and then breathe out slowly through your mouth with pursed lips to the count of eight like blowing a bubble. (Do this with your client a couple of times.)

Then breathe normally while paying attention to the feeling of the breath.

Now start counting each time you breathe out. This is called the exhale. Hold out one finger on your right hand for each breath. (Do this with them)

When you have counted four exhales, hold one finger out on your left hand and count that as one set of four.

Count another four exhales counting with the fingers on your right hand again and hold out a second finger on your left hand, thereby counting a second set of four.

Continue to do this for several minutes.

Every time you notice that your attention has wandered from counting your breaths and you have started to focus on some other thought or feeling or distraction, simply accept it, dismiss it, and return your attention to counting your exhales.

See how many sets of four exhales you can count on your fingers before you realize you have stopped counting. If you use your fingers to count as above you can tell how many sets by how many fingers you are holding out on your left hand. Typically they are still holding the position after you have forgotten to count.

For beginners 10 sets is a lot.

Tool 6-11: Journal About Breathing

BACKGROUND: Journaling can be an effective way for clients to process and integrate their experiences while learning mindfulness. Some clients will love to journal. Others will not. If a child cannot yet write, ask them to tell you what they want to put in their journal and do it with them. Many clients would rather draw so ask them to draw a picture that represents something about their experience with mindfulness of breathing. If they don't want to journal, you might still ask them the following prompts and process their verbal responses.

SKILL BUILDING: Ask the client to respond to the journal prompts in Handout 6-11 about how the breathing exercises in this entire chapter have affected their life. Do it with younger kids. Help them write if they can't write yet. Encourage them to draw. You might read the prompts aloud and wait for them to write, draw, or tell you their answers.

REFLECTION: Ask your client if they want to share their journal entries with you or with the group if in a group setting. Discuss what they write. Normalize any difficulty they are having with focusing or being self-critical about learning mindfulness. Help them process the feelings that they express during this process.

JOURNAL ABOUT BREATHING

Journal Prompts:

- What happened when you practiced breathing meditations?

- What did you think about?

- How did you feel?

- Was it hard or easy to pay attention to breathing?

- Did you teach anyone else to breathe?

- How did you feel when you focused on breathing?

- What did you notice about your breathing?

- Did you notice your mind wandering?

- How did you bring your attention back to breathing?

- Which breathing skills do you like the best and why?

- When have you used the mindfulness of breathing skills?

- When could you have used them?

- How has practicing these breathing exercises changed your day?

- What did you like most about breathing exercises?

- What did you like least about breathing exercises?

- Have you noticed any changes in your stress level?

- Have you noticed any changes in your ability to concentrate?

- Has anything changed for you?

Picture Prompts

- Draw a picture of you breathing

- Draw a picture of your brain before and after you practice breathing

Chapter 7
Present Moment Awareness

MINDFULNESS OF SURROUNDINGS

Tool 7-1: Mindfulness of Surroundings—Indoors

BACKGROUND: One of the basic concepts of mindfulness is to increase the ability to be aware in the present moment. This can include self-awareness of body, breath, thoughts, emotions, sounds, smell, and touch. It is often easier and less threatening to kids and teens to start teaching this process by helping them become aware of their physical surroundings as opposed to internal awareness. This tool provides a method for leading kids and teens to pay attention to what's around them indoors and to stay focused on the present moment.

SKILL BUILDING: Older kids and teens will benefit from an explanation that this brief mindfulness meditation teaches the ability to stay totally present in this moment. Engage in a discussion about what the present moment is. Ask them to describe the present moment. With younger kids, just do the process and then help them reflect on what it was like for them (see below). Explain to clients that although you will be asking questions, you don't want a verbal response. Explain that clients should just listen to the questions and answer them in their head as they explore their surroundings. Tell them it is normal to be distracted and for thoughts to wander and that as soon as they notice this has happened they can dismiss the thought or distraction and bring their attention back to being aware of their surroundings.

Read Handout 7-1 aloud to lead the client through a guided Mindfulness of Surroundings meditation. Use the same process in any room but change the statements slightly to reflect what is actually in the room. You might say "pay attention to the wall in front of you. Now pay attention to the windows (or pictures, etc.) on the wall."

Encourage kids and teens to practice a brief version of this skill when they first arrive in new surroundings such as when they get to school or their part-time job (teens), a store, a friend's house, the movies, each time they change classes, or perhaps when they sit down to do their homework to help them transition and bring their focus to their present surroundings.

REFLECTION: Ask your client what happened for them during the meditation. Ask them: What did you notice? Did you notice anything new in the room that you never noticed before? How did your body feel? What was going on in your mind? Was it hard to pay attention to the room? Were you distracted and if so, by what? How did you bring your attention back to your surroundings?

MINDFULNESS OF SURROUNDINGS

Find yourself a comfortable position in your chair with feet flat on the floor, back resting gently against the back of the chair, thumb and middle finger connected in a loop, and hands resting gently palms up on your thighs. Keep your eyes open and look at what is around you in the room.

Look all around. Pay attention to what you see. Is it bright or dark? Are you alone or with others? Are there windows in the room? Can you see outside? Can you see the sky? Is there light, or sunshine shining in the window? If so, does it light up an area on the floor or the wall? Or if it's dark outside can you see lights or the moon?

Look at what is in front of you. Is there a wall, door, window, curtains, artwork, light switches, furniture, bookshelves? What is beside you? Can you see behind you? Look all the way around you. Observe. When your mind wanders, notice it, accept it, and then bring your attention back to looking around the room again.

Notice the temperature around you. Is it warm, cold, just right? Is the air moving or still? Do you smell any odors or smells? Are they comforting or distasteful? Are they new smells or are they familiar?

What can you hear? Is it quiet? If there is noise what sounds are there? Where are they coming from? Are they loud, soft, sharp, soothing, or annoying? Do you want to keep listening to the sounds or do you want them to stop?

Is anything moving in the room? What is moving? What is staying still? Are things moving through the room, coming and going?

Pay attention to your body sitting in the chair. Feel where your bottom is touching the chair. Is the chair hard, soft, cushiony, or solid? Is the back supporting your back? Is the chair too big for you? Do your feet touch the floor or swing above it? Do your knees bend at the edge of the chair? Do you fill the seat side to side?

Look around and find something that particularly attracts your attention. Notice what shape it is, where it is located, what color it is, its texture, its purpose. Observe why it draws your attention. Does it remind you of something else? Do you know what it is? Is it common, or unusual? When you notice you are not thinking about the room around you and about this present moment, notice these thoughts, accept them, and let them go. Tell them, "not now." Bring your awareness back to your surroundings.

Become aware of yourself in this space. How do you feel? Do you feel safe? Do you want to be here? Does this place feel familiar or does everything seem new to you? Have you been someplace else that reminds you of this place? Do you feel good, bad, or neutral here?

Now that you have spent some time completely focused on being in this moment, bring the awareness you have gained back with you as you resume your regular life. Practice this exercise whenever possible to keep yourself present in the moment. You will concentrate better, get more done more quickly and feel calmer.

Tool 7-2: Mindfulness Outside in Nature

BACKGROUND: Being aware of the present moment is one central aspect of mindfulness. This mindfulness tool teaches kids and teens the skill of being totally present in this moment while focusing on all the details of natural surroundings. It uses as many of the senses as possible for an integrated awareness. This tool incorporates awareness of surroundings with the well-known healing, calming effect of being outside in nature. It also provides a way to be mindful while moving.

SKILL BUILDING: If at all possible take kids and teens outside to practice this skill. Find a park, playground, beach, lawn or other location where they will be safe. This tool can be done while going for a walk which is great for kids and teens who have trouble sitting still. If not walking someplace, encourage the kids to move around the defined space to look at everything they can see around them. The skill can also be done indoors by asking the client to close their eyes and imagine someplace outdoors that they have been.

Use the process on Handout 7-2 as the basis for this skill but modify it to suit your particular surroundings. Help clients stay focused by guiding them where to look and what to notice.

Encourage the client to practice this skill for a few minutes whenever they are outside. One great time might be every morning while they are waiting for the school bus or walking to school.

REFLECTION: After leading this skill, ask your client what it was like for them to pay such close attention to the nature around them. If outside, what did they notice for the first time? If indoors, were they able to use their imagination to pretend they were outside? Was it difficult to stay focused? What distracted them? How did they bring their attention back to the present moment? Were they able to practice it themselves during the week when they were outside? What did they notice when they did it? How did they feel before, during, and after the exercise?

MINDFULNESS IN NATURE MEDITATION

Whenever you are outside, practice being in the present moment by noticing your surroundings.

Ask clients to close their eyes and imagine they are outside someplace they've been or, better yet, take the client outside to practice this skill with eyes open.

Let's start by looking at the sky. What color is it right now? Is it clear? Are there clouds? What do the clouds look like?

Is the sun shining? Is it behind the clouds? Is it daylight or after dark?

Look around and see what's around you. Can you see some trees? If so, look closely at one of the trees. Is it covered with leaves or are the branches bare? What color are the leaves or the branches? Are there buds on the branches or seed pods or flowers? Does it have needles and pine cones? Is the tree perfectly still or is it moving in the breeze?

Slowly inhale and notice what you smell. Is there a fragrance or odor? Is it pleasant or distasteful? Is it natural or man-made? Does it remind you of something or of another time in your life?

Can you see grass? What color is it? Is it lush and green or dried out and brittle? Is it long or nicely groomed? If you can, reach down and touch the grass. What does it feel like?

Are there any flowers blooming? Notice their colors and shapes. Smell them if you can.

Are there any rocks in view? Look at their shape and color. Touch them and notice their texture.

Can you see a lake or the ocean? Pay attention to the water. Is it calm and still or moving and full of waves? What color is the water? Is there a beach?

Listen. What do you hear? Are there birds singing? Do you hear the sounds of civilization such as cars, trucks, planes, motors, horns, sirens? Can you hear the breeze blowing in the trees? Is there a sound from a stream or a waterfall or ocean surf?

Pay attention to the temperature. Is it hot, cold, warm, or chilly? Is the air still or is there a breeze, or perhaps a strong wind?

Now that you have spent some time focusing completely on your natural surroundings, bring your awareness with you as you resume your daily activities.

Note: Encourage kids and teens to practice this skill every time they are outside, whether it's to go for a walk, to sit on the deck, or on the playground or waiting for the school bus.

AWARENESS OF OBJECT

Tool 7-3: Beginner's Mind with Any Object

BACKGROUND: To see the richness of the present moment, we need to cultivate what has been called "beginner's mind." According to Jon Kabat-Zinn, beginner's mind is a mind that is willing to see everything as if for the first time, with openness and curiosity. This tool is a present moment awareness exercise that uses awareness of any object to practice using beginner's mind to see the object as if for the first time.

SKILL BUILDING: Explain to older kids and teens that two of the basics of mindfulness are beginner's mind and present moment awareness. Explain that this exercise helps them use beginner's mind, which is a mind that is open and willing to see everything with curiosity, as if for the first time, as they practice present moment awareness. Ask them to name some times they were beginners at something. Even very young children can do this exercise, but the explanation may not be needed.

Use the process described in Handout 7-3 with any object that is small enough to be held. Some examples of objects to use include a pencil, an eraser, a piece of paper, a cup, a fork, a ball, a toy, a smartphone, ear buds, a tablet, a stuffed animal, a coin. Use whatever you have handy. Hold the same type of object yourself and follow the instructions as you lead the exercise. In a group try to provide all group members with the same or similar object. Vary the length and detail of the exercise depending on the age and cognitive capability of the client. Each time you do this skill with the same client, lengthen the practice time a bit.

This is also a Mindful Seeing (Chapter 9), Mindful Touching (Chapter 12), Mindful Listening (Chapter 8) and perhaps Mindful Tasting (Chapter 10) and Mindful Smelling (Chapter 11) skill.

REFLECTION: Ask the client what it was like for them to do this exercise. Did they notice anything about the object they hadn't noticed before? Did their mind wander? How did they bring their attention back to the object? Was it boring? Did they notice any change in how they were feeling as they focused on the object? Do this process several times with the same object over a few weeks and see if the client gets better able to pay attention with practice.

AWARENESS OF OBJECT

Choose an object that is small enough to pick up easily and hold in your hand. Hold it in one hand and pass it to the other hand. Notice how heavy or light it is in your hand. How big is it? Rub your fingers over the surface. Are the edges rough or smooth? Observe the shape, color, and texture of the object. Feel any bumps or dents in the surface. Pay attention to whether it feels smooth, or rough. Does it feel cool or warm to your fingers? Is it sticky, greasy, slippery, wet, or dry?

Look closely to see if there is anything written on it. Are there words on it? Are there designs drawn or printed on it?

If your mind wanders or you start thinking about how bored you are, just bring your awareness back to the object. Squeeze it between your fingers. Is it squishy, flexible, hard, or solid?

How does it sound when you tap on it with your finger or scrape it with your fingernail? Does it echo, thud, click, thump, rattle? Rotate it in your hand. How does the light reflect off it? Is it shiny or dull? Does it reflect light, like a mirror? Is the color solid, opaque, transparent? Can you see through it? Is it solid or hollow? What material is it made out of?

Hold it up to your nose and smell it. Does it have an odor? Is it stinky or fragrant or neutral? Can you drop it on the table? Does it stay still or roll around or rock back and forth? What sound does it make as you move it around the table? Does it slide easily or stick in one place? Look closely and find something you didn't notice before.

Tool 7-4: Water Glass Game

BACKGROUND: This tool is another present moment awareness skill using a glass of water as the object to observe. Using water allows the client to engage all five senses: sight, touch, smell, taste, and hearing. This tool gives an excellent example of engaging "beginner's mind" to observe the glass of water. It is a great active skill that kids and teens enjoy.

SKILL BUILDING: Explain to clients that you will lead them in a present moment awareness exercise using a glass or cup of water as the object of their attention. Use Handout 7-4 as a guideline. After you have read through the handout yourself and understand the concept, put it down and hold a glass (or cup) of water in your own hand and do the exercise yourself as you lead the meditation. Ask the client to open their mind and look at the glass of water like they've never seen one before. For safety, use clear plastic cups with young kids. This skill can be done with paper cups but the client will not be able to look through the water as with a clear plastic cup or glass. Be prepared for kids to play with the water, splash it a bit, or drink it all. That's okay. They are having fun while learning mindfulness. Perfect!

REFLECTION: Ask the client what this was like for them. What did they notice about the glass/cup? How did it feel to pay attention to the glass/cup and then the water? What did they notice about how the water looked and moved? What did they notice about the taste or the smell? Were they able to follow the water as it went down their throat? How did they handle distracting thoughts? Do they feel any different now compared to before the exercise?

PRESENT MOMENT AWARENESS: WATER GLASS

Give the client a glass (or clear plastic or paper cup for younger kids) filled half full of water. Lead them in the following process. Do it with them. Take some time with each step. Engage their curiosity and have some fun.

Guided Script:

Look at the glass/cup as it sits on the table. Notice the shape, color, and size. Pick up the glass and look at it from all sides. Is there anything written on the sides or bottom? Rub your fingers across each surface of the glass/cup. Is it smooth, rough, sticky, slippery? Is it curved or squared? Are there any rough edges?

Can you see through the glass/cup? Move the glass back and forth and notice what happens to the water inside. Does it move? Move the glass in circles and watch the water swirl around the edges of the glass. Now hold it still. What happens to the water?

Tap on the glass below the water line. What does it sound like? Now tap on the glass above the water line. Does the sound change? Tap on the bottom and then on the rim. How does the sound differ?

Bring the glass up toward your nose and sniff it. Is there any odor? Is it pleasant, unpleasant, familiar, or perhaps surprising?

Take a small sip of water and hold it in your mouth. What does wet feel like? Is it hot, cold, silky, or rough? What does it feel like as you move it around your mouth? Swallow.

Take another sip and notice how the water feels as it comes into your mouth. Swallow it and pay attention to how it feels as it flows down your throat and into your stomach. Where do you lose track of it?

Bring your awareness back to the room.

OPEN FOCUS

Tool 7-5: Can You Imagine the Space Between?

BACKGROUND: Open Focus was developed by Les Fehmi (Fehmi, 2007, 2010, 2012). Its practice helps to develop attentional skills, the most basic skill in mindfulness. Open Focus attention training encourages awareness of how you attend to the wide array of sensory experiences and the space between those experiences. It helps clients put things in perspective and helps to relieve stress, manage physical pain, regulate emotions, and set the stage for peak performance and transcendent moments (teens and adults). For more information, see *The Open Focus Brain: Harnessing the Power of Attention to Heal Mind and Body* (Fehmi, 2007*).*

SKILL BUILDING: Explain that Open Focus is a present moment awareness tool that trains wide versus narrow attention in the present moment. Engage kids and teens in a discussion about what the difference is between narrow and wide focus. Narrow focus might be to look at someone's eye, while wide might be looking at their whole head or body. This skill is designed to help clients put things in perspective. For example, when they feel worried about school on a particular a day, to put it in perspective and remember that they have felt better about school and will again soon. One day is not everything and is less significant in the context of a whole month or year.

Ask clients to find a comfortable position and close their eyes if they feel comfortable. Then read through the Open Focus meditation (Handout 6-5). Use the whole meditation for older kids and teens and start with the second part of the meditation for younger kids to make it shorter and easier. Once you get the idea of alternating between large and small spaces, modify it to suit the needs of your client. Many of my young clients visibly calm down while listening to this exercise and often ask me to "do that thing again, Miss Deb."

REFLECTION: Ask your client what this experience was like for them. Were they able to visualize the space "between"? Did they notice any change in their body or their mind? Do they feel more relaxed now? What did they like/dislike about this exercise? Were they able to stay focused? Did they notice the difference between large and small spaces?

OPEN FOCUS: CAN YOU IMAGINE THE SPACE BETWEEN?

Start Here for Older Kids and Teens

Bring all your awareness to the space between your eyes.

Get a feeling of the space.

Imagine seeing the space.

Hear the silence between the eyes.

Think about the space.

Have a sense of newness between the eyes.

After seeing it, imagine feeling the space.

Put your thumbs together.

Can you imagine the space between the thumbs?

Can you imagine the shape?

Imagine what's around the thumbs.

Imagine what's outside the thumbs.

Feel nothing—absence of thumbs.

Can you feel the space around the thumbs?

Can you feel the sense of presence on your thumbs and index fingers?

Can you feel the space between the fingers and thumbs?

More of the brain's cortex is devoted to your awareness of this area of your body than any other part of the body.

Can you imagine feeling the space between the other fingers as well?

Can you imagine that throughout this exercise you will use this example of space to imagine what other spaces feel like during the exercise?

Effortlessly allow your imagination do all the work.

You will try to consciously grip the space which is not grippable.

You will focus more on how you are paying attention to it.

It occurs on an unconscious level.

You will release a lot of tension.

You will loosen and your focus will open.

When you are open you diffuse stress and tension.

When you are not open you accumulate tension.

If an unpleasant feeling occurs it is just a small thing in the totality of your total focus.

This practice builds a kind of refuge that helps you deal with things.

This provides a way for normalizing physiology.

Sit gently erect to avoid dropping out or sleeping.

(Adapted with permission from www.openfocus.com) (Fehmi, 2007, 2007, 2010)

Start Here for Younger Kids:

Can you imagine the space inside your head?

Can you imagine the space between the top of your head and the bottom of your feet?

Can you imagine the space between your left ear and right ear?

Can you imagine the space between your shoulders and your toes?

Can you imagine the space inside your mouth?

Can you imagine the space between your back and the back of the chair?

Can you imagine the space between your fingers?

Can you imagine the space between your shoulders and your hips?

Can you imagine the space between your mouth and your nose?

Can you imagine the space between your hips and your toes?

Can you imagine the space between your ankles and your heels?

Bring your focus back to the room.

JOURNAL

Tool 7-6: Journal About How Present Moment Awareness Changes My Day

BACKGROUND: Journaling will help kids and teens consolidate what they have learned about present moment awareness as well as point out where they may need more guidance.

SKILL BUILDING: Ask kids and teens to answer the journal prompts on Handout 7-6 in their journal or verbally. Use the second set of prompts for younger kids. Explain that this will help them understand what they learned about present moment awareness.

REFLECTION: Review the client's answers to the journal prompts with them. Discuss their answers or pictures and help them clarify what they have learned. Use this as an opportunity to answer their questions.

Journal About How Present Moment Awareness Changes My Day

Journal Prompts:

For Older Kids and Teens

- Describe what Present Moment Awareness (PMA) is.

- Give some examples of when you did or could have practiced this.

- How can you practice PMA while answering these prompts?

- How has your ability to be aware in the present moment changed?

- What have you noticed about your body when you practice this skill?

- What have you noticed about your emotional state when you practice this skill?

- When might you have practiced this skill that you didn't?

- How has your life changed now that you practice present moment awareness?

- How have you practiced using "beginner's mind"?

- What distracts you most when you are trying to focus on the present moment?

- What helps you return you attention once you have been distracted?

- List three example of narrow focus.

- List three examples of wide focus.

For Younger Kids

- Draw three things you see around you.

- Draw a picture of yourself paying attention to something in the present moment.

- Draw a picture of the water glass/cup.

- Draw a picture of a child learning something new.

Chapter 8
Mindfulness Listening

Tool 8-1: Listen to the Bell

BACKGROUND: Mindful listening is a skill often included in mindfulness programs for kids and teens. (Schonert-Reichl, & Lawlor, 2010; Kaiser Greenland, 2010; Hawn Foundation, 2011). Mindful listening can be used as a way to quiet the mind as well as a way to train the ability to pay attention and stay focused. This tool uses the meditation bell as the focus of attention. A meditation bell typically continues to ring for many seconds before it fades. The intention of this tool is to increase the ability to calm down and focus. It is an external awareness skill.

SKILL BUILDING:

1. Use the meditation bell to get the attention of a group of kids or teens. Ring the bell to signal that you want their attention. In a group setting you can also teach the kids and teens to ring it if they feel overwhelmed and need the group to quiet down and focus. See Tool 3-6 for more detail.
2. Use the meditation bell to begin and end various mindfulness skills throughout this workbook. The sound of the bell will quickly become a signal to kids and teens to calm down, quiet their mind and pay attention.
3. To use the bell as a mindfulness exercise, explain to kids and teens that you are going to ring the meditation bell (can be readily purchased from amazon.com) and that you want them to listen closely to the sound the bell makes and then to raise their hand when they can no longer hear the sound. Watch to see when they raise their hand. Repeat this several times and use the bell often as an effective way to help kids and teens tune in.

REFLECTION: Ask kids and teens if they could hear the bell. Ask them if they were distracted or had trouble paying attention to the sound until it stopped. How did they bring their attention back to the sound? Did other sounds distract them? Notice if they raise their hand next time you use the bell to get their attention.

Tool 8-2: Listen to the Sounds in the Room

BACKGROUND: As mentioned in Tool 8-1, mindful listening is a great way to teach kids and teens to calm their minds and to focus. This tool uses the sounds in the room as the focus of attention.

SKILL BUILDING: Ask the client to make lots of noise for a few moments. Then ask them to take a deep breath and be perfectly quiet while they listen to the sounds they can hear in the room. Allow about 30 seconds of silence—more or less time depending on the age of the client. Then discuss what sounds the client heard in the room or outside the room during the silence. If you heard sounds that they didn't hear, tell them what you heard, do the exercise again and see if they can hear what you heard now that you have directed their attention. In one group of kids who did this exercise, all we heard was the sound of their sneakers squeaking as they wiggled while sitting on the floor. The next time we were silent I asked them to see if they could keep their sneakers quiet. Even the 3-year-olds did it!

REFLECTION: Ask the client if they heard any sounds while they were being quiet. Had they noticed these sounds before? Did the sounds seem louder or quieter when they kept silent? Did they recognize what was making the sounds? Did they hear different sounds the second time they did the exercise? Were they making any of the sounds themselves and, if so, were they able to quiet them?

Tool 8-3: Dance Until the Music Stops

BACKGROUND: This skill provides another way to help kids and teens be mindful while listening to music and dancing. This tool provides a simple way to get kids and teens up and moving while practicing a mindfulness skill.

SKILL BUILDING: Be mindful of choosing a selection of upbeat music that matches your client's age and preference and that kids and teens will enjoy dancing to. Tell them you are having a dance party. Play a couple of songs and encourage them to dance to the music. Dance with them. Make it fun.

Now tell them to listen to the music and that when they hear the music stop to pretend they have been sprinkled with 'freeze dust' and to freeze in place until the music starts again. Play, dance, and have fun with them. Start and stop the music quickly, then slowly. Encourage them to freeze in funny positions. You get the idea.

The classic game of musical chairs could also be used to practice this skill but since it is a competitive game it changes the dynamics of the free-flowing, non-judgmental atmosphere of simply dancing. Sprinkle it in occasionally to prevent boredom if necessary.

REFLECTION: Ask the client what it was like for them to dance. Did they enjoy it? Did they feel self-conscious? What happened when the music stopped? Were they able to freeze in place? What did being sprinkled with 'freeze dust' feel like? How long did it take them to notice the music stopped?

Tool 8-4: Can You Hear the Ocean?

BACKGROUND: Kids of all ages have listened to hear the ocean when placing a conch shell up to their ear. This tool uses the same concept to help kids and teens tune in and pay attention to what they hear.

SKILL BUILDING: Tell clients that you are going to play a game to see if you can hear the ocean. In an ideal world you would have an actual conch shell to use for this skill. If not, then use a metal travel mug or hard plastic cup or glass without the cover. Demonstrate the skill by placing the conch shell/cup/glass up to your ear and listening. Ask the client to do the same and ask them if they can hear anything. Does it sound like the ocean? If no conch shell is available use one of the other items listed. When you place it completely over your ear you will hear nothing. When you tip it a little so the ear is not completely covered, you will hear a whooshing sound much like the ocean. Play with it and see how the sound changes.

This exercise may prompt a discussion of whether the client has ever been to the ocean and if so, what it sounded like. This is further practice with tuning into and being mindful of sounds. Use this as an opportunity to explore other sounds the client is familiar with.

REFLECTION: Did the client hear anything inside the conch or other item? Did it sound like the ocean? Did it sound like something else? Have they heard the actual ocean? What did it sound like? What makes the sound of the ocean? Does the sound of the ocean stay the same or change with the waves? What other sounds has the client noticed?

Tool 8-5: Listen to the Music

BACKGROUND: This tool provides another way for kids and teens to practice mindful listening. Music is a universal language across all cultures, races, and ethnicities. Much like a music appreciation class, this tool teaches the client to focus on the sounds in a piece of music and notice certain things about it.

SKILL BUILDING: Use a variety of styles of music to match the age and developmental level of the client. Play a piece of music and ask the client to listen to the music. Play with this as you see fit. You might ask the client to raise their hand when they hear someone sing, or when the drums stop beating, or when they hear a flute or a piano. Or play three different types of music and ask them to raise their hand when they hear music that calms them, or revs them up, or, makes them happy, or sad. Encourage them to clap their hands to the beat.

With teens, ask them which bands or singers they enjoy and play some of those songs. Also, play music of different genres including Top 40, Country, Rock and Roll, Classical, Jazz, Calypso, Alternative, and Folk Music. Ask them to listen to the songs and identify differences between the styles, their own likes and dislikes, and whether the music is familiar or not. Ask them to notice how they feel inside when different songs play.

REFLECTION: Was the client able to stay focused on the music being played? What distracted them? How did they bring their attention back to listening? Were they able to notice when: the singer sang, the drums stopped, or the flute or piano played? Were they able to notice how they felt when listening to different songs?

Tool 8-6: Let's Drum Together

BACKGROUND: It is quite easy to pay attention to the sound of a drum. Drums have a long and important history dating back to 5500 BC and have been used in cultural rituals, communication, motivation, war, spirituality, and music. (Wikipedia, 2013) This skill involves beating a drum or drum substitute in various rhythms while listening to the sounds.

SKILL BUILDING: There are several ways to do this mindful listening skill.

1. Play music that has a heavy drumbeat and ask clients to clap their hands along with the drum.

2. Allow kids and teens to beat on a drum or drum substitute. A variety of hand held instruments can be used—basically anything that shakes, rattles, or clacks when shaken or hit. Tell them to make as much noise with their drum (or substitute) as possible. Then ask them to be silent when you raise your drumstick in the air. Direct their attention to the sound of the silence. Then ask them to notice how it sounds when they are all beating their drum again (in a group). Then ask for silence again. Now ask them to beat their drum all together with the same rhythm: beat, beat, beat, beat. Ask them to notice how this sounds different than when they were all playing different beats.

3. Then beat a simple rhythm and ask them to copy it. Go back and forth making the beat more difficult as they master easier ones. Play and have fun. Vary the rhythm such as:

   - Beat, beat, beat, beat
   - Beat, hold, beat, beat
   - Beat, beat, hold, beat
   - Beat, hold, hold, beat
   - Beat, beat, beat, hold
   - Hold, beat, beat, beat.

REFLECTION: Ask clients: Were you able to hear the drum in the music? What did you notice when you played along with the music? What did you notice when everyone was beating at once? How did it sound different when you all had the same beat? What did it feel like to be silent? Did you have any trouble paying attention? Was it easier to pay attention before or after you learned the new beat being played? What helped you stay focused?

Tool 8-7: Listen Relay Game

BACKGROUND: This mindful listening activity requires the client to tune in and listen to sounds being made by passing an object from person to person. It is a great way to have fun while practicing mindful listening. It combines mindful listening with mindful touch as kids and teens use listening skills to tell where the object is and to know when it is being passed to them and mindful touch to feel the object being passed to them and then to the next person.

SKILL BUILDING:

Do this activity in stages and vary the difficulty depending on the age of the client. Start with passing an object that makes a lot of noise such as a bell, jingle-bell, maracas, or crumpled up piece of paper. Then make it more challenging by using objects that make less noise such as a Nerf ball, or small stuffed animal. For teens, pass a smartphone or iPod that is playing music. Then pass it while it is turned off.

1. Ask clients to sit in a circle and pass an object around the circle. Now ask them to close their eyes and pass it while using their ears to know where the object is and when it is being passed to them. If you are working with an individual child or teen instead of a group, ask them to pass the object from one hand to the other and then to you. You will pass it to your other hand and then back to them in a continuous circle.

2. Add a second object and pass it in the other direction so now the kids and teens must pay attention to where two objects are and when either one is being passed to them.
3. Avoid boredom and loss of focus by periodically asking the kids and teens to point to where they think the object is as it moves around the circle.
4. Try using water balloons to make this activity a little more exciting. This option is probably best done outside in warm weather.

REFLECTION: Ask the client if they could tell where the object was as it was passed around the circle. What sounds did they hear? How did they know when it was being passed to them? How did they find the object in order to take it? How did they find the hands of the client they were passing the object to? How did they let the next person know they were passing the object if they weren't ready? Did they use any other senses besides hearing?

<h1 style="text-align:center">Chapter 9</h1>

Mindful Seeing

Tool 9-1: Awareness of Object

BACKGROUND: Mindful seeing is an external awareness skill that involves paying attention to what the child or teen is seeing. It uses the sense of sight to observe the intended target of attention. This tool is a fun way to see how much more we notice about what we see when we are really paying attention to it. It uses the Mindfulness of Object Tool 7-3. Tool 7-4, Water Glass Game is another excellent Mindful Seeing exercise.

SKILL BUILDING:
1. Give the client an object and ask them to look at it closely for about 30 seconds and then hand it back to you. Put it out of sight. Ask them to describe or draw the object with as much detail as they can remember.
2. Give the object back to the client and use the Mindfulness of Object Tool 7-3 to guide them to look at it very closely.
3. Now ask them to describe or draw the object again.
4. Ask them if they noticed anything about the object after doing the Mindfulness of Object exercise that they didn't notice before doing it.

REFLECTION: Help clients reflect on this process. Did they notice anything after the mindfulness skill that they hadn't noticed the first time they looked at the object? Were they surprised they had missed some things about it the first time? How did they feel while doing the skill? Did they have trouble paying attention? How did they bring their attention back to the object when their mind wandered? What might they pay attention to during the week to practice this skill?

Tool 9-2: Remember the Objects

BACKGROUND: Mindful seeing is visually paying attention to something in particular. This tool provides a mindful seeing skill in the form of a game. It also demonstrates how being mindful while paying attention enhances our memory of what we paid attention to. This exercise is often played as a memory game.

SKILL BUILDING: Use the mindful seeing exercise on Handout 9-2. You can use actual objects or the photo provided, or another photo to your liking. Make sure the objects are things the client would recognize.

REFLECTION: How many objects did the client remember the first time? Did they remember more the second time after doing the exercise? Were they able to stay focused and if not what distracted them? How did they stay on task?

REMEMBER THE OBJECTS

Name or Draw the Objects

- Cover a tray or plate filled with various small objects

- Place it in front of clients and remove the cover

- Tell them to look at it for 10 seconds

- Then cover it up

- Ask them to list the objects they saw or draw them

- See how many they remembered

- Now lead them in a Mindful Seeing exercise with the objects (see Tool 7-3)

- Again, ask them to list the objects they saw or draw them

- Did they remember more this time?

Here's an example of a plate full of objects. Use this picture in place of actual objects. Or use any other picture of many objects.

Tool 9-3: Describe or Draw

BACKGROUND: This tool provides another exercise for kids and teens to practice mindful seeing and to become aware how much more they notice when they set their intention to pay attention to a familiar room.

SKILL BUILDING:

Use Handout 9-3 as a guideline for asking kids and teens to describe or draw a picture of someplace they are very familiar with. In this example we use their bedroom. This may be a great option for teens especially those with a messy room. Feel free to substitute other familiar places in the client's life such as their classroom, their kitchen, their bathroom, or your office. It's fun to see how much more they notice after they really look at the room. Be mindful to avoid asking a victim of abuse to describe a room where abuse may have taken place.

You can modify this exercise and ask the client to describe or draw your office without peeking at it. Then ask them to take a good look around and describe or draw it again. You might lead them in a mindfulness of surroundings exercise to help them notice more detail about the room. Clients who have trouble following through at home may benefit from doing this with them right there in your office.

REFLECTION: How much detail did the client remember the first time? Did they follow through and look at the room as you encouraged them to do between sessions? Did it work better for this particular client to use your office instead of a room in their home? Did they notice more after looking at the room mindfully? What distracted them? How did they bring their attention back to the exercise?

DESCRIBE OR DRAW

Draw Your Bedroom/Kitchen/Classroom

- Ask kids or teens to describe or draw a picture of a familiar room such as their bedroom, kitchen or classroom from memory

- Tell them to take a good look at that room next time they are in it

- Next time they come in ask them to describe or draw it again

- Notice how the descriptions or pictures differ

- Did they include more detail the second time?

Draw your picture here:

Tool 9-4: Hi, I See You

BACKGROUND: Another great way for kids and teens to practice mindful seeing is to look at a person and notice something about them such as what they are wearing, their hair, or their eyes. This is also a great way for practicing social skills and mindful relationships. This tool provides a simple exercise to really look at someone and pay attention to something about them.

SKILL BUILDING: Use the exercise provided on Handout 9-4. This works great in a group but can be modified to use with individual clients as well. Some kids and teens may feel very self-conscious and vulnerable when they look closely at another child or make eye contact, particularly if they are shy or have symptoms of autism. Some may close their eyes to allay their discomfort. If so, that's okay. Encourage them to say "I see your eyes are closed." For clients with extreme discomfort, relieve their stress and encourage them to look at the person's hair or shirt instead and say what color that is. This may be less anxiety provoking. As their comfort increases encourage them to try looking at eye color.

Set the stage for non-judgment by avoiding correction of the color or item identified. For example, encourage clients to accept whatever color is named as the color seen by that client. If Jill says "Hello, your shirt looks orange" to Bill and you see Bill's shirt is blue, just accept it. If Bill says "no, my shirt is blue" just smile and say "your shirt looks orange to Jill today." This exercise often results in giggles and intense focus and connection.

When doing this exercise in a group encourage the clients to speak loudly enough so everyone in the group can hear them. Instruct the group members to listen closely to the color or item being named and to raise their hand if they can't hear it. This will engage them all in mindful listening and keep them involved in the exercise while they await their turn.

This exercise can be done with an individual client simply between them and you.

REFLECTION: Ask the client what happened when they looked at another person closely enough to name something about what they saw? Were they able to make eye contact? Did they feel comfortable or self-conscious? Did it feel different when they were naming what they saw than when someone was naming what they saw about them? What did you notice about their body language? Did they have trouble paying attention? How did they bring their attention back if they were distracted? Did they name colors accurately?

Hi, I See You

- Ask kids and teens to sit in a circle or do this with your individual client

- Tell the first child to look at the second child and say "Hi – I see you _____" have them fill in the blank with something they see when they look at the child such as what they are wearing, the color of their hair, their eye color, if they are wearing glasses, if they have a barette in their hair, or if they are smiling, etc.

  - Examples:
    - Hi, I see you are wearing a blue sweater

    - Hi, I see you have blond hair

    - Hi, I see your eyes are blue

    - Hi, I see you have your shoes on

- Then have the second child do the same back to the first child filling in the blank

- Go around the circle

- If a child is shy and looks away the other child can simply say "Hi– I see you are looking away"

- For kids and teens who have trouble making eye contact suggest they start with something else and gradually try looking at eye color.

- Ask all the participants in the circle to listen to what is being named and raise their hand if they can't hear it. This will keep them engaged instead of bored and distracted.

Tool 9-5: Simon Says

BACKGROUND: The classic childhood game of Simon Says is a wonderful mindful exercise. It combines several mindfulness skills as it requires the players to engage in mindful seeing to see what movement to make and mindful listening to tune in to make sure they hear the phrase "Simon Says" before they move. It is also a mindful motion practice and addresses impulse control. This tool provides a great way to use this game as a mindfulness exercise.

SKILL BUILDING: Explain to clients that you want to play a game that uses their mindful seeing and mindful listening skills. Teach them the classic Simon Says game.

Assign the role of "Simon" either to yourself or to a child or teen if working with a group. Instruct "Simon" to give instructions (usually physical actions such as "hop on one leg" or "touch the floor") to the other participants. "Simon" should demonstrate the actions when giving the verbal instructions and may simply say "Simon says, do this". Tell them to follow "Simon's" instruction only if they hear the phrase "Simon says". For example, "Simon says, jump up and down" vs "Jump up and down". Ask participants to sit out of the game if they follow instructions that are not immediately preceded by the "Simon says" or if they fail to follow an instruction which does include the phrase "Simon says".

It is the ability to be mindful of when the command is valid or invalid, rather than physical ability, that usually matters in the game; in most cases, the action just needs to be attempted. This combines mindful seeing and mindful listening.

The object for the player acting as Simon is to get all the other participants out as quickly as possible. The winner of the game is usually the last person who has successfully followed all of the given commands. Occasionally however, two or more of the last players may all be eliminated by following a command without "Simon Says", thus resulting in Simon winning the game.

After playing for a while, help the clients reflect on what it was like to use their mindful seeing and mindful listening skills.

REFLECTION: Was the client eliminated from the game quickly? Ask them what it was like to listen to the command while watching the action. Was it easier to listen to the words or watch the action? Did they have trouble paying attention and giving priority to the words they heard instead of the action they saw? Did they get distracted? How did they bring their attention back to listening and seeing?

Chapter 10
Mindful Tasting

Tool 10-1: Taste Tester
Tool 10-2: Mindful Flavors Matching Game
Tool 10-3: Mindful Eating

Tool 10-1: Taste Tester

BACKGROUND: Mindful tasting is simply paying attention to what you taste. It is an external to internal awareness skill and is an excellent way to practice being mindful of the present moment. Jon Kabat-Zinn's Mindfulness Based Stress Reduction Program is famous for mindfully tasting a raisin. (Stahl & Goldstein, 2010) This tool provides a fun exercise to practice being mindful of taste.

SKILL BUILDING: Use Handout 10-1 to guide clients in a mindful tasting exercise. Tell them you want them to pretend to be a taste tester like the people that test the flavor of foods or wines to see if it tastes the way it should. Ask them to close their eyes and use their sense of taste and see if they can guess what each food is. Do this with several different foods with different textures and tastes.

Encourage them to use this skill every time they eat.

Use caution when giving food to children due to possible food allergies, some of which may be life threatening. Always check with parents or guardians beforehand. Parents may want to provide food for this exercise that they know is safe. Tools 10-2 and 10-3 do not involve actually eating food, just imagining it.

REFLECTION: Guide clients to reflect on what this exercise was like for them. Did they guess what the food was? What did they notice about the texture, temperature, aroma, and flavor of the food? Was it familiar to them or not? Did they like the taste or not? Did they notice anything about a familiar food that they never noticed before? Did they get impatient with the process? Were they able to go slowly? How were the foods different from each other? Which one did they like the best and least?

Taste Tester Game

Gather a collection of foods (4 or 5 different kinds) in bite size pieces. Examples: grapes, cherry tomatoes, apple slices, crackers, lemon, M&M candy, bread, cookies, cheese, popcorn, candy, oranges, raisins, pretzels, olives.*

Guided Script:

We are going to pretend that we are all taste testers. You know, they are the people that test the flavor of foods or wines to see if it tastes the way it should.

If it is okay with you, close your eyes. I am going to place a small piece of food in your hand. Hold onto it and wait for me to start.

We are going to eat this food mindfully. We are going to teach our brains to pay attention to what we eat and how we eat.

First hold it in your fingers. Notice if it is soft, hard, squishy, smooth, bumpy, wet, dry, warm, or cold.

Slowly put it up to your nose and take a sniff. Is there any smell? Now take a lick. Notice what it feels like on your tongue.

Now put it in your mouth but don't bite yet. Just move it around your mouth with your tongue.

Focus on how the food feels in your mouth. Is it changing, melting, or softening?

Now take a little bite. Notice what it tastes like. You are a taste tester and it's your job to really pay attention to how the food tastes. Notice whether it's crunchy, silky, soft, hard, hot, cold, scratchy, wet, or dry. Is it sweet, sour, salty, or spicy? Chew it slowly and pay attention to how it feels in your mouth. Notice how it feels on your teeth, on your tongue, on the roof of your mouth.

When you have chewed it enough, swallow it and notice how it feels sliding down your throat into your stomach. How far down does it go before you can't feel it anymore? How does your mouth feel now that the food is gone? How does your stomach feel?

When they have finished that food, ask "what did you notice about your body as you mindfully tasted the food? What did you notice about how the food tasted? What was the food?"

Then give them another food and repeat the process with up to four foods that have different characteristics such as textures, flavors, etc.

*Use caution when giving food to children due to possible food allergies, some of which may be life threatening. Always check with parents or guardians beforehand. Parents may want to provide food for this exercise that they know is safe.

Tool 10-2: Mindful Flavors Matching Game

BACKGROUND: Mindful tasting is an excellent way to help clients be mindful in the present moment. It is an external-to-internal awareness process. This tool provides a fun matching game to help clients increase their awareness of taste.

SKILL BUILDING: Use Handout 10-2 to help clients think about how different foods taste. Help younger kids understand what the words mean by naming or giving them examples of foods that are sour, sweet, crunchy, etc. This tool can readily be combined with the Taste Tester Tool 10-1. After the client completes the worksheet, initiate a discussion about tastes that kids and teens like, dislike, which foods are sweet, spicy, crunchy, chewy and so forth.

REFLECTION: Did the client understand the words for the various flavors? Were they able to complete the worksheet accurately? Were they able to identify different foods that were sweet, sour, crunchy, minty, salty, spicy, cold, or hot? What did they learn about tastes? What distracted them while they were completing the worksheet?

MINDFUL FLAVORS MATCHING GAME

Draw a line from the flavor to all the foods that match it.

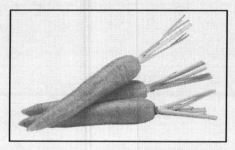

SWEET

SOUR

SPICY

CHEWY

CRUNCHY

COLD

MINTY

HOT

SALTY

Tool 10-3: Mindful Eating

BACKGROUND: Paying attention to eating while eating is a great way to practice being mindful throughout the day. This is an external-to-internal awareness skill. It combines mindfulness of intention, mindfulness of touch, seeing, smelling and taste. This tool provides a way for kids and teens to use their imagination to pretend they are eating their favorite food in a mindful way. It teaches them a mindful process they can use when they are actually eating.

SKILL BUILDING: Explain to clients that one great way to practice being mindful is to set their intention to pay attention to eating. Explain to kids and teens that setting an intention in mindfulness is simply deciding what to pay attention to—in this case, eating. Ask them to close their eyes and pretend that they are eating their favorite food while you read the Awareness of Eating guided imagery to them on Handout 10-3.

Another great way to do this exercise is to give clients a small piece of actual food such as a grape, a raisin, or an M&M as in the Taste Tester Tool 10-1. This could be incorporated at the beginning of having a snack.*

Encourage clients to slow down and practice this mindfulness skill when they first sit down to eat at every meal.

*Use caution when giving food to children due to possible food allergies, some of which may be life threatening. Always check with parents or guardians beforehand. Parents may want to provide food they know is safe. If food allergies are an issue, use the tools that use the imagination to pretend food is being eaten instead of real food as in Handout 10-3.

REFLECTION: Guide clients to reflect on what it was like to imagine they were eating while listening to the Mindful Eating guided imagery on Handout 10-3. Could they imagine the taste, smell, and feel of the food? What was it like to slow down the process of eating and to pay attention to every detail? Did they get distracted? How did they bring their attention back to imagining they were eating? Ask them to practice awareness of eating whenever they eat and discuss what happens when they do so.

AWARENESS OF EATING

Close your eyes and pretend that you are eating. Set your intention to pay attention to everything about eating. Whenever other thoughts arise that are not about eating, notice them, dismiss them, and remind yourself of your intention to pay attention to eating.

Imagine you can see your favorite food. Notice how the food looks as it sits on your plate. Be aware of the food's smell, color, and shape. What food is it?

Before you start to eat, notice how your stomach feels. Does it feel hungry, empty? Is it comfortable, uncomfortable? Can you connect how it feels with hunger? Tune in to how your stomach feels and make sure you are hungry before you eat.

As you put the food on your fork, notice how heavy it is. Take a sniff to see what it smells like.

As you place the food in your mouth, notice if the food is warm or cold and how it feels in your mouth. Pay attention to how it feels when you chew the food. As you chew, focus on the flavor, and whether it is crunchy, chewy, soft, or hard. Notice if it is tender, tough, slippery, smooth, rough, salty, tangy, sweet, sour, spicy or plain. Be aware of whether it sticks to your teeth.

If your mind wanders, just remember your intention and bring your attention back to eating.

Again notice the feeling of the food in your mouth, on your teeth, on your tongue, on your lips. Chew until it is completely ready to be swallowed. Pay attention to how the food feels as you swallow and it leaves your mouth and slides down your throat. Notice how far down it goes before you can't feel it any more. Notice if there is any food still in your mouth or if it's empty now. Tune in to how your stomach feels. Notice how it feels different after you have eaten a little food and then after you have eaten a lot of food. Repeat this process until your food is gone or until you feel full.

Chapter 11
Mindful Smelling

Tool 11-1: Imagine That Smell

BACKGROUND: Mindful smelling uses the sense of smell to practice being mindful. It is an external to internal awareness skill. The sense of smell is often strongly associated with memories and other information. As with other mindfulness skills, mindful smelling increases the kid's or teen's ability to observe, enjoy and engage in their experiences. It boosts their self-awareness and self-control. This tool uses the power of the imagination to remember and focus on familiar scents.

SKILL BUILDING: Use Handout 11-1 to guide clients to imagine that they are smelling various familiar scents. Pause to allow them time to imagine and remember the scents as you go through the exercise. Reflect on what this was like for them.

REFLECTION: Guide clients to reflect on what this exercise was like for them. Were they able to imagine the various scents? Were there any they had trouble with? Did imagining the scents remind them of anything in their life? Was the memory positive or negative? Engage them in a discussion of when they smelled the various scents.

IMAGINE THAT SMELL

Take a deep belly breath in through your nose and let it out slowly through your mouth.

Now I want you to use your imagination to pretend you are using your nose to remember how different things smell. The first thing I want you to imagine is the smell of fresh popcorn. Mmm can you smell it?

Now imagine someone just mowed the grass. Can you smell the freshly mowed grass smell?

Imagine you are eating an orange. What does it smell like?

Now pretend you are biting into a lemon. What do you smell?

Pretend you are by the fireplace or the campfire and the smoke blows into your face. Can you imagine what the smoke smells like?

Do you have a dog or a cat? Imagine how they smell.

Imagine that someone in your house is using fingernail polish. Do you know what that smells like?

If you have been swimming in a pool remember what the chlorine smell is like from the pool water.

If you have been to the ocean, remember the smell of the salt air or perhaps the seaweed.

If someone you know wears perfume imagine that you can smell the fragrance of the perfume.

Pretend you are holding a bouquet of flowers. Imagine you can smell the flowers.

Can you remember the smell of fresh coffee?

How about peppermint candy?

Imagine you are enjoying the delicious smell of your favorite soup.

Now take another deep breath and then open your eyes and bring your attention back to the room.

Which smells were you able to imagine? Were they good, neutral, or bad? Did they bring back any memories?

Tool 11-2: Name That Smell

BACKGROUND: This tool provides another way for kids to increase their mindfulness skills by using their sense of smell. It is a fun activity that kids and teens, as well as adults, enjoy. Some younger kids might need some help to learn how to smell something by breathing in through their nose. See Tool 6-2 for practice using flowers.

SKILL BUILDING: Explain to clients that you are going to play a game to see if they can recognize different smells. Place a piece of food or other scented item in the bottom of a small paper cup. Then place another paper cup inside that cup on top of the item. The fragrance will seep out of the bottom cup while the top cup hides the item from view. Make sure the cups themselves are fragrance-free.

If you have a group larger than 3 or 4 kids or teens, you may need to make several sets of each fragrant item to speed things along. For example, label 3 or 4 cups with the number 1. Then put a wintergreen lifesaver in each of the 3 or 4 cups. Then place an empty cup inside each of these cups, on top of the wintergreen. Now label another 3 or 4 cups with the number 2. Place a chai tea bag in the bottom of each of these cups and place an empty cup inside these cups on top of the tea bag. Then label another 3 or 4 cups with the number 3. Place some fresh or instant coffee grounds in each of these cups. Then place an empty cup inside these cups on top of the coffee grounds.

Use Handout 11-2 to lead the game. Hand out each of the cups in set #1 and ask the kids and teens to sniff the cups without removing the top cup and peeking. Ask them to write down #1 and what they think the item is. Collect the first set of cups. Then hand out set #2 and ask them to write down #2 and what they think is in the cup #2. Repeat for as many different sets of fragrant items you have prepared.

REFLECTION: Ask clients: Were they able to recognize the various scents? Were some scents easier to recognize than others. Did the scents remind them of anything? For example, the spicy fragrance of the chai tea bag reminds some clients of Christmas. Did they have trouble staying on task? What distracted them? How did they bring their attention back to the smelling game?

NAME THAT SMELL GAME

Gather about 4 -5 foods or items that have a distinct smell. Some examples are listed below. See the skill building section for how to organize this game if you have a group of more than a few kids or teens.

Place a small fragrant food or other item in the bottom of a paper cup. Place an empty paper cup inside this cup on top of the fragrant item to hide it from view.

"We are going to play a mindful smelling game. I will come to each of you one at a time and hand you a cup containing something that has a smell. "Please take a slow breath in through your nose and tell me what you smell." Be careful not to remove the top cup and peek. When everyone has had a turn I will see who guessed the smell."

Repeat with 3 or 4 more fragrant items. Here are some that work well.

Popcorn	Apple Juice
Perfume	Bananas
Oranges	Wintergreen Lifesavers*
Tomatoes	Coffee*
Bread	Flowers
Cheese	Play Doh
Lemon	Chai tea bags*
Pickles	Cinnamon
Strawberries	

Use any other food or object that has a distinct smell that kids will recognize.

*These are my favorite because they hold their scent, are portable, and non-perishable.

Tool 11-3: What Kind of Smell

BACKGROUND: A smell can trigger a flood of memories, and influence a child or teen's mood and academic performance. The olfactory bulb, where our sense of smell is located, is part of the brain's limbic system (where the amygdala resides) (See Tool 3-13). This is an area so closely associated with memory and feeling that it is sometimes called the "emotional brain". Therefore smell can call up memories and powerful responses almost instantaneously. This tool uses the imagination to remember smells and the emotions associated with them.

SKILL BUILDING: Use Handout 11-3 to lead kids and teens to imagine different smells and to notice what emotions and memories are evoked by the smells. Use this exercise as a springboard for a discussion about smells; which one they like or dislike, what different smells remind them of; memories that are linked in their brain to certain smells.

REFLECTION: Ask clients: Were you able to imagine the different smells? What feelings came up when you imagined different smells? Did any smells bring up bad memories? Did any of them trigger good memories? Did you have trouble paying attention to imagining smells? How did you bring your attention back when it wandered?

WHAT KIND OF SMELL

- Ask kids and teens to imagine different smells one at a time, some that smell good and have good connotations and some that smell bad or may be dangerous.

  "Close your eyes and use your imagination to pretend you are smelling strawberries. Can you smell them? What kind of smell is it? How do you feel inside when you smell them? Is it a good feeling? Does it feel safe? Is it something you want to smell?"

- Repeat this with other smells. Examples:

✓ Strawberries	✓ Pizza
✓ Smoke (campfire, forest fire, house fire)	✓ Coffee
✓ Manure or dog poo	✓ Freshly baked chocolate chip cookies
✓ Fingernail polish	✓ Pumpkin pie
✓ Shampoo	✓ Gas fumes
✓ Popcorn	✓ Paint
✓ Freshly cut grass	✓ Play Doh
✓ Flowers	✓ Finger paints
✓ Dirty diaper	✓ Soup
✓ Garbage can	✓ Mint candy

- Initiate a conversation about different smells they like or dislike and the memories and emotions evoked.

Chapter 12

Mindful Touching

Tool 12-1: Ice Cube Game

BACKGROUND: Holding an ice cube in your hand is often included as an effective distress tolerance skill in dialectic behavior therapy (DBT) (Linehan, 1993). Rather than reacting impulsively to the stinging cold (or to a distressing event or emotion), the goal is to bring attention to the discomfort and tolerate it rather than reacting by putting it down, and to notice how after a while the discomfort turns to numbness. This tool uses an ice cube as the focus of attention for teaching mindfulness of touch and for increasing distress tolerance. Kids and teens have fun holding the ice, noticing how it stings, and feeling it melt and start dripping while increasing their mindfulness of touch as well as their distress tolerance.

SKILL BUILDING: Use Handout 12-1 to lead clients in the Ice Cube Game. Have fun with this game. Encourage clients to hold the ice as long as they can but create an accepting environment for those who need to put it back in the cup. Coach them to keep trying. Direct their attention to all the sensations they feel in their hand from the freezing cold ice.

After they have done it once, start over again and ask them to see how holding the ice is different the second time.

Use caution and avoid injury by telling the clients not to hold the ice for longer than a minute or two. For older kids and teens find out if they have heard of the dangerous ice and salt challenge and educate them that holding the ice too long might cause frostbite and that combining salt with ice causes burns. Use your judgement about which clients you use this skill with.

REFLECTION: Ask clients what feelings they had about holding the ice. Did they give up and put it back in the cup? Did they keep holding it but feel dumb or ashamed because they felt so uncomfortable? Did they feel a sense of accomplishment or pride that they kept holding the ice? Did they notice any change in how it felt? Did their hand get numb? Was the ice easier to hold after a little while? How did they handle getting wet as the ice melted?

ICE CUBE GAME

Give each child a cup with an ice cube in it and a napkin.

Guided Script:

Pay attention to your hand. Just notice how it feels. Is it warm, cold, hot, sticky, wet, dry, comfortable or uncomfortable?

Now let's look at the ice cube in the cup and then reach into the cup and take the ice cube out of the cup and hold it in your hand.

Notice how your hand feels now with the ice cube in it. Put the ice in the palm of your hand and fold your fingers over it.

If it feels too uncomfortable, that's OK. Simply drop it back into the cup. As soon as your hand warms up a bit, take it out again.

Notice what happens as you hold the ice cube. Does it feel cold? Does it begin to sting? Does it burn? Is it melting? Is it dripping?

Do you notice any feelings in the rest of your body? Does your body feel uncomfortable, neutral, or comfortable?

What happens after a little while? Does your hand start to feel numb? Can you feel the ice anymore?'

Put the ice in the cup and warm your hand for a moment.

Pick up the ice again, only this time with the goal of doing what it takes not to react physically or mentally to the discomfort from the ice. See if you can hold it longer this time.

Put it down after holding it for a maximum of 1 or 2 minutes.

Adapted from (Linehan, 1993) and (Kaiser Greenland, 2010)

*Use caution and avoid injury by telling the clients not to hold the ice for longer than a minute or two. For older kids and teens find out if they have heard of the dangerous ice and salt challenge and educate them that holding the ice too long might cause frostbite and that combining salt with ice causes burns. Use your judgement about which clients you use this skill with.

Tool 12-2: Textures Game

BACKGROUND: Kids and teens love to touch. From infancy, kids use their sense of touch to explore and learn about their world. Focusing full attention on the sense of touch can be a great way to practice mindfulness and increase self-regulation skills. This tool provides a fun game that encourages the players to focus on how various textures feel in their hand.

SKILL BUILDING: Use Handout 12-2 to lead the kids and teens in a game that focuses their attention on the sense of touch. Discuss what the word "texture" means and give some examples of items with different textures.

REFLECTION: Reflect on what this game was like for clients: Did the client stay focused on how the item felt in their hand? What did they notice about how the item felt? Did they have any trouble identifying the texture? What came up for them while they focused on different textures? Did any of the textures remind them of other things they have touched before? Were they able to identify the item? Did they like how some textures felt better than others? Were any of the items unpleasant to touch? Did they get distracted and, if so, how did they bring their attention back to the feel of the item? Did anything about the feel of the item change after they opened their eyes?

TEXTURES GAME

Gather a collection of items with a variety of textures. Some examples include: sandpaper, satin, burlap, smooth wood, pine needles, rock, water, suede, pretzels, lettuce, strawberries, Kleenex, fleece, cooked noodles, Play-Doh, small toys with interesting shapes.

"We are going to play a Mindful Touching game called Textures. Does anyone know what a texture is?"

(Discuss this with them and give examples of different textures. Ask them what the difference is between something that feels soft vs rough, or hot vs cold, or soft vs hard. Tailor this to the age of the client.)

"This game is more fun if you close your eyes so if you are comfortable doing so, close your eyes now. I am going to give you a small item. Just take it and hold it in your hand without looking at it.

Play with it between your fingers and your thumb. Pay attention to how it feels. Tap on it. Squeeze it. Slide your fingers over it. Is it smooth or rough? Does it feel prickly, dry, wet, soft, hard, solid, sticky, or bendable?

Notice how your fingers feel as you touch the texture of the item in your hand. Is the feeling pleasant or not pleasant? Have you felt this texture before? Does it remind you of anything you have touched before? Do you like touching it or would you rather put it down?

What do you think the item is?"

(Let them guess.)

"Okay. Now open your eyes and look at what you are holding. Is it what you thought it was? Does it look the way you expected it to look? Feel it now while you look at it. What do you notice about how it feels now that you can see it?"

Repeat several times with items with various textures.

After doing this game with several items ask which items felt the best, or the worst to them.

Tool 12-3: Guess the Objects Game

BACKGROUND: The sense of touch activates different areas of the brain from the sense of smell or sight and is a very tangible way for kids and teens to increase their awareness. This tool provides kids and teens a game that engages them in being mindful of their sense of touch in an effort to guess what the items are they are holding in their hand. We used to play this game in elementary school when we finished our work.

SKILL BUILDING: Use Handout 12-3 to lead clients in using their sense of touch to guess what object they are holding in their hand. This can be done with an individual client or in a group. Use a variety of different objects that clients might be familiar enough with that they can guess what it is.

REFLECTION: Help clients reflect on what this game was like for them: What did the object feel like? Did it feel familiar? Were they able to guess what it was? What happened to their awareness as they focused on their sense of touch? Were they distracted? How did they bring their attention back to the object in their hand? What were they thinking about while they tuned in to the feel of the object?

GUESS THE OBJECT GAME

Gather a collection of small items that can be held in the palm of the child or teen's hand. Some examples are: grapes, raisins, erasers, pretzels, rocks, shells, tiny toy animals, a wad of Play-Doh, marbles, cotton balls, pecans, wet sponges, feathers. Make some of them slippery, some smooth, some rough, some hard, some soft, different shapes.

"We are going to play a Mindful Touching game call Guess the Object. If you are comfortable close your eyes and put your hands out so I can place something in your hand."

Now place an object in each client's hand.

"What does the object feel like? What shape is it? What do you think it looks like? Is it hard or soft, smooth or rough, sticky or slippery? Can you guess what it is?"

Give each client a chance to describe what they are holding and to listen as all the clients (in a group) describe what they are holding.

Repeat with a variety of items.

Tool 12-4: What Is It?

BACKGROUND: Kids and teens love to play guessing games. We played this game as kids at Halloween with slimy things like pasta and hard boiled eggs that made us think we were touching eyeballs and brains. This tool provides another variation on using the sense of touch to increase mindfulness.

SKILL BUILDING: Use Handout 12-4 to guide clients to use their sense of touch to guess what the different items are in a small bag or box. A simple brown paper bag works well. Be creative. Just for fun, with younger kids, I use small felt bags decorated with animals that I found at a craft store to hold and hide the items. Teens might enjoy bags decorated with favorite bands, sports teams, or celebrities.

Encourage them to reach into the bag and feel around until they can pick out one item and hold it in their hand without looking at it. You might put 10 different tiny items in the bag and see how many of them the client can guess. For a group, use several bags full of items so the clients are not waiting very long to participate. Otherwise they get bored and easily distracted.

REFLECTION: Help the client reflect on what this game was like for them: How many items did they guess correctly? Did they have trouble with certain items? Which ones were easy to guess? What were they thinking about while they were touching each item? Were they distracted? How did they refocus? Did any of the items feel familiar, unfamiliar, pleasant, icky to touch?

WHAT IS IT? GAME

Place a variety (between 5 and 10) of small objects in a small bag or box. Examples include: pencils, erasers, plastic paper clips, tiny toy animals, furry fabric, marbles, balloons, sandpaper, dice, AA battery, whistle, feathers, tiny toys, keys, package of Post Its. Use your imagination.

"We are going to play a Mindful Touching game called 'What Is It? Put your hand in the bag (or box) and without looking at it, pick up an item and describe it.

What does the object feel like? What shape is it? What do you think it looks like? Is it hard or soft, smooth or rough, sticky or slippery? Can you guess what it is?"

You might place 10 items in a bag and ask the client to see how many of them they can correctly guess.

Another way to do this is to put common foods in separate containers and use foods such as grapes, hard boiled eggs, strawberries, cooked noodles, mashed potatoes, ice cubes, prickly fruit, etc. and ask them to touch the items without looking and guess what they are.

Be cautious with very young kids to avoid choking hazards.

Chapter 13
Mindful Motion

Tool 13-1: Walk Mindfully

BACKGROUND: Walking meditation is a great alternative to sitting meditation for active kids and teens. Walking meditation is a mindful practice during which close attention is paid to the feeling of each part of the body as it takes part in walking. This type of walking meditation is not thinking or contemplating while walking (that's a different form of walking meditation). It is being mindful of the muscles of your body, the placement of your feet, balance, and motion. Walking meditation can be practiced anywhere.

In walking meditation, we focus on the movement of each step and on the body as we move. Since walking is part of our daily lives, walking meditation is a great way to increase and practice mindfulness. And it is a great alternative to mindfulness skills that require clients to sit still. Kids and teens can do it anywhere and anytime they walk. It can help them feel connected to the earth and fully present in their body. It can help them calm the busy chatter of their mind and allow a clearer presence. This is a great mindfulness exercise for clients who have trouble sitting still such as those with ADHD or anxiety or who just do better when they are moving.

SKILL BUILDING: Find a place where clients have room to walk about 20 steps. If there is no room, just do this exercise walking in place. Use Handout 13-1 to lead clients in a walking meditation. Encourage clients to practice this whenever they walk during their day, even if it's just on the way to the kitchen or bathroom. Play with it and make it fun. The goal is to help clients pay attention to every component of walking and to every part of their body as it participates in walking.

For added intrigue, walk on a labyrinth. Labyrinths are often used in more contemplative walking meditations but the walking meditation described here can be easily adapted to be done on a labyrinth pattern. There is a portable labyrinth available which is printed on a huge plastic sheet and thus can be used anywhere there is a big enough space, inside or out. Very cool. These can be found by searching for "portable labyrinth" on the internet.

REFLECTION: Help clients reflect on how they felt during the walking meditation. Were they able to feel their feet, legs, hips, back, shoulders, and neck? What was it like to slow down their steps? Did they lose their balance when they walked slowly? Was it easier to walk quickly or slowly? Did their mind wander? How did they stay focused on walking?

WALKING MEDITATION

Find a place where you have room to walk back and forth, about 10 or 20 steps in length. Walk in place if there is not enough room to walk.

Place your hands either behind your back, at your sides, or in front.

Notice your breath for a moment as it flows easily in and out. Now pay attention to what it feels like to be standing. Notice how your feet feel touching the ground. Notice what muscles in your body are working to hold you up and keep you from losing your balance or falling over. Feel your hands hanging down, your shoulders, your lower back, and your belly, each having its own part in keeping you upright in the standing position.

Lean to the right and notice how your legs feel. Does your right leg feel lighter or heavier than your left leg? How does your right foot feel compared to your left foot? Now lean to the left and notice what feels different in your legs. Now stand up straight again.

Now bend your knees. Pay attention to your feet, your ankles, your knees. Now stand up again. Feel the difference. Just notice and allow without judgment.

Now let's begin to walk. Very slowly lift your left foot off the ground and move it forward and place it on the ground. Pay attention to your left foot and put your weight on it. Now pay attention to the right foot. Lift it, swing it forward, and step onto it. Notice how your legs feel from your waist all the way down to your ankles and feet. Continue stepping slowly. Keep noticing how your body feels. When you get to the end of the path, stop and turn around. Take a deep breath, and be aware of the first step as you begin again.

Now walk faster but keep noticing how your legs and feet feel. Now slow down again. Now pretend you are an Indian who is walking so quietly no one can hear him walk. Remember to move mindfully. As your mind begins to quiet, you will see how you notice more when you move slowly. Your mind becomes clearer. You tune into the connection between your mind and body.

If it helps you stay focused, you can say to yourself "walking/walking" or "step/step," or "right/left." Use these words to encourage the awareness of the sensations of walking.

Slow down a little and, as you walk, notice when you lift your foot, swing it forward, and then, when you place it down. You might say "lift" as you lift and swing, and then "place." Go a little slower, but not so slow that you lose your balance. Lifting, placing, stepping. Feel the stepping, feel the lifting. Lift and place, it is very simple, you are really just being with walking.

Tune into the motion of walking. Whenever your mind wanders, allow the thoughts, dismiss them, and focus back on the practice of mindful walking.

When you are done, take a quick scan of your body. Notice how it feels. Notice how clear and calm your mind is. Enjoy the calmness. Bring the feelings with you as you get back to your day.

Practice Mindful Walking as often as you can as you walk from here to there during your day. Resist the urge to be thinking, thinking, thinking while you walk. Allow the clear mind that results from choosing to pay attention to the walking itself.

Tool 13-2: Mindful Movements

BACKGROUND: Moving the body mindfully is a great way to engage active kids and teens in being mindful. They love to move. This tool teaches them to direct their attention to the feeling of the movement using various repetitive movements. It increases their self-awareness and self-regulation. Thich Nhat Hahn's book *Mindful Movement* is a great resource for more detail on this concept. (Thich Nhat Hanh, 2008)

SKILL BUILDING: Demonstrate each movement on Handout 13-2 to clients. Lead them in doing each movement slowly and repeat it 4 times. Then go on to the next movement and repeat it 4 times. Try to include at least 4 different movements during each session. Ask kids and teens for suggestions of movements they would like to use and incorporate their ideas for variety and fun. The goal is to pay attention to the feeling of each of the movements while breathing slowly in and out.

REFLECTION: Help clients reflect on what being mindful while moving was like for them: What did you notice while you moved slowly? How did your body feel? Was this easy or difficult for you? What was it like to breathe slowly while you moved? What happened when you repeated the same motion over and over? What was going on in your mind while you did this? Did you notice any change in your mind before and after doing this exercise? Does your body feel and different after doing this?

Sitting Motions

Lead the client(s) in doing various movements while seated.

- Put your hands down to your side. Take a breath in and raise your arms out to the side and straight up over your head. Now breathe out gently like blowing a bubble while lowering your arms back to your side. Repeat 4 times.

- Place your feet flat on the floor. Now breathe in and raise your feet straight out in front of you. Slowly breathe out and lower your feet to the floor. Repeat 4 times.

- Take a deep breath in and straighten your neck like a string is pulling your head up to the ceiling. Now blow out gently and lower your chin down to your chest. Repeat 4 times.

 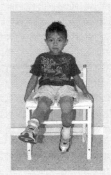 

Standing Motions

Stand up and lead the client(s) in these motions.

- Place both arms at your side. Breathe in slowly and raise your left arm up in front of you until it is level with your shoulders. Blow out gently and lower it back down. Breathe in gently and raise your right arm up in front of you until it is level with your shoulder. Blow out gently and lower it back down. Repeat 4 times.

- Place your hands on your hips, lean forward, breathe in and circle to the right all the way around. Now breathe out and circle to the left all the way around. Repeat 4 times.

- Breathe in and raise your right foot out in front of you while pointing your toe. Blow out gently and lower your foot. Breathe in and raise your left foot out in front of you with pointed toe. Blow out gently and lower your foot. Repeat 4 times.

 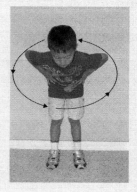 

Tool 13-3: So You Think You Can Dance

BACKGROUND: Dancing has been part of human life since ancient times and has been used for celebration, worship, cultural rituals, and just plain fun. Kids love to dance and most teens do too, especially when you remove all judgment, as teens tend to be self-conscious. This tool uses dance to increase self-awareness and self-expression and self-regulation. It is a great active mindfulness option.

SKILL BUILDING: Use Handout 13-3 to encourage kids and teens to just let go and dance. Emphasize to them that this is 'free' dancing with no judgment allowed and that there is no right or wrong way to dance. Guide them to feel the music in their body and to move how the music tells them to move. Do it with them. Have fun. Use age appropriate music and be sure to include some top 40's artists for teens. Try using a peaceful classical song and then a heavy metal song and ask clients how these two kinds of music felt different to them.

REFLECTION: Ask clients to reflect on how their body moved with the various songs. Discuss how they moved differently to the first, second, and third songs. Ask them how they feel differently with different music. Explore what they noticed about how their body felt and moved while they danced and paid attention to how they moved. Discuss feeling self-conscious or embarrassed and connect this with the concept of non-judgment (even self-judgment) that is central to mindfulness.

So You Think You Can Dance

Guided Script:

I'm going to play some music, and I want you to just listen for a moment.

Now let's dance and move with the music. There is no right or wrong way to dance. Just feel the music and then dance and move like the music is inside you.

Move however you feel like moving.

Now pretend you are a mirror showing the world what the music looks like.

Notice where you feel the music in your body.

Pay attention to how it feels to move while you listen.

Instructions

Play several different songs with different beats and different styles. Try using a song that is only drumming. For teens play some of their favorite artists.

Tool 13-4: The Voice

BACKGROUND: This tool asks kids and teens to use their voice to make noise. It combines mindful motion (singing) with mindful listening and mindfulness of physical body. Kids and teens love to make noise. This exercise helps them use their voice and listening skills to increase self-awareness, as well as awareness of the sounds being made by others. See? Mindfulness does not have to be about sitting still for long periods of time.

SKILL BUILDING: Use Handout 13-4 to lead clients in using their voice to make lots of chaotic noise followed by noise that is synchronized with other voices. It provides a fun way to teach them to pay attention to the sounds they make as well as the sounds around them. It will help to increase their internal awareness of what they notice when the sounds are discordant versus synchronized.

For older kids and teens this tool can be used as a springboard for discussing what goes on in the brain when it is full of worry, anger, or distraction—the discordant sounds. Compare this to a brain that is being mindful, calm, clear, and focused—the synchronized sound.

REFLECTION: Engage clients in a discussion about what it felt like to do this exercise: What did you notice when everyone was making noise and singing their own favorite song? What did you notice when everyone sang the same song at the same time? Can you think of a time your brain sounded like when everyone made different sounds? What did you feel like then? Can you think of a time when your brain sounded more like when everyone sang the same song? What did you feel like then? How can you calm your brain?

THE VOICE

This exercise fits in several categories including: mindful motion, listening, and mindfulness of physical body.

Guided Script:

First I want you to use your voice to make as much noise as you can. Go ahead. Make noise.

Ok. Great! Now take a break and breathe quietly.

Now make lots of noise again and listen to the sound around you.

Wonderful!

Now take a break and breathe quietly.

Now all of you sing your favorite song all at the same time as loud as you can and pay attention to the sound.

Now take a break and breathe quietly.

Now let's all sing together with me like this "I am happy, I am happy, I am happy. . . ." (this works to the tune of "I Am Pretty" from West Side Story, or just make up your own tune). How was that different than the first few times?

Now sing "Row, row, row your boat gently down the stream." What was that like? Did you feel any different inside your body? How about inside your brain?

Now sing 'Aaahhhh' together with me. Take a breath when you need to but then just come back in. Keep the sound going. Terrific!

Take a break and let's talk about what this was like for you and what you noticed.

Tool 13-5: Journal about Mindful Motion

BACKGROUND: Kids and teens love to move. Now that they have practiced Mindful Movement using Tools 13-1 – 13-4 this tool will provide another way for them to increase mindfulness of movement by writing and/or drawing about their experience with it.

SKILL BUILDING: Ask clients to respond to the journal prompts on Handout 13-5. Ideally they will write or draw their answers but, if they cannot do so, just ask them to tell you their answers.

REFLECTION: Review journal entries with clients. Ask them more about their answers and help them explore and expand their increasing awareness of movement.

JOURNAL ABOUT MINDFUL MOTION

Journal Prompts

- What did you like most about mindful movement?

- Do you have a favorite exercise from the ones we did?

- Were you able to feel the music in your body?

- What did it feel like to move with the music?

- What did you notice when you used your voice?

- Have you been walking mindfully during your day?

- Which movements felt the best to you?

- Do you have more control over your body's motions now?

- What was it like to slow down and walk mindfully?

Picture Prompts

- Draw a picture of yourself walking mindfully.

- Draw a picture of yourself dancing.

- Draw a picture of yourself using your voice.

- Draw a picture of yourself moving mindfully.

<h1>Chapter 14</h1>
<h1>Mindfulness of Thoughts</h1>

Tool 14-1: Lazy River

BACKGROUND: We all have a steady stream of thoughts and feelings. One of the basic skills in mindfulness is noticing thoughts, feelings, or sensations, dismissing them without engaging in them, and bringing our attention back to our intended target of attention. This tool provides an effective way to practice dismissing them and noticing the next ones that come along.

SKILL BUILDING: Use Handout 14-1 to guide clients in a simple guided imagery to help them learn to notice and dismiss thoughts without engaging in them. Explain that you are going to pretend that thoughts, feelings, and bodily sensations are riding in rafts or boats on a lazy river. The goal is to notice them, but to just let them float by without getting in the boat or raft (engaging with them). They can picture words written on the side of the boat or raft if they like.

One of my clients used skill this to stop obsessing about a mean classmate. She imagined her classmate's name written on the side of a raft and just watched it float by without "getting in the raft." She was able to allow thoughts about the classmate to go without getting into all the feelings of anger she had been experiencing. Using this process, the client was able very quickly to stop the obsessive thoughts.

After clients have practiced this imagery you might add a step where they find a boat or raft with something positive written on it. When they see the positive one come by they can imagine that they get in that boat or raft and float with the positive thoughts or feelings that go with it. For example, they let go by the boats or rafts that have something in them that upsets them, but they can get in a boat or raft that is associated with something that feels good. In other words, let the "anger" boats go by but get in the "happy" boat.

REFLECTION: Help clients reflect on what this exercise was like for them: Were they able to imagine the lazy river? Did they imagine boats or rafts or both? Did they notice any thoughts or feelings or bodily sensations riding in the rafts or boats? What came up for them while they did this exercise? Did any of the rafts or boats have words written on them and, if so, what were they? Were they able to let the rafts and boats float by? Did they get in any of the rafts or boats and, if so, which one(s)? This exercise can be a great doorway to a discussion of what the client is holding onto that may need to go.

LAZY RIVER

Guided Script:

Get comfortable in your chairs. Close your eyes and clear your mind.

I want you to picture a river with tiny boats and rafts of all different sizes, shapes and colors flowing continuously by. Some water parks call these lazy rivers.

Now picture yourself standing beside the river, watching everything coming towards you.

Imagine that what you are watching for are your thoughts, wishes, feelings, or bodily sensations. Watch them come downriver.

You might notice a word written on the side of the raft or boat that represents your thought or feeling.

As they come closer to you, I want you to just watch them come and go and look to see what comes down the river next. Do not get in any of the rafts or boats. Just let them go by.

Try not to attach to or push away what you notice on the river. Just let it all come and go.

Tool 14-2: Blank White Board

BACKGROUND: Being able to notice distracting thoughts that are not about your intended target of attention is a basic concept of mindfulness. This tool provides an effective way for kids and teens to practice noticing the steady stream of thoughts, acknowledging them and dismissing them without engaging with them.

SKILL BUILDING: Use Handout 14-2 to guide clients in an exercise to use their imagination to practice noticing their thoughts, writing them on a blank white board, and then dismissing them as they vanish from the board. Explain that this skill will help them pay attention to what they are supposed to be paying attention to (for example, their breath or a task) by getting rid of distracting thoughts. Vary the time of the silence at the end depending on the age and skill level of the client. Start with about 10 seconds for very young kids. Work up to 5 to 10 minutes for more experienced and skilled clients.

REFLECTION: Help clients reflect on what happened when they did this exercise: Did thoughts get written on the board? Were you able to erase them? Did the same thought keep coming back? How did you keep your mind from wandering? Were any of the thoughts about the process of doing this skill?

Blank White Board

Close your eyes and take a deep cleansing breath in through your nose and out through your mouth. Do it again. Inhale peace and comfort, exhale tension and stress. Allow the breath to come and go effortlessly. Be aware of the ease with which your breath comes and goes.

It is normal while you focus on your breath that thoughts will arise. They will come and go in a steady stream. For this mindfulness of thoughts meditation notice each thought as it arises.

Imagine you are looking at a blank white board right up in front of you. As you notice each thought, imagine that the thought is being written on the white board in bright red letters. As soon as it is written there imagine that it simply vanishes off the board, poof. The board is white and blank again.

Pay attention to your breathing.

When another thought arises, notice it, watch it get written on the white board and again, watch it vanish with a poof. Gone.

You let it go. No need to pay attention to the thought or to judge it. Just notice it, watch it get written on the board and watch it vanish.

Pay attention to your breathing.

Do this over and over as the parade of thoughts continues. Enjoy the process of awareness of thoughts followed by their instantaneous disappearance. In between the thoughts bring your awareness back to your breath.

Continue this process on your own for the next 2 minutes. (** Note: Vary this time according to age and skill level, starting at 10-20 seconds on up to 5-10 minutes for more experienced clients.)

Silence.

Tool 14-3: Get In-Between Thoughts

BACKGROUND: Get In-Between Thoughts is a tool based on Wayne Dyer's "Getting in the Gap" meditation (Dyer, 2002). It is a practice based on visualizing two words and paying attention to the space between the words. It is a way for kids and teens to slow down their busy brain, focus on the gaps as opposed to the thoughts, clarify the thoughts, and get in touch with their inner awareness as well as with God. This tool combines this practice with positive affirmations.

SKILL BUILDING: Use Handout 14-3 to explain the process to your client. Choose or ask the client to write a positive affirmation that applies to their situation and then use their affirmation to do the meditation as outlined on the handout.

REFLECTION: Ask your client what they noticed when they did this meditation. What did they like about it? Were they able to pretend they were in a swing hanging down between the two words? Were they able to visualize the words and focus on the gap between them? How did it feel to sing "AHH"? How did they feel about the affirmation? How did this meditation compare to the other ones they've done so far?

GETTING IN-BETWEEN THOUGHTS

Adapted from Concept in *Getting in the Gap* by Wayne Dyer

The Getting In-Between Thoughts meditation involves learning to focus on the gap between thoughts for a brief moment. It can be compared to the rest in music. It quiets the mind, clarifies the thoughts and increases concentration. Sample affirmations:

Learning to be mindful:

- "I am learning to be mindful"
- "My mindfulness skills are improving."
- "I am getting better at mindfulness"
- "Mindfulness helps me feel good"

Depression:

- "I can find a thought that feels better"
- "I am learning how to feel better"

Anxiety:

- "I am replacing worry with calm thoughts"
- "I am learning to worry less"

ADHD:

- "Mindfulness helps me concentrate and stay calmer"
- "Being mindful is getting easier"

Sleep Disorder:

- "Mindfulness helps me sleep better"
- "I fall asleep easily now"

THE PROCESS

Substitute the words in the affirmation for your particular client.

Picture the first word in your affirmation in your mind's eye. Now that you can see it, move it to the left of your field of vision in your imagination. Now picture the second word in your mind's eye. Move it to the right of your field of vision.

Now imagine that you are between the two words and focus on the space between the words. Take a deep breath and say "AHHH" as you exhale. Take another deep breath and say "AHH" as you exhale.

Now picture the second word and move it over to the left to replace the first word. Now picture the third word and place it to the right.

Again, focus on the space between the two words. Take a deep breath and say, "AHHH" on the exhale. Do it again. "AHH."

Now move the third word to the left and place the fourth word on the right.

Again, focus on the space between the two words. Take a deep breath and say. "AHHH" on the exhale. Do it again. "AHH."

Now move the fourth word to the left and place the fifth word on the right.

Repeat this process until all the words in the affirmation have been done.

EXAMPLE using a four word affirmation, 'Mindfulness helps me concentrate'

Picture the word 'Mindfulness' in your mind's eye. Now that you can see it, move it to the left of your field of vision in your imagination. Now picture the word "helps" in your mind's eye. Move it to the right of your field of vision.

Now imagine that you are sitting on a swing that is hanging down between the two words with "Mindfulness" on the left and "helps" on the right. Focus on the space between the words. The swing helps you stay put. Take a deep breath and say, "AHHH" as you exhale. Take another deep breath and say "AHH" as you exhale.

Now picture the word "helps" and move it over to the left to replace the word "Mindfulness." Now picture the word "me" and place it to the right. Imagine that you are sitting on a swing between "helps" on the left and "me" on the right. Focus on the space between the two words.

Take a deep breath and say, "AHHH" on the exhale. Do it again. "AHH."

Now move the word "me" to the left and place the word "concentrate" on the right.

Again, focus on the space between the two words. Take a deep breath and say, "AHHH" on the exhale. Do it again. "AHH."

Adapted and used with permission from (Dyer, 2002)

Tool 14-4: Changing the Channel

BACKGROUND: Most kids and teens don't realize that we can deliberately choose what we want to think about. This tool uses the concept that the current content of our thoughts is the channel we are watching. Kids and teens easily get this concept as most are very familiar with the channels on TV. For example, we may be watching our worry, anger, sad, or stressed channel. We can change the channel to a happy, calm, relaxed, or fun channel and thereby change the contents of our thoughts and subsequently our feelings. This aligns with the cognitive behavioral concept that what we think about affects our feelings and our behavior and vice versa. And that we can choose a thought that feels better.

SKILL BUILDING: Explain to clients the concept that for this mindfulness skill their thoughts indicate what channel they are watching, such as the happy, sad, worried, angry, calm, or stressed channel. Help your client identify the thoughts and the channel they are currently watching. Ask them to think about what they would put on their happy/peaceful/relaxed channel. Help them come up with at least 4 positive ideas based on what you know about their interests and hobbies. Kids and teens often choose activities such as dance, skateboarding, swimming, or other sports. Help them identify things that feel good to them. Follow the process in Handout 14-4. Encourage them to use this tool whenever they need to shift their thoughts or feelings.

See the Case Example described in Tool 22-4 for how a 7-year old client eliminated her anxiety using this tool.

REFLECTION: Ask clients when they used this tool during their day. How was it helpful? Were they able to identify negative/unpleasant thoughts in the moment? What did they put on their happy/peaceful/relaxed/feel good channel? What did they notice about their thoughts or mood when they used it? Do they need several different positive channels or is one enough?

CHANGING THE CHANNEL

Did you know that you can choose what you want to think about? You can only have one thought at a time so make sure it's a good one.

Imagine that what you are thinking about is like watching a TV channel.

What are you thinking about right now?

Are your thoughts calm, happy, sad, worried, angry, painful, good, or bad? This is the channel you are watching now.

Think about what you would put on your happy/peaceful/relaxed/feel good channel. Be specific. Choose 4 different things you could put on 4 different channels that feel good to you. What are these 4 things? Some examples might be petting your cat or dog, swimming, dancing, playing sports, skateboarding, your favorite music or band, a warm bath, your favorite food, playing your favorite game, or whatever feels good to you. What 4 things could you use for your channels?

If your thoughts feel bad or are negative, then pretend you are picking up an imaginary remote control and using it to "change the channel" to one of your happy/peaceful/relaxed/feel good channels and imagine you are watching what you already decided would be on that channel.

Practice "changing the channel" in your mind to a more positive channel.

Do you feel better watching this channel?

Use this process any time you have negative or unpleasant thoughts or feelings.

Tool 14-5: Replace Those ANTs (Automatic Negative Thoughts)

BACKGROUND: Many kids and teen are already experts at generating a steady stream of automatic negative thoughts. This is particularly true in depression, anxiety, ADHD, and trauma. Many of these negative thoughts originate from false core beliefs that get programmed into the brain very early in childhood, ostensibly for survival.

Often, kids and teens internalize the negative messages that they receive from their world. A 6-year-old boy told me he knew his new ADHD medicine was working because "no one yelled at me all day." Already, at 6, he felt bad about himself and experienced negative self-talk. Cognitive behavioral therapy works to identify and change these automatic negative thoughts. Daniel Amen calls these automatic negative thoughts "ANTs" and categorizes them into "species of ANTs" (Amen, 1998). This tool uses Amen's framework to identify automatic negative thoughts (ANTs) and to exterminate or kill the ANTs by replacing them with realistic thoughts that feel better.

SKILL BUILDING: Explain to kids and teens that have developed the pattern of automatic negative thinking that in order to get rid of an automatic negative thought (ANT), we must first identify the ANT and then exterminate or kill it by replacing it with a more positive reality-based thought. For younger kids, use the words, "get rid of the ANT" or "kill the ANT". Perhaps relate it to spraying for ants or bees. Review Handout 14-5A with clients and help them identify some of their automatic negative thoughts. Help them label their thought by ANT species. Then help them exterminate the ANT by replacing it with a positive thought that feels better. Read the example from Handout 14-5A and ask them what species that thought is. Then ask them to kill the ANT by coming up with a thought that feels better. Use Handout 14-5A as a guideline for examples. Encourage them to post the ANT graphic on Handout 14-5C someplace to remind them to be mindful of, and exterminate, their ANTs.

REFLECTION: Ask clients what ANTs they have become mindful of. Help them discover if they have a pattern of negative thinking. What species of ANTs have they identified? Help them identify the species if they cannot. Explore how they have begun to replace the ANTs with thoughts that feel better. What have they noticed about how they feel after they kill the ANT by replacing the negative thought with a thought that feels better? Where did they post the ANT graphic?

SPECIES OF AUTOMATIC NEGATIVE THOUGHTS (ANTS)

- **All-or-nothing thinking.** You see everything as entirely good or entirely bad. For example if you don't do something perfectly, you've failed.
- **Always/Never thinking.** You see a single negative event as part of a pattern. For example, you *always* lose your homework.
- **Mind-reading.** You think you know what people think about you or something you've done without asking them—and it's usually bad.
- **Fortune-telling.** You are certain that things will turn out badly.
- **Magnification and minimization.** You exaggerate the significance of minor problems while trivializing your accomplishments.
- **Guilt-beating with "should" statements.** You focus on how things *should* be, leading to severe self-criticism as well as feelings of resentment toward others.
- **Personalizing.** You take everything personally.
- **Focusing on the negative.** You see only the negative aspects of any experience.
- **Emotional reasoning.** You assume that your negative feelings reflect reality. Feeling bad about your job means "I'm doing badly and will probably fail this course."
- **Comparative thinking.** You measure yourself against others and feel inferior, even though the comparison may be unrealistic.
- **Labeling.** You attach a negative label to yourself or to someone else.
- **Blaming.** You blame someone else for your own problems. It's always someone else's fault.

Species	Example	Kill the ANT
Always/Never Thinking	Nobody likes me.	Julie talked to me today.
Blaming	It's all your fault my homework is late.	Homework is my own responsibility so next time I will get it done on time.
Personalizing	She was rude to me.	Maybe she ignored you because she was in a hurry.
Labeling	I'm stupid.	I didn't do well on this test, but I get better grades when I study longer.
Guilt-beating	I shouldn't feel so upset.	There is a good reason why I am so upset.
Mind-reading	My teacher hates me.	Maybe my teacher doesn't know me very well.
Fortune-telling	No one will invite me to the dance.	There is still time to ask someone myself if John doesn't ask me first.
Focusing on the negative	I got 2 wrong on the test.	Yes, but I got 98 of them right.

Expanded from (Amen, 1998)

Copy the ANT and hang it up where you will see it to remind yourself to be mindful of your own ANTs.

Tool 14-6: Past, Present, Future Game

BACKGROUND: One major goal of mindfulness is to cultivate the ability to stay in the present moment. This tool provides a game to help kids and teens learn to identify whether thoughts are about the present, the past, or the future.

SKILL BUILDING: Explain to clients that we can think about something that is happening right now in this moment (the present), something that already happened (the past), or something that hasn't happened yet (the future). Use the scenarios on Handout 14-6 as a springboard for helping kids and teens learn to identify thoughts that are of the past, present or future. Modify the statements as appropriate for different age groups. Read the statement and ask them whether it is about the past, present, or future. Then encourage them to find a thought that is about the present moment based on that scenario (see example in first scenario). After practicing with the scenarios on the handout, ask the client to tell a story about the past, then one about the future, then one about the present.

Next, ask the client to identify what they are thinking about right now and identify whether it is about the past, present, or future. If it is not about the present, encourage them to find a relevant thought that is or identify the present moment of the thought. Encourage them to notice how they feel when the thought is not about the present compared to when it is.

REFLECTION: Help clients reflect on what this game was like for them. Did they learn (or already know) the difference between thoughts about the past, the present, or the future? Were they able to correctly identify them? What did they notice about how they felt when the thought was about the present versus the past or the future?

PAST, PRESENT, FUTURE GAME

Are these statements about the past, the present, or the future?

- Jen is worried about her math exams that she must take next week. Example: A present moment thought might be "Jen is studying her math today so she will do well on her exams next week."

- Sally is angry because Joe bumped into her yesterday and knocked her books on the floor.

- Sophie is thinking about how beautiful the flowers are on the table in front of her.

- Jada loves her nursery school teacher.

- Jim worries that his brother will get sick like he did last year.

- Jordan is enjoying the story that his mother is reading to him.

- Susan can't stop thinking about how rude Jane was to her.

- Bill is sure that the kids he will meet at camp won't like him.

- Jose is noticing how happy he feels today.

- Preston is paying attention to doing his homework.

- Steve is trying to study but keeps thinking about his girlfriend.

- Jordan is worrying about getting into college.

Tool 14-7: Meditation for Concentration

BACKGROUND: A number of studies have found that mindfulness improves concentration. Refer to Handout 3-21, Summary of Mindfulness Research for Kids and Teens for more detail. (Semple, et al, 2010), (Napoli, 2005), (van de Oord, 2012) and (Flook, et al, 2010). Most of the tools in this workbook can be used to improve concentration. This tool describes a technique that helps kids and teens use their imagination to pretend they are in a tree being mindful of their surroundings. It is a guided imagery that leads their attention to notice what's around them. This type of practice, when done repeatedly, gradually improves their ability to stay focused when they are doing a task. See Chapter 23 for more tools to improve concentration for ADHD. One special education teacher uses a number of these meditations in class and has found that her students particularly like the one about sitting in a tree.

SKILL BUILDING: Explain to clients that you are going to ask them to use their imagination to pretend they are sitting in a tree. For older kids and teens, explain that this type of exercise helps their brain learn to pay attention, stay focused and be more mindful. The brief mindfulness meditation provided in Handouts 14-7A and 23-1 can be used for kids and teens. Read the meditation to your client and ask them to reflect on what came up for them during the exercise. It will increase the effectiveness of this exercise if you can repeat it a number of times over the course of a few weeks. Recommend that they remember the exercise when they need to concentrate on something to remind themselves to notice when they are distracted and to bring their attention back to what they need to be paying attention to. A similar meditation is available on the Meditations for Concentration CD available at www.PESI.com and www.TheBrainLady.com.

REFLECTION: Explore what this guided imagery was like for your client: Were you able to imagine the tree? Could you see it in your imagination? What did it feel like to imagine sitting in the tree? What did you notice while you were sitting in the tree? Were you distracted by anything? How did you stay focused on being in the tree? Could you feel the tree or hear the birds? What did you see in the tree? Were you able to concentrate on pretending you were in the tree? Did it almost seem real? When have you told yourself "not now" when you are distracted to help yourself pay attention?

IN THE TREE

Find yourself a comfy place to sit for a few minutes. Close your eyes and listen to my voice. I want you to use your wonderful imagination.

Let's pretend you are standing on the ground underneath a giant tree. Pretend you can see the tree in your mind. Can you see it? What does it look like? Are there leaves on the tree? What color are they? Listen for the sounds of the branches as they wave in the wind. Notice how the air smells here under the tree. Reach up and touch the trunk of the tree. Is the trunk rough or smooth? Can you feel it?

Look for a place to put your foot up on the trunk and slowly climb up onto a branch. Keep climbing until you find the perfect spot to sit on a branch. Let your feet hang over the branch while you hold on with both hands.

Now that you are sitting comfortably and safely, look out and see what you can see from up here in this tree. What do you see? Can you see the sky? How about the clouds? Are you really high up or just a little ways off the ground? Are the leaves in your way so all you can see are the leaves? Maybe you can see another tree. How does it look from way up here?

If your mind wanders and you are thinking about something besides sitting in this tree, that's okay. Just say "not now" and bring your attention back to imagining you are sitting in the tree.

How do you feel being held by a tree way up in the air? Is the bark rough on your hands? Does the tree move with you in it? What sounds can you hear up here? Is there a dog barking? How about a car horn or a fire truck siren? If you notice you are thinking about something else, just say to yourself "not now" and bring your attention back to being in the tree.

Maybe a bird perches next to you. Do you see its nest? Look around. Do you see any people or animals on the ground? How big are they? Can you see a long way or just a little way?

Look at your hands, then look out and see as far as you can see. Now look at your nose and then look straight down. Can you see the ground from here?

Continue to imagine you are in the tree for a little while. If your mind wanders, just tell it "not now" and bring your attention back to being in the tree.

Silence. (Vary from 10 seconds to 5 minutes depending on the age and skill level of the client.)

When you are done being in this tree, climb down.

Tool 14-8: Journal About Mindfulness of Thoughts

BACKGROUND: One key aspect of mindfulness practice is to notice thoughts and then let them go without engaging. Another component of mindfulness is increasing awareness of the content of the thoughts and the ability to change negative thoughts to thoughts that feel better. The tools in Chapter 14 provide experience with both of these concepts. This tool will help kids and teens explore this process through journaling.

SKILL BUILDING: Explain to clients that mindfulness practice starts with noticing thoughts and dismissing them without engaging, which eventually increases the ability to monitor the thought content and gradually change the automatic negative thoughts (ANTs) to thoughts that feel better. Ask the client to respond to the journal prompts in Handout 14-8 and discuss their answers.

REFLECTION: Explore the client's answers with them. If they didn't write anything, go over the questions with them in session and discuss their responses. Help the client identify how mindfulness practice is helping them.

Mindfulness of Thoughts

Journal Prompts:

Older kids and teens

- What's it like for you to notice thoughts and just let them go?

- Do you notice any change in how you feel when you dismiss thoughts during mindfulness practice?

- Have you experienced any calming during mindfulness practice?

- Do certain thoughts tend to recur?

- Have you noticed any change in your ability to let go of thoughts while practicing mindfulness?

- Do you have ANTs (automatic negative thoughts)?

- What's your sense of where this pattern started in your life?

- What species of ANTs have you identified?

- Describe an example of when you had success with finding thoughts that feel better.

- What did you put on your "feel good" channels?

- Give an example of a thought from the past, one from the present, and one from the future.

- How have the Mindfulness of Thoughts meditations helped you?

For Younger Kids

- Draw a picture of yourself and your thoughts.

- Draw a picture of yourself watching the rafts or boats float by you. What thoughts are riding in them?

- Draw a picture of yourself in the tree.

- Draw a picture of yourself watching your happy channel.

- Draw a picture of a thought from the past, the present, and the future.

- Draw a picture of your happy channel.

- Draw a picture of yourself saying "not now" to a distracting thought.

Chapter 15
Mindfulness of Emotions

Tool 15-1: Awareness of Emotions Process

BACKGROUND: In addition to being mindful of thoughts, mindfulness may involve being aware of feelings or emotions. Younger kids are typically not yet skilled at labeling emotions. Older kids and certainly teens are better at this. Clinicians often use feelings charts and games to help them learn to identify their emotions. (See Tool 15-4 for younger kids.)

There are three basic components to an emotion that older kids and teens can be mindful of:

- Thoughts or the story behind the emotion.

- Bodily sensations: how the emotion shows up in their body. All emotions have some physical component. This is often the first and easiest way for kids and teens to notice that they are having an emotion. For example, when they are angry they may feel hot or like their chest is going to explode.

- Emotional mood in the mind. This can be difficult to identify for young kids but is easier for older kids and teens.

We can teach kids and teens to pay attention to any of these aspects of the emotion in mindfulness. The thoughts or the story that accompanies the emotion often tends to pull them in so that they lose their mindfulness. These thoughts or stories usually pertain to the past or future—not the present—and hence distract them from being mindful of the present. Use Tool 14-6 to help clients identify if a thought is from the past, present, or future.

This tool provides a simple process for being mindful of emotions, identifying the emotion without judging and examining the present moment of the feeling without getting pulled into the past or future.

SKILL BUILDING: Start a discussion with older kids and teens about what an emotion is. Ask them to give you some examples of when they felt afraid, angry, worried, happy, excited, etc. Then use the process outlined on Handout 15-1 to help older kids and teens identify their feelings, observe them without judging or trying to change them, notice where the emotion manifests in their body, and clarify what is present versus past or future. If the client states that they aren't feeling anything in particular in the moment, then ask them to explore the process by remembering an emotion they experienced recently. For example, if they had an episode of anger at their teacher or worry about an exam, ask them to remember how they felt then and use the process on the handout. You might also tell or read a story and follow the process on Handout 15-1 to help clients tell you what feeling the characters in the story might be feeling.

REFLECTION: Ask clients what it was like to focus on their emotions as an observer. Where they able to identify and name the emotion? Where did the emotion show up in their body? Where they able to identify the present component of the emotion as well as the past or future components? What thoughts triggered their emotion? What was their story behind the feeling? Have they felt this way before?

AWARENESS OF EMOTIONS PROCESS

Notice the feeling.

- Identify the feeling—name it.
- Notice how and where it shows up in your body.

Observe the feeling as:

- Feels good, feels bad, neither good nor bad

Accept the feeling—don't judge it or try to change it.

Investigate the present moment of the feeling.

- Notice the part of the emotion that is present as well as those aspects that are past or future aspects of the feeling.

Stay present with it.

Don't identify with the feeling.

- Your emotion does not equal you.

What are the thoughts and the story behind the feeling?

What caused you to feel this way?

When have you felt this way before?

Tool 15-2: Meditation: Mindfulness of Emotions

BACKGROUND: Basic mindfulness practice involves letting go of thoughts and emotions that arise during practice. This more advanced tool for older kids and teens goes a step further to help the client tune into an emotion as it arises, observe it, examine it, and notice how and where it shows up in their body. By cultivating such mindfulness of emotions, we can build our resiliency to handle the intense experiences associated with daily life. We can decrease our tendency to get hijacked by emotions, which can sidetrack us and lead us to undesired places (like going to the wrong classroom).

SKILL BUILDING: Explain that the purpose of this exercise is to increase the client's ability to tune in and identify an emotion or feeling when it is happening, observe it without judging, and notice where and how it shows up in their body. When learning about emotions, kids and teens often find it easier to identify how their body feels when they are having an intense emotion such as anger or fear. Ask the client to find a comfortable position and close their eyes if they feel comfortable doing so. Read the Mindfulness of Emotions Meditation in Handout 15-2. Then help them reflect on what came up for them. Use the handout as is for older kids and teens. Use it as a guideline to encourage a discussion about what emotions are and how clients know how they are feeling.

Take caution with kids and teens. Be sure to let them know there is no right or wrong way to feel. Avoid implications that they should have any particular feelings either positive or negative towards other people. And avoid implications that they should feel compassion or forgiveness towards someone who harms them.

REFLECTION: Ask clients what this exercise was like for them. Did they notice an emotion that arose during the practice? Where they able to identify it? What was it? Where did they notice it in their body? Give them some examples such as stomach ache, muscle tension, changes in heart rate or body temperature. Were they distracted and, if so, how did they bring their attention back to their emotion? What triggered the emotion? When have they experienced it before? What was the story behind the emotion? Was it past, present, or future?

MINDFULNESS OF EMOTIONS MEDITATION

We all have feelings or emotions throughout the day. These often start as a small nudge, gradually get stronger, and then slowly go away. This is much like the waves in the surf at the ocean shore. They start slowly offshore, build as they come into shore, and then slowly recede only to be replaced by new waves in a continuous cycle.

This exercise will help you tune into your emotions, your judgments about them, and how they come and go like waves.

Take a few moments to pay attention to your breathing.
Just notice your breathing without changing it.
(Pause)
Notice how you feel inside right now in the present moment. Are you happy, sad,
worried, calm, excited, relaxed, curious, proud?
Without judging just be aware of how you feel.
What feeling are you experiencing?
Name the feeling or emotion.
It is pleasant or unpleasant?
Notice if it feels good or not good.
Is the feeling staying the same or coming and going?
Is it getting stronger or weaker?
How is it changing?
Gently keep your attention on your emotion.
Have you felt this way before?
Is it coming from the past or the present?
What is the present moment of the feeling?
How are you breathing?
How does your posture match the feeling?
How does the emotion show up in your body?
Is there any part of your body that is uncomfortable?
Have you noticed this body sensation before?
Are your muscles tight and tense or relaxed?
What is your facial expression: smiling, frowning, relaxed?
As you notice thoughts, simply accept them, dismiss them and bring your attention back to your emotion.
Allow and accept instead of judging.
As one emotion goes away and another emotion arises simply repeat the process.
Allow, accept, and name the feeling.
Remind yourself that you are not your emotion.
Find the present moment of the emotion.
Do you tend to hold onto certain emotions?
Do you reject others?
How can you replace a negative emotion with a positive one?
Bring your attention to your breath.
Reflect on what came up for you during this meditation.

Inspired by Jonathan Kaplan, PhD (Kaplan, 2008)

Tool 15-3: "I Feel" Game

BACKGROUND: Mindfulness of feelings is an important component of mindfulness and is an internal awareness skill. Young kids are not typically able to identify how they feel. But they can use the mindfulness of feelings skills to learn and improve their ability. Many clinical hours are typically aimed at helping kids and teens identify how they feel using a variety of feelings games. This tool uses the format of a game to ask clients to tell how they are feeling right now. It has several variations that can be used for kids and teens of all ages.

SKILL BUILDING:

- Explain to kids and teens that you are going to play a game called 'I Feel' to help them tune in to how they feel right now. Practice it with them and start by telling them how you feel. Tell them to look at you (or another client if in a group) and say "hello". Then say how they are feeling right now. "Hello, I feel -----".

For example:
  "Hello, I feel confused about what we are doing."
  "Hello, I feel glad that my friend invited me over after school."
  "Hello, I feel silly doing this."
  "Hello, I feel happy to be here today."
  "Hello, I feel afraid I might do this wrong."
  "Hello, I feel excited because my dog just had puppies."
  "Hello, I feel angry because my mom made me come here."
  "Hello, I feel embarrassed doing this."
  "Hello, I don't know how I feel." "I don't know" is okay, but prompt the client with some further questions to help them understand how they feel.

Encourage clients to notice how they feel right now and, if they name a feeling they had earlier today or that is about something in the past of future, help them sort out how they feel about it in this moment, the present component of the feeling.

- Another option is to read a story aloud and then ask kids to say how they think each character in the story feels at each point along the way in the story. Or ask the client how they feel after hearing the story.

- Another variation on this is to name a feeling and ask clients when they felt that way or when they might feel that way.

For example, say:
  "When did you (or might you) feel HAPPY?"
  "When did you (or might you) feel EXCITED?"
  "When did you (or might you) feel AFRAID?"
  "When did you (or might you) feel SAD?"

REFLECTION: Ask clients what it is was like for them to notice how they felt. Were they able to notice how they felt? Were they able to name the feeling? Did they feel uncomfortable or embarrassed? Were they able to find the present moment of the feeling?

Tool 15-4: Name That Feeling

BACKGROUND: Being mindful of feelings is an essential component of mindfulness as well as of good mental health. Kids, teens, and even some adults often have difficulty putting a name to a feeling they may experience. This tool uses a common feelings chart containing faces expressing different feelings to help kids and teens improve their ability to notice, recognize, and name various feelings.

SKILL BUILDING: Use the feelings charts on Handout 15-4 to help clients name various feelings. Point to each picture and ask them what that child is feeling. Cover the text and ask them again. Then ask them to tell you about a time that they felt that way or when someone might feel that way. For example if they name the feeling "sad", ask them if there was a time they felt sad and if so why. If not, ask them when someone might feel sad. Tell them about a time when you felt sad.

You might ask them to make a sad or happy face, or any of the other feelings. You might make a sad, scared, worried, or silly face and ask them to name the feeling. Give them a mirror and ask them to look in the mirror and make a happy face in the mirror, then sad, then worried, etc. Ask them to draw a scared face or a face showing any of the other feelings.

There are "feelings" card games available that can be used for this purpose. One of them uses the rules of "Go Fish" to collect sets of 4 cards of each different feeling. Other play therapy games include this concept as well.

REFLECTION: Was the client able to correctly identify feelings based on facial expressions on the chart? Could they name a time when they felt a particular feeling? Ask older kids and teens what it was like to think about their feelings. Was it hard or easy to name the feelings on the chart? Did they have trouble with any of them?

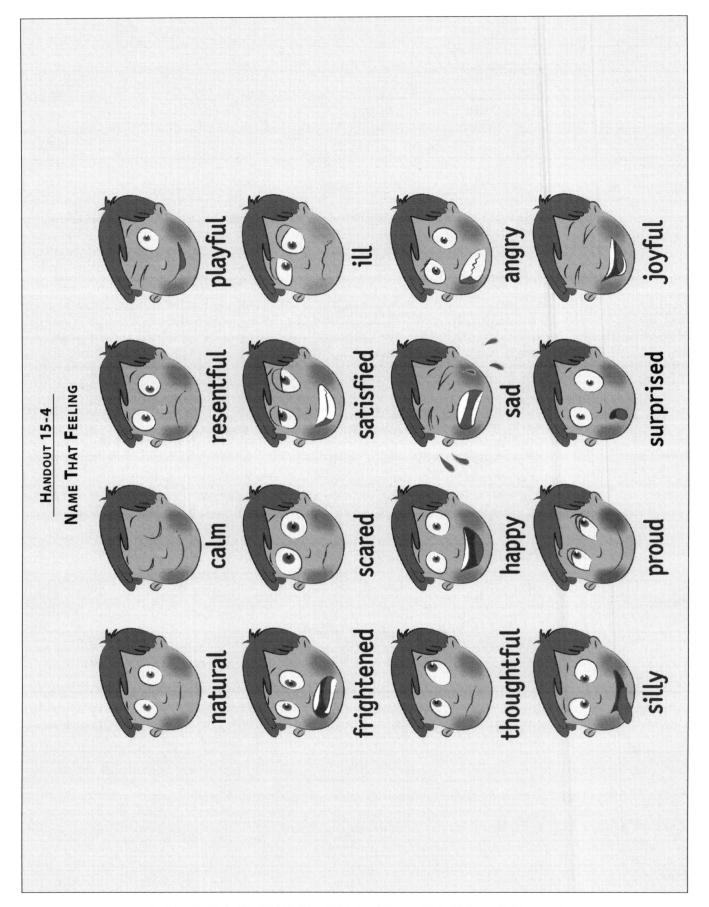

playful

ill

angry

joyful

resentful

satisfied

sad

surprised

calm

scared

happy

proud

natural

frightened

thoughtful

silly

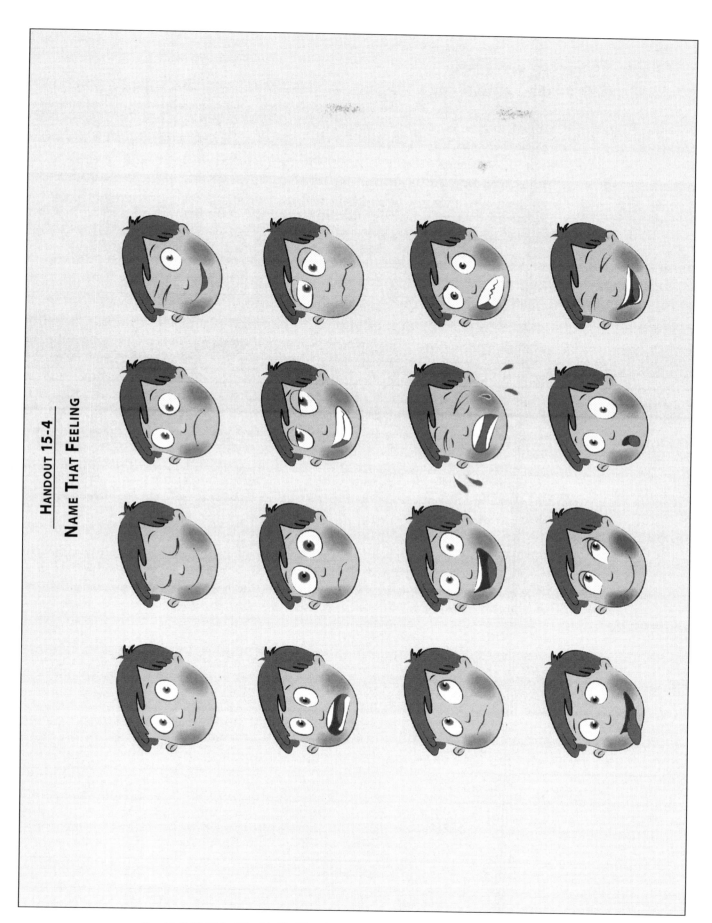

Tool 15-5: Core Heart Feelings

BACKGROUND: This mindfulness skill is based on being mindful of the core heart feelings of appreciation, gratitude, loving or caring. Doing so while imagining that you are breathing through your heart changes the variability of your heart rate in healthy ways called coherence. Studies have shown that depression and anxiety improve when people practice putting their heart into coherence. (Childre et al., 1999). One commercially available computer program, HeartMath's EmWave™ program (HearthMath, 2013), allows you to see your heart rate variability improve as you imagine feelings of appreciation, gratitude, love, or caring. This tool provides the basic technique that has been proven to put the heart into coherence. Kids and teens can become quite good at this practice. It is especially fun to use the EmWave™ system to show them how well they are doing but this is not necessary for it to work.

SKILL BUILDING: Explain to older kids and teens that for best health we want our heart to beat at a rate which varies somewhat. Not enough variation isn't good, nor is too much variation. Explain that we can change heart rate variability in very positive ways by simply focusing on the heart area, imagining we are breathing through our heart while remembering a feeling of appreciation, gratitude, love, or caring. Use Tool 3-16 to teach them how to take their pulse which is how they can feel their heart rate. Engage them in a discussion about times they felt grateful or thankful, or times they appreciated something or someone. Help them identify a time they can remember when they felt grateful, appreciation, love or caring. Read Handout 15-5 to your client and reflect on what came up for them. Ask them to practice this during the week.

Note: this tool will work just fine without all the explanation so if it's appropriate for your client, skip the explanation and just do the exercise. Use the graphic as a nice reminder to do this practice.

REFLECTION: Help clients reflect on what this mindfulness practice was like for them. What feeling of appreciation, gratitude, love, or caring did they remember? What did it feel like to focus on their heart area? What changes in their breathing, or physical sensations, did they notice? How did they feel different after doing the exercise?

CORE HEART FEELINGS

HERE IS A SIMPLE EXERCISE TO PUT YOUR HEART INTO COHERENCE.

Find a comfortable position

Close your eyes, take a few deep breaths in through your nose to the count of 4 and breathe out slowly through your mouth like you are blowing a bubble to the count of 8

Clear your mind and bring your attention to your heart area

Pretend you are breathing slowly through your heart for a while – pause

Now remember a time when you were thankful for someone or something positive in your life. Perhaps remember the feeling of love or care for someone it's easy to love. Stay with the feeling.

Send that thankful feeling to yourself and others

As other thoughts pop into your mind, just dismiss each thought and bring your focus gently back to the area around your heart

(Adapted from HeartMath Workshop) (Childre et al., 1999)

Tool 15-6: Journal About Mindfulness of Emotions

BACKGROUND: Mindfulness of emotions practice improves the ability to notice emotions as they arise. It increases emotional self-regulation and resiliency. Now that your client has practiced these skills, journaling will help them consolidate their learning.

SKILL BUILDING: Tailor an explanation to the age of your client about why journaling is an important way to increase the effectiveness of their practice. Ask them to respond to the journal prompts in Handout 15-6, either in writing (or with drawing) or verbally.

REFLECTION: Review your client's answers to the journal prompts with them. Ask them what they have learned from practicing the mindfulness skills and journaling about their experience.

JOURNAL ABOUT MINDFULNESS OF EMOTIONS

Journal Prompts:

Older kids and teens

- What feelings and emotions did you notice arising during this practice?

- Were you able to notice where the emotion showed up in your body?

- Were you able to observe without judging the emotion?

- Did you identify the trigger for the emotion?

- What was the story behind it?

- What was it like to sort out the present moment of the emotion from the past or future component?

- What did you do to stay present?

- How did you handle distracting thoughts?

- What feelings can you name?

- Do you have trouble naming any feelings?

- What feelings do you notice you have a lot?

- How do you want to feel?

- What feeling of appreciation or gratitude did you remember?

- What did you notice about how you felt inside when you breathed through your heart and remembered a feeling of appreciation?

- How did you feel after practicing the core heart feelings meditation?

- How is your mindfulness practice helping you?

Younger kids

- Draw a picture of you feeling: sad, angry, happy, silly, etc.

- Draw a picture of you breathing through your heart.

- Draw a picture of how you feel right now.

- Draw a picture of how your mom, your dad, or your teacher, feel.

- Draw a picture of how you want to feel.

Chapter 16
Mindfulness of Physical Body

Tool 16-1: Progressive Muscle Relaxation

BACKGROUND: Progressive muscle relaxation is a systematic technique for achieving a deep state of relaxation. It was developed by Dr. Edmund Jacobson more than 50 years ago (Jacobson, 2012). Dr. Jacobson discovered that a muscle could be relaxed by first tensing it for a few seconds and then releasing it. Tensing and releasing various muscle groups throughout the body produces a deep state of relaxation, which Dr. Jacobson found capable of relieving a variety of conditions, from high blood pressure to ulcerative colitis.

Keep in mind that the body can be relaxed at the same time the brain is alert. This is the definition of peak performance. Practicing progressive relaxation will help kids and teens reduce their arousal state and relax and calm down their brains and bodies. It will also give them the ability to evoke a physical relaxation on demand, in a few moments, just by remembering how their body felt at the end of the relaxation meditation and doing two or three deep cleansing breaths to invoke it.

SKILL BUILDING: Explain to kids and teens that progressive muscle relaxation is a way for them to calm their brain and body and achieve a deep state of relaxation. Encourage a discussion of what it means to be relaxed. Ask them to describe a time when they felt relaxed and another time when they didn't feel relaxed.

For older kids and teens explain that Dr. Jacobson's progressive muscle relaxation involves tensing and relaxing, one after the other, 16 different muscle groups of the body. The idea is to tense each muscle group hard (without straining) for about 10 seconds, and then to let go of it suddenly. Then relax for 15 to 20 seconds, noticing how the muscle group feels when relaxed in contrast to how it felt when tensed, before going on to the next group of muscles. Make sure they understand what it means to tense a muscle, demonstrate it by scrunching up your eyes and eye lids, and watch them try it. Have them practice tightening and then relaxing a couple of muscles with you such as pretending to be a bodybuilder by flexing their biceps in their upper arm.

Explain that you are going to lead them in an exercise to tighten and relax 16 muscle groups (shorten this number for very young kids). Suggest that while they do the exercise they might also say to themselves: "Relaxing, relaxing," "Letting go, letting go," "Letting go of everything that needs to go," or any other relaxing phrase during each relaxation period between successive muscle groups.

Encourage them to keep paying attention to their muscles and that when their attention wanders, they can simply say to themselves "not now" and bring their attention back to the particular muscle group they are working on.

For younger kids, simplify your explanation or omit it completely and just read and demonstrate the progressive relaxation on Handout 16-1. Make sure they do all the motions. Make it fun.

Read Handout 16-1 to kids and Handout 16-2 to teen clients and demonstrate each muscle group for them as you go along. You might use either of these handouts for any age group depending on their developmental level and maturity.

Reflect on their experience afterward. Encourage them to practice this at home on their own.

REFLECTION: Ask clients to reflect on what it was like for them to do the Progressive Muscle Relaxation Meditation. Were they able to notice the difference between a tense muscle and a relaxed muscle? Did they feel more relaxed at the end of the meditation? How did they handle distracting thoughts? Did they experience any particular emotions during the exercise? In what ways does practicing this mindfulness technique help them? When might they practice this during their day?

PROGRESSIVE MUSCLE RELAXATION FOR KIDS

Find yourself a comfortable position.

1. **To begin, take three deep belly breaths (like blowing up a balloon in your belly), breathing out slowly, like blowing a bubble, each time.** As you breathe out, imagine that your body begins to relax and get limp.

2. **Imagine picking up a sponge in each hand.** Now pretend that you put the sponge in water and it gets full and heavy with water. Now lift it out of the water and squeeze it tightly. Squeeze all the water out of the sponge. What do your hands feel like? Now let go and drop the sponge back in the water. How do your hands feel now? Do it again. Fill the sponge with water and then squeeze it tight, tight, tight. Squeeze out every last drop of water. How do your hands feel when they are so tight? Now let go and drop the sponge. Which feels better, when you are squeezing the sponge or after you drop it?

3. **Now pretend you are a body builder and you are making your arm muscles really strong.** Imagine that you pick up two small weights, one in each hand. You might picture using cans of soup or bottles of water or even two small balls as weights. Now turn your hand so your fingers are pointing up and bend your elbows and bring the weights right up to your shoulders and "make a muscle". Hold it while I count to 7. 1-2-3-4-5-6-7. Now straighten your arms and relax while I count to 10. 1-2-3-4-5-6-7-8-9-10. Do it again. Bring the weight up to your shoulders and squeeze tight while I count to 7. 1-2-3-4-5-6-7. Great. Now straighten your arms and put the weights down.

4. **Imagine you are a big gray elephant and your arms are the elephant's trunk.** Stretch your trunk out straight in front of you and reach as far as you can. Hold that stretch while I count to 7. 1-2-3-4-5-6-7. Okay, now curl your trunk and let it relax while I count to 10. 1-2-3-4-5-6-7-8-9-10. Stretch it out straight again and hold. Now curl it up and relax.

5. **Let's pretend you are a clown and you are making a clown face.** Raise your eyebrows up as far as you can just like on a clown face. Hold while I count to 7. 1-2-3-4-5-6-7. Now drop your eyebrows and take your own face back while I count to 10. 1-2-3-4-5-6-7-8-9-10.

6. **Imagine you are taking a shower and the water in the shower is spraying on your face.** Quick close your eyes as tight as you can to keep the water out while I count to 7. 1-2-3-4-5-6-7. Now open them while I count to 10. 1-2-3-4-5-6-7-8-9-10.

7. **Now pretend you are a baby bird and your mother bird is feeding you.** Open your mouth as far as you can so you can get some food while I count to 7. 1-2-3-4-5-6-7. Okay, great. Now you've had enough food so close your mouth while I count to 10. 1-2-3-4-5-6-7-8-9-10.

8. **Imagine there is a pretty picture on the ceiling or a brightly colored bird in the sky.** Tilt your head way back so you can look up at it while I count to 7. 1-2-3-4-5-6-7. Now tilt your head down while I count to 10. 1-2-3-4-5-6-7-8-9-10.

9. **Imagine that you are balancing a basket full of toys on top of your head.** Is it heavy? Now pretend you put it down. Does your head feel lighter?

10. **Pretend you are a turtle sunning yourself on a rock.** Something splashes in the water next to you so you pull your head into your shell by raising up your shoulders while I count to 7. 1-2-3-4-5-6-7. All is clear. Now bring your head out of your shell and look around by lowering your shoulders back down while I count to 10. 1-2-3-4-5-6-7-8-9-10.

11. **Imagine you are a beautiful butterfly with great big wings.** Flap your wings and then bring them all the way back and hold them there while I count to 7. 1-2-3-4-5-6-7. Now let your wings fall forward while I count to 10. 1-2-3-4-5-6-7-8-9-10.

12. **Pretend you are going for a swim. Take a deep breath in and hold your breath while you imagine putting your head under the water.** Hold it while I count to 7. 1-2-3-4-5-6-7. Okay. Come out of the water and breathe again while I count to 10. 1-2-3-4-5-6-7-8-9-10.

13. **Imagine someone putting a stuffed animal on top of your belly.** Rock the animal to sleep by moving it up and down with your belly. Now lower the animal down as far as you can and pull in your belly muscles while I count to 7. 1-2-3-4-5-6-7. Now let the animal sleep and relax while I count to 10. 1-2-3-4-5-6-7-8-9-10.

14. **Pretend you are a dog and your master tells you to sit.** Now he is holding a tasty treat above your head. Lean way back to grab your treat as your master holds it just above and behind your head while I count to 7. 1-2-3-4-5-6-7. Okay, got it. Now relax and enjoy your treat while I count to 10. 1-2-3-4-5-6-7-8-9-10.

15. **Imagine you are a cute kitten.** Stretch your legs out as straight as you can while I count to 7. 1-2-3-4-5-6-7. Ok, kitten. Relax your legs while I count to 10. 1-2-3-4-5-6-7-8-9-10.

16. **Pretend you are standing in a puddle.** Stand on your heels and pull your up toes towards you to get them out of the water while I count to 7. 1-2-3-4-5-6-7. Great, now splash them back down in the water while I count to 10. 1-2-3-4-5-6-7-8-9-10.

17. **Imagine you are standing barefoot in the sand at the beach.** Curl your toes down into the sand and grab hold of some sand while I count to 7. 1-2-3-4-5-6-7. Now let go of the sand while I count to 10. 1-2-3-4-5-6-7-8-9-10.

18. **Now imagine a wave of relaxation slowly spreading throughout your body, starting at your head and slowly going into every part of your body all the way down to your toes.**

PROGRESSIVE MUSCLE RELAXATION FOR TEENS

Find yourself a comfortable position.

1. **To begin, take three deep belly breaths (like blowing up a balloon in your belly), breathing slowly, like blowing a bubble, each time.** As you breathe out, imagine that tension throughout your body begins to flow away.

2. **Clench your fists.** Hold for 7–10 seconds and then let go for 15–20 seconds. Use these same time intervals for all other muscle groups.

3. **Tighten your biceps by drawing your forearms up toward your shoulders and "making a muscle" with both arms.** Hold . . . and then relax.

4. **Tighten your triceps—the muscles on the undersides of your upper arms—by extending your arms out straight and locking your elbows.** Hold . . . and then relax.

5. **Tighten the muscles in your forehead by raising your eyebrows as far as you can.** Hold . . . and then relax. Imagine your forehead muscles becoming smooth and limp as they relax. Say to yourself "relaxing, relaxing".

6. **Tighten the muscles around your eyes by clenching your eyelids tightly shut.** Hold . . . and then relax. Imagine sensations of deep relaxation spreading all around them.

7. **Tighten your jaw by opening your mouth so widely that you stretch the muscles in your cheeks.** Hold . . . and then relax. Let your lips part and allow your jaw to hang loose.

8. **Tighten the muscles in the back of your neck by pulling your head way back, as if you were going to touch your head to your back (be gentle with this muscle group to avoid injury).** Focus only on tensing the muscles in your neck. Hold . . . and then relax. Since this area is often especially tight, it's good to do the tighten–relax cycle twice.

9. **Take a few deep breaths and tune in to the weight of your head.** If you are thinking about something besides relaxing, that's okay. Just say to yourself "not now" and bring your attention back to your muscles.

10. **Tighten your shoulders by raising them up as if you were going to touch your ears.** Hold . . . and then relax.

11. **Tighten the muscles around your shoulder blades by pushing your shoulder blades back as if you were going to touch them together.** Hold the tension in your shoulder blades . . . and then relax. Since this area is often especially tight, you might repeat the tighten–relax sequence twice. Say to yourself "letting go, letting go".

12. **Tighten the muscles of your chest by taking in a deep breath.** Hold for up to 10 seconds . . . and then release slowly. Imagine any extra tension in your chest flowing away when you breathe out.

13. **Tighten your stomach muscles by sucking your stomach in.** Hold . . . and then release. Imagine a wave of relaxation spreading through your belly.

14. **Tighten your lower back by arching it up.** Hold . . . and then relax.

15. **Tighten the muscles in your bottom.** Hold . . . and then relax. Imagine the muscles in your hips going loose and limp.

16. **Squeeze the muscles in your thighs all the way down to your knees.** You will probably have to tighten your hips along with your thighs, since the thigh muscles attach near the hips. Hold . . . and then relax. Feel your thigh muscles smoothing out and relaxing completely.

17. **Tighten your calf muscles by pulling your toes toward you (flex carefully to avoid cramps).** Hold . . . and then relax.

18. **Tighten your feet by curling your toes downward.** Hold . . . and then relax.

19. **Now imagine a wave of relaxation slowly spreading throughout your body, starting at your head and gradually going into every muscle group all the way down to your toes.**

This exercise was adapted from Jacobson (2012).

Tool 16-2: Relaxation Response

BACKGROUND: The term "relaxation response" was coined by Herbert Benson, M.D., at Harvard Medical School (Benson, 2000). This meditation invokes the relaxation response, which effectively decreases the stress response. Although many of the mindfulness tools may foster the relaxation response, the meditation included here was designed specifically for this purpose.

SKILL BUILDING: Explain to kids and teens that this mindfulness meditation invokes the relaxation response, which is a term created by a famous heart doctor, Herbert Benson, M.D., at Harvard Medical School. The relaxation response is a way to completely relax your mind and body and it lowers the effects of stress. Encourage clients to discuss what relaxation and stress are. Ask them when they felt relaxed or stressed.

Ask clients to find a comfortable position and then lead them using the meditation from Handout 16-2. Depending on your client's age, maturity level and experience with meditation, vary the length of the pause in the meditation between 30 seconds and several minutes. For young kids, make sure they know all the words used for parts of the body such as calves and shins. Make sure they understand the meaning of "inhale", "exhale", and "tension". You might replace the words inhale and exhale with breathe out and breathe in. Have a discussion about what the word "awareness" means.

REFLECTION: Help clients reflect on what they experienced during this meditation. Did they notice a feeling of relaxation? What did it feel like? Is this a new feeling or a feeling they have had before? Did they feel drowsy or fall asleep? Did they notice any particular sensations in their body? Did their body seem to become numb, float, or disappear from awareness? Were they able to maintain their attention for the whole time or were they distracted? Could they do it for a longer period of time, or was this already too long? What would it be like to relax like this for a few minutes every day? Did any feel afraid or worried when they tried to relax?

RELAXATION RESPONSE

The relaxation response is a simple practice that, once learned, can help lower stress and tension. Learning and putting into practice such techniques can significantly improve your mental, emotional, and physical health.

The term relaxation response was created by a famous heart doctor, Herbert Benson, M.D., at Harvard Medical School (Benson, 2000).

Read the following meditation to clients to effectively invoke the relaxation response. Depending on the client's age, maturity level and experience with meditation, vary the pause near the end between 30 seconds and several minutes.

Find yourself a comfortable position either sitting in a chair with feet flat on the floor, hands on thighs with palms facing up; or lying on your back with arms and legs uncrossed and arms lying by your side palms up.

Now take a deep breath in through your nose to the count of 4 and then breathe out through your mouth like you are blowing a bubble, to the count of 8. Do it again. Breathe in relaxation and peace. As you breathe out relax your mind and let go of stress and worry. Do it one more time, breathe in a cushion of healing energy and, as you breathe out, relax your body.

Now bring your attention to your feet. Notice what you carry there in your toes, the bottoms, heels, and tops of your feet. Let go of anything that needs to go and let it flow down through the ends of your toes and onto the floor.

Now focus on your ankles. Notice if there is anything uncomfortable there and let it flow down through your feet, right through the ends of your toes and onto the floor.

Now bring your attention to your calves and shins. Just notice what's there and let go of anything that needs to go. Let it flow down through your ankles, through your feet, and right out through the ends of your toes and onto the floor.

Now pay attention to your knees. Notice what's there and let healing energy flow down from your knees through your calves and shins, through your feet, and right through the ends of your toes and onto the floor.

Now bring your awareness to your thighs, fronts, backs, sides, and insides. Release anything that needs to go and let it flow down through your knees, through your calves and shins, through your feet, and right through the ends of your toes and onto the floor.

Concentrate on your bottom. Move back and forth ever so slightly to let go of any tightness stored there. Let it flow down through your thighs, through your knees, through your calves and shins, through your feet, and right through the ends of your toes and onto the floor.

Now focus on your entire legs and feet. Take a slow, deep breath and fill your legs and feet with a cushion of healing energy. As you exhale slowly let anything that needs to go flow gently out with your breath.

Now pay attention to your lower back. Lots of stuff gets carried here and you just don't need any of it. Let it flow down through your bottom, through your thighs, through your knees, through your calves and shins, through your feet, and right through the ends of your toes and onto the floor.

Pay attention to your belly and notice how it feels. Let go of any tightness or discomfort and let it flow down through your thighs, through your knees, through your calves and shins, through your feet, and right through the ends of your toes and onto the floor.

Now bring your awareness to your stomach area. Picture in your mind's eye a huge rope that is twisted, coiled and tied in a tight knot. As you watch this rope it un-ties, uncoils, untwists until it is hanging limply. Imagine this happening to your stomach area as your release tension there and let it flow down through your abdomen, through your thighs, through your knees, through your calves and shins, through your feet, and right through the ends of your toes and onto the floor.

Now focus on your chest. Take a deep breath and fill your lungs with a cushion of healing air and as you breathe out let go of anything that needs to go. Do it again, inhale peace and comfort and, as you exhale, relax your mind and body.

Bring your focus to your heart. Imagine you are breathing in through your heart and imagine feelings of thankfulness and love.

Spend a moment here.

Now bring your attention to your back, your middle and upper back. Lots of tension gets stored here and you don't need it. Let it flow down through your lower back, your bottom, your thighs, your knees, your calves and shins, your feet, and right through the ends of your toes and onto the floor.

Now focus on your shoulders, throat and neck. Move your head back and forth ever so gently to let go of the tension stored there. Let it flow down through your back, your lower back, your bottom, your thighs, your knees, your calves and shins, your feet, and right through the ends of your toes and onto the floor.

Now pay attention to your hands including your fingers, thumbs, palms, and the backs of your hands. Notice what you are carrying there and let go of anything that needs to be let go. Let it flow right through the ends of your fingers and onto the floor.

Pay attention to your arms from your shoulders, upper arms, elbows, forearms, and wrists. Let any tightness stored there flow down through your arms and wrists, hands and right through the ends of your fingers and onto the floor.

Bring your attention to your face and jaw. Tighten up your checks into a huge smile and hold for a few seconds then let go.

Now scrunch up your forehead and close your eyes tight, tight, tight, and then release.

Relax your jaw, open your mouth a little bit and let your jaw drop and hang loosely. Place your tongue lightly on the bottom of your mouth behind your lower teeth. Pay attention to your scalp from your forehead down to your ears and around to the top of your neck in back. Let any tension that was stored in your face, jaw and scalp flow down through your chest, abdomen, legs, feet, and right through the ends of your toes and onto the floor.

Now look around inside your body with your mind and notice any areas of discomfort or tightness. Take a deep breath in through your nose and fill those areas of your body with a cushion of healing energy and let it flow out as you blow out slowly through your mouth. Do it again. Inhale a cushion of light and healing and then exhale anything that needs to go.

Now that your whole body is relaxed, know that every part of your body is working exactly as it was designed to work. Blood and energy are flowing freely bringing healing, oxygen, and nutrients to every part of your body. Tune in to this feeling of total relaxation.

Enjoy this warm, safe place for a few minutes.

Pause. (Vary the length of the pause to suit client's age, maturity level, and experience)

When you are ready, slowly bring your awareness back to the room. Open your eyes when you are ready.

Bring this relaxed feeling with you as you return your attention to the room. Remember this feeling any time you need to get calm and relaxed.

Tool 16-3: Body Scan for Kids and Teens

BACKGROUND: The Body Scan Meditation is usually included in studies on the effectiveness of mindfulness for adults, teens and kids (Biegel, et al., 2009). It is a component of most formal meditation practices such as Kabat-Zinn's Mindfulness Based Stress Reduction Program (Stahl & Goldstein, 2010). It involves focusing your full attention on each part of the body, noticing whatever sensations arise, accepting them, and sending kind and compassionate thoughts to each area of the body. Through regular practice, it can help kids and teens enter deep states of relaxation, accept their body as it is, work effectively with their body sensations and feelings of discomfort and pain, and increase powers of concentration and mindfulness.

SKILL BUILDING: Explain to kids and teens that a body scan is the process of paying attention to each part of their body one area at a time. It is a common part of many formal mindfulness mediation practices. It is designed to help them enter a deep state of relaxation, to accept their body as it is, to work with discomfort and pain, and to increase concentration and mindfulness. Read through Handout 16-3 with your client lying on their back if at all possible, or sitting comfortably in a chair. Encourage them to practice this between sessions. If they become uncomfortable or emotional at any point, ask them if they want to continue or to stop. Be prepared to process what comes up with them. Shorten the practice for young kids to start and gradually lengthen it. For young kids, discuss what the word "notice" means before doing the body scan.

REFLECTION: Help clients reflect on how they felt during and after practicing the Body Scan Meditation. What did they notice about their body? Were they able to stay focused? Did they fall asleep? Did they become more relaxed or more agitated? What was it like for them to simply observe and accept? Did they feel any pain? Did any pain they felt get better or worse? Did any thoughts or emotions arise when they focused on specific areas of their body? If so, process these and help them connect them to past experiences. It is not uncommon for kids and teens who have experienced trauma to remember deeply buried feelings or thoughts when they focus on certain parts of their body. If they need to stop, process what came up for them. Help them to integrate the past memory with the safety of this moment.

BODY SCAN FOR KIDS AND TEENS

Let's begin. Breathe in slowly through your nose to the count of 4: 1-2-3-4 and breathe out even more slowly like you are blowing a huge bubble, through your mouth to the count of 8: 1-2-3-4-5-6-7-8. Now just breathe normally.

Bring your attention to your left foot. Just notice your left foot, including your toes, heel, bottom of your left foot, top of your left foot. Notice what it feels like.

Then move up to your left ankle. Notice how your left ankle feels. Pay attention to whether there is any pain there, is it cold, or hot, does it feel light or heavy?

Then pay attention to your left leg starting at the bottom, up to your knees, and thighs, all the way to your hips at the top of your leg. Notice if your left leg feels tight or relaxed, warm or cold, light or heavy.

Now pay attention to your right foot. Just notice your right foot including your toes, heel, bottom of your right foot, top of your right foot. Notice what it feels like.

Then move up to your right ankle. Notice how your right ankle feels. Pay attention to whether there is any pain there. Is it cold, or hot, does it feel light or heavy?

Then pay attention to your right leg starting at the bottom, up to your knees, and thighs, all the way to your hips at the top of your leg. Notice if it feels tight or relaxed, warm or cold, light or heavy.

Now pay attention to both legs from your toes up to your hips. Be still, breathe and send your legs some kind and loving thoughts.

Now move your attention to your belly. Just notice what's there. Feel how your belly feels. Let it be the way it is. Send love and kindness to your belly.

Now pay attention to your back starting with your low back all the way up to your shoulders. Notice how your back feels. Sit for a moment just noticing your back.

Now give your attention to your fingers, thumbs, wrists, arms and shoulders. Just notice how your arms feel.

Now pay attention to your neck and throat. Swallow and notice how your neck and throat feel.

Now pay attention to your face: your chin, your mouth, your cheeks, your eyes, your eyebrows, your forehead and finally your ears.

Now bring your attention to your head, including your hair and scalp and your brain inside your head.

Now take a big belly breath and fill your whole body with a cushion of air. Blow the air out gently like you are blowing a huge bubble and let go of anything that needs to go.

Open your eyes and bring your attention back to the room.

Tool 16-4: Listening to My Body

BACKGROUND: An important aspect of self-awareness involves being aware of your body. This ability to sense the state of our body takes place in the insula (see Tool 3-15). This can include noticing how your body feels, your heart rate, your gut, and pain or discomfort. This tool provides a mindfulness exercise to help kids and teens tune into their bodies and practice being aware of the state of their body and perhaps what their body needs in the moment.

SKILL BUILDING: Explain to clients that being able to tune in to their bodies is an important mindfulness skill. This is helpful for monitoring their body state for many things such as realizing they need to use the bathroom, or that their body is in pain, or that they are freezing and need to put a coat on. It can also assist them in tuning in to how emotions show up in their body.

Use Handout 16-4 to help clients tune in to their body state. Make it fun and play with the process to notice and then change their body state. For older kids and teens use Handout 3-15 to review the location and function of the insula which is involved in sensing our body state.

REFLECTION: Help clients reflect on what it was like to pay attention to their body. Were they able to pay attention to their body? What did they notice about how their body felt? Did they like paying attention to their body? Did they get distracted and if so how did they return their attention to their body? Do they already pay attention to their body? Have they ever not noticed they had to go to the bathroom until it was almost too late? Did they ever eat when they already felt full? Have they ever ignored their body when it was in pain, tired, or ill? How does their body let them know they are upset?

LISTENING TO MY BODY

Let's practice tuning-in and paying attention to our body.

Close your eyes, take a nice deep breath in and blow out gently.

Now pay attention to how your body feels.

Is it hot or cold or just right?

Can you feel your heart beating? Is it fast or slow? Where in your body can you feel it beating?

Is there any part of your body that hurts right now?

How does your stomach feel? Does it feel empty, hungry, full, calm, upset, tight?

Is any part of your body making any noise?

Take a nice deep breath and pay attention to how your chest and your belly feel. Did they move when you filled them with air? Did they move easily or did they have trouble moving? Can you hear yourself breathing?

Is your nose clear or stuffy?

Swallow and notice how your throat feels.

Is your mouth wet or dry?

Is any part of your body itchy?

Does your body feel full of energy? Does it want to move?

Does your body feel tired? Does it want to rest?

How heavy does your body feel?

Is your body warm or cool?

Is your body feeling like you need to go to the bathroom soon?

Pay attention to how it feels to smile and then frown.

Pay attention to how it feels to stand or sit down.

Does your body have something to tell you?

Optional: Now let's stand up and jump up and down for a moment.

Great! Now let's do the same exercise again and see what changed after jumping up and down.
(Go back to the beginning and repeat.)

Variations:

Put a warm coat on and pay attention to how your body feels when it is warmer. Take it off and pay attention to how it feels when it is cooler.

Pay attention to how your stomach feels before a snack or a meal. Then notice how it feels differently after you eat.

Tune in to your body first thing in the morning and then again at bedtime and see what's different.

Pay attention to how your legs feel when you dance or run.

Tool 16-5: Let It Snow

BACKGROUND: Mindfulness involves awareness without engaging, reacting, or judging. This tool engages the imagination of kids and teens to pretend they are sitting outside when snow is falling gently. It provides practice tuning in to their body while observing and not engaging or reacting.

SKILL BUILDING: Use Handout 16-5 to lead kids and teens in a guided imagery exercise. Most kids and teens can imagine snow even if they have no experience with it, but you might substitute rain or glitter for the snow if not. Engage them in a discussion about what they felt like when they did the exercise. Explore what they would do if they were actually sitting outside in the snow.

REFLECTION: Guide clients in a discussion to reflect on what this exercise was like for them. Were they able to visualize and imagine the snow? Could they feel it on their face and head? Could they imagine the feel of the snowflakes on their nose? Did they have the urge to get out of the snow? What did the snow feel like to them? Did it get harder or easier to imagine sitting in the snow after a while?

LET IT SNOW

This exercise practices tuning in to the body while observing and not reacting.

Guided Script:

Close your eyes and pretend you are sitting outside in the winter time in the northern mountains where it snows a lot. Imagine it is a cold winter day and, as you sit quietly, it begins to snow. You are wearing a jacket but you do not have a hat on so you notice how it feels when the snow starts to land on your head, your face, your nose, your cheeks and even your chin. It lands on your jacket, but you don't feel that.

In real life you would get up and go inside or at least put on a hat. But today just use your imagination to sit completely still as you notice how the snow feels.

Pay attention to each flake as it lands on your face. Can you feel it land on you? Is it light and fluffy or hard and frozen like ice? Notice how it feels as the snow falls on you. Check in with your nose as a big flake lands there. What does it feel like? Is it light like a feather? Is it hard to tell it's there? Does it tickle?

Perhaps some of the flakes are melting? How do they feel different now on your skin? Are they cold? Wet? Soft? Is your face getting covered with snow? Is your face freezing? Is it burning from the cold? Is the wind whipping the snow onto your head and face or is the air still with the flakes gently falling?

Sit quietly and notice how your body feels as you use your imagination to allow the snow to cover your head and face.

Now shake off the snow and open your eyes.

Let's talk about what that felt like.

Tool 16-6: How My Body Feels Game

BACKGROUND: Being aware of your body is a great way to practice mindfulness. This tool teaches kids and teens to check in with their body and to tell someone else how their body feels. It encourages them to make eye contact with the person, tune into their body, and translate their body awareness into words.

SKILL BUILDING: Use Handout 16-6 to guide kids and teens to tune into their body and notice what it feels like. Ask them to make eye contact with the person they are telling what their body feels like. It is okay if they cannot find anything to say but encourage them to tune into their body by asking them specific questions such as: How does your stomach feel right now? How does your face feel?

To keep all the kids or teens engaged in a group as others take their turn, ask them to listen to what each one is saying around the circle and to raise their hand if they could not hear what was said. This will practice mindful listening and help them from getting bored.

For variety, you might expand the exercise to include anything the kids or teens notice in the room using any of their senses. Use this exercise to increase self-awareness and also to encourage social skills such as eye contact, listening, repeating what they just heard, and sharing how their body feels.

REFLECTION: Ask clients to reflect on what it was like for them to do this exercise. Were they able to feel their body? Did they name how their body felt? Did they have trouble finding something to say about their body? Were they self-conscious or shy about making eye contact or sharing how their body felt?

HOW MY BODY FEELS GAME

Ask the kids or teens to sit in a circle.

Guided Script:

> We are going to play a Mindfulness of Body game called "How My Body Feels."
>
> Take a moment to notice how your body feels. Look at the person next to you and tell that person how some part of your body feels. That person will repeat back what you said.
>
> Let me give you some examples to start: My fingers feel warm. My feet feel tired. My stomach feels hungry. My head feels hot. My hands feel wet. My throat feels scratchy. My leg feels achy. My shoulders feel relaxed. My skin feels itchy. My heart feels happy. My legs feel comfortable.
>
> I will start. I look at you and say, "my knees hurt from sitting on the floor." Now you look at me and say, "your knees hurt from sitting on the floor". Then you look at the next person and tell them something about how your body feels.

Now just go around the circle. To keep all the kids or teens engaged as others take their turn, ask them to listen to what each one is saying around the circle and to raise their hand if they could not hear what was said. This will practice mindful listening and help them from getting bored.

You might expand this exercise to include all the senses. In this case, kids and teens can say anything they notice in the room using any of their senses.

Note: For individual clients just go back and forth taking turns between you and the client.

Tool 16-7: Balancing Chips Game

BACKGROUND: One great way to practice mindfulness is to focus attention on your body. This tool uses the process of balancing chips on the body to see how long the kids or teens can stay still without knocking the chips off. It teaches self-awareness and mindfulness of body, and may help hyperactive clients train themselves to be less hyper.

SKILL BUILDING: Use Handout 16-7 to teach clients how to play this mindfulness of body game. Vary the number of chips used depending on the client. Use a timer and challenge them to see how long they can balance the chips before one falls off. Make it fun. Show them how long you can do it, too. Encourage them to practice at home. Suggest that when they notice they are really hyper that they take a breath, say to themselves: "balancing chips", and remember how they felt while balancing the chips.

A brief version of this exercise can be done by placing a chip on the backs of the client's hands and asking them to see how long they can balance them before they fall off.

CASE EXAMPLE

A 4 year-old boy who was diagnosed with ADHD was extremely hyperactive. We played this Balancing Chips Game one week in session. He loved playing it so much that each time he came in for his therapy session he said, "Miss Deb, can we play that chip game again?" Over the course of several weeks of playing the game in session he was able to calm his body more and more, and each week his time increased before a chip fell off. His mother commented that she noticed he seemed less hyperactive at home.

REFLECTION: Help clients process what it was like to play this game: "What did it feel like to balance the chips on your body? Was it hard or easy? Was it fun? Could you feel the chips? How did you know when they were about to fall off? Did you feel how still you kept your body? Did it get easier with practice?"

BALANCING CHIPS GAME

Use the chips from a game such as Checkers, Othello, or Connect Four. Take them out and place them where you and the child can reach them.

Guided Script:

>We are going to play a Mindful Body game called Balancing Chips. Please sit down on the floor. Let's get the wiggles out. Do it with me, wiggle every part of your body for a few moments. Wiggle your feet, your legs, your arms, your hands, your fingers, your head, your mouth, and your eyelids. (Do it with them).
>
>Ok, now take a belly breath in through your nose and blow out like you are blowing a bubble.
>
>Now I will give you a chip. Take the chip and place it on your leg just above your ankle and balance it there. Now put this next chip on the other leg. Now put this next chip on your leg above your knee and this next chip on the other leg.
>
>Lie down on the floor on your back with your arms and legs straight. If it is okay with you I will put the rest of the chips on. I will put one chip on the back of each hand and then another chip on each arm between your wrist and your elbow. I will put a chip on each shoulder. Now I will put a chip on each side of your forehead above your eyes. And I will put this last chip on your chin.
>
>Now I will time how long you can balance all of these chips without moving and knocking any of them off. Pay attention to your breathing. Let yourself relax and sink into the floor. If you feel like you need to move, just let go of that thought and bring your attention back to how it feels to breathe and keep balancing the chips.

Keep track of how long they balance the chips. Let them try several times. Have fun with them and enjoy the process.

Let them play the game for a few minutes each week for a few weeks. Then let them play later on after learning and practicing more mindfulness skills. They may start to decrease hyperactivity and gain more control over their body movement.

Tool 16-8: Remembered Wellness for Kids and Teens

BACKGROUND: Herbert Benson, M.D., coined the term "remembered wellness" (Benson, 1996). "Remembered wellness" is what happens when you allow the body and mind to recover its memory of wholeness and completeness, of innate order, balance, harmony, and flow. Remembered wellness involves remembering a time when we felt well and reimagining what it felt like. Studies have shown that the body reacts to imagination and visualization as it does to an actual event, so it doesn't know the difference between an imagined wellness and a real wellness. It is a process of invoking good feelings, of feelings of well-being, to reduce stress, anxiety or pain.

This Remembered Wellness Tool helps kids and teens tap into the power of their imagination through remembering a time when they felt well in order to create wellness in the present. This is a powerful practice for kids and teens who are struggling with chronic mental or physical illness, pain, or injury.

SKILL BUILDING: Explain to kids and teens that we can help our bodies heal by remembering in our imagination a time when we felt really well. (Hauss, 2011) Discuss how our brain doesn't know the difference between imagining feeling well and being well. For older kids and teens you might explain more detail about the concept of remembered wellness. Discuss the power of using the imagination to recreate previous wellness in the present. Read the Remembered Wellness Meditation in Handout 16.8 to your client. Help them reflect on the results. Encourage them to use this skill whenever they want to improve their current physical or emotional health, and repeatedly if dealing with chronic illness. A recording of this meditation is available on the *Mindfulness Toolkit for Kids and Teens* CD at www.PESI.com or www.TheBrainLady.com.

REFLECTION: Ask clients to reflect on how they felt during and after this meditation. Were they able to remember a time they felt well? How did they feel different than they do now? What did they notice in their feeling of wellness when they completed the meditation? Some clients become quite emotional during this meditation as they remember how good they used to feel and they get in touch with losses they have incurred due to decreases in physical or emotional health. Therefore, be prepared to process these feelings with them.

REMEMBERED WELLNESS MEDITATION

Take a deep relaxing breath and focus your attention within.

Go inside.

Let your mind choose a time in your life, no matter how brief it was, when you felt really good.

Even if you had unpleasant things going on at the same time, just choose the memory of when you felt really well.

Be picky.

Choose only the best.

Remember that time.

Remember how you felt then.

Your muscles are in peak condition.

Your body is in excellent health.

You feel really good.

Everything is working exactly as it was designed to work.

Your thoughts are positive and happy.

You experience a profound sense of well-being.

Your mood is content, calm, blissful, peaceful.

Use whatever the words are that best describe that state for you.

Breathe that memory in now.

Let it grow and get stronger.

Remember it.

Feel it.

Allow it.

Build an inner wave of joy.

Smile.

Enjoy the memory as it spreads throughout your mind and body.

Notice how for the moment your brain doesn't know the difference between then and now.

Every cell, every muscle, every neuron, every fiber of your brain and body is remembering.

As you remember wellness, notice that it starts to spread.

Your body knows how to heal.

We've all fallen down and scraped ourselves, or cut ourselves, and then healed.

Our bodies know absolutely how to heal.

You're remembering that peak state,

In your body; in your feelings; in your mind; in your brain; and in your spirit.

Imagine bringing that feeling from the time you remember to right now.

Almost like a copy and paste from then to now.

Let your body and mind feel, right now, that peak wellness.

Your memory is guiding your brain to function now like it did when you were well.

You might like to imagine a color that represents this incredible wellness.

What color would you choose?

The color anchors the feeling.

Imagine that color now.

Notice that there's a certain way you breathe that is all part of that healing process.

Begin to notice everyday all the ways your body shows you it knows how to heal.

Eating, breathing, sleeping, laughing, peeing, sweating, playing.

Ask for a word or phrase that represents your peak wellness.

Allow every change that is part of this peak health.

Find a place to be grateful for the way things are.

Be thankful that your body remembers wellness.

When you are ready, let yourself come gradually back to the room, and slowly all the way out.

Bring your remembered wellness with you.

Know that the remembered wellness starts a process that continues throughout the day, night, weeks, months, and on into your future.

As you return to the present, know that your remembered wellness has been switched on and is now operating in the present.

Tool 16-9: Journal About Awareness of My Body

BACKGROUND: These Mindfulness of Physical Body tools promote self-awareness and physical and emotional relaxation. They provide an excellent way to counter the stressors encountered in daily life. This journaling tool will help kids and teen review what they have noticed while doing these meditations and increase their awareness of the positive benefits.

SKILL BUILDING: Ask clients to respond to the journal prompts in Handout 16-9 either in writing, verbally or pictorially.

REFLECTION: Review the client's journal responses with them. Process any emotional response they may have experienced during the meditation. Help them explore their new-found ability to relax as a tool they can use to deal with stress and worry. Encourage them to practice tuning in and listening to their body.

JOURNAL ABOUT AWARENESS OF MY BODY

Journal Prompts:

- What has changed for you about the way you notice your body?

- Has your ability to observe and accept discomfort or pain changed?

- What does it feel like to completely relax?

- Is relaxation a new feeling or a familiar one?

- Are you better able to relax your muscles at will?

- Did any particular feelings arise when you paid attention to your body?

- Did you remember previous intense emotions or trauma?

- How did you handle these emotions as they arose?

- Where you able to feel safe being mindful of your body?

- Are you able to remember the feeling of the relaxation response when you start to feel stressed?

- What happens when you sit still?

- What stresses you out during your day?

- How can you de-stress?

Picture Prompts

- Draw a picture of yourself relaxing your muscles.

- Draw a picture of yourself when you are all revved up.

- Draw a picture of yourself sitting quietly and being very still.

- Draw a picture of yourself playing the Balancing Chips Game.

- Draw a picture of a snowflake landing on your nose.

- Draw a picture of your body.

- Draw a picture of yourself being completely healed.

Chapter 17
Mindfulness of Relationships

Tool 17-1: Mindful Greeting
Tool 17-2: Relationships
Tool 17-3: Mindfulness of Relationships - Kids
Tool 17-4: Mindfulness of Relationships - Teens

Tool 17-1: Mindful Greeting

BACKGROUND: The first step in being mindful in relationships for kids and teens is to greet one another. This can be done at the beginning of each session or used alone as a skill to teach social skills, self-confidence, and mindfulness of others.

SKILL BUILDING: In a group, sit in a circle and ask one of the kids and teens to look at the person to their right and say, "Hello, my name is _____. What's your name?" Then the person they greeted will say "Hello, I hear that your name is _____. My name is _____. Nice to meet you." The first person says back "Hello, I hear your name is _____. Nice to meet you, too." Then the next person in the circle does the same until everyone in the circle has had a turn. Encourage them to look at each other while speaking and listening. Ask all the kids and teens to listen and raise their hand if they cannot hear what the two who are speaking are saying. If a hand is raised, ask them to repeat louder. This will keep everyone engaged while they practice mindful listening.

For an individual client, do the same process between them and you.

REFLECTION: Help clients reflect on what this exercise was like for them. Were they shy or embarrassed or comfortable doing this? Did they make eye contact? What did it feel like to tell someone their name? What did it feel like to have someone's undivided attention if only for a moment? Did they learn anyone's name they didn't know? Did they speak loud enough for everyone to hear? When might they practice this in their life?

Tool 17-2: Relationships

BACKGROUND: The ability to create and sustain relationships begins in early childhood and is an important task of childhood and adolescence. This tool helps kids and teens understand what a relationship is and increases their mindfulness in relationships they already have or would like to have.

SKILL BUILDING: Encourage older kids and teens to engage in a discussion about relationships by asking them what they think a relationship is. Start by explaining that a relationship is simply a connection between two people. Discuss the various kinds of relationships such as parent/child, sibling, friends, teachers, and others in their lives. Ask them to make a list of people they have a relationship with including: family, friends, teachers, coaches, scout leaders, you, etc. Then ask them to make a list of people they would like to have a relationship with.

Then, ask them to identify what makes a good relationship. Explore their thoughts about such things as:

What makes a good friend?
What makes you feel good in a relationship?
What makes you feel accepted?
What makes you feel appreciated?
What makes you feel liked?
How can you be kind to someone?
Does it help you feel connected if you have things in common?
How does it feel if someone calls you stupid?
How does talking to someone make the relationship better, or worse?

Even 3-year-olds can do a simple version of this exercise. Just use words they can understand and relate it to their parents, siblings, and caregivers. Ask questions such as:
Do you like it when Mommy smiles at you?
What do you feel like when Daddy gives you a big hug?
How does mommy take good care of you?
    Helps me get dressed
    Cooks food I like to eat
    Reads to me
    Hugs me
What do you feel like if your brother hits you?
Do you enjoy playing with your sister, mother, father, or friend?
What does it feel like if a friend takes your toys away?

REFLECTION: Help clients reflect on the relationships in their life: What relationships do you have? Which relationships do you like the best? Is there anyone you have a relationship with that is mean to you or hurts your feelings? Do you have more relationships than you thought (often true for teens)?

Tool 17-3: Mindfulness of Relationships - Kids

BACKGROUND: An excellent opportunity to be mindful is in relationship to others. Kids typically learn relationship skills from how they are treated starting from birth on up and by observing others. Many kids did not receive what they needed from parents or they may experience symptoms such as the inattentiveness of ADHD or social disconnection of autism that interfere with their processing. These kids may struggle to notice and observe social cues and thereby do not develop adequate social skills. This tool helps kids practice some basics of interacting with others and being mindful in relationships.

SKILL BUILDING: Depending on the age of the child, engage them in a discussion by asking them what a relationship is. Explain that a relationship is the way two people are connected. Ask them who they have a relationship with and encourage kids to name the people that are in their life such as parents, siblings, friends, teachers, and therapists. Discuss the type of relationship they have with each of these people. For example, they have a mother and daughter relationship, or a brother and sister relationship, or a friend relationship, or perhaps a fun, hard, or worried relationship.

Teach clients some basic social skills. Ask them to look at you, or another child if in a group, and tell you something they notice about you or the other child such as the color of your eyes, hair, glasses, or shirt.

Do a role-play where you pretend to be distracted by your smartphone or by looking around the room while your client tells you a story. Then look at them and pay attention to them while they tell you a story. Explore what they felt like when you paid attention versus when you were distracted. Reverse roles and have them pretend to be distracted while you talk and then to pay attention.

Make different facial expressions and ask them to tell you if you look happy, sad, angry, or worried. Ask them to look sad, happy, angry or worried. Play a feelings game such as the one in Tool 15-4 Name That Feeling or in Tool 15-3 "I'm Feeling" Game.

Use Tool 17-1 Mindful Greeting to help kids practice looking at someone and saying "hi."

Ask them how they know someone in their life shows them they are interested in them. Ask them how it feels if someone asks them about something or mentions something they remember about them. Compare this to when someone doesn't pay attention to them and they feel ignored or misunderstood.

Discuss when they did something fun together with someone. Explore how that connected them.

You might also use Tool 9-4: HI, I See You to help kids be mindful in relationships.

REFLECTION: Help kids reflect on what it was like for them to think about their relationships and do these exercises. Did they know what a relationship was? Were they able to name people they have relationships with? Were they able to make eye contact and be present with another person? How did they feel when you were distracted versus paying attention to them?

Tool 17-4: Mindfulness of Relationships - Teens

BACKGROUND: Being mindful in relationships is essential to building healthy connections throughout the life span. Teens are particularly focused on building relationships with friends, girlfriends or boyfriends, and to a lesser degree, teachers, and coaches as they strive for independence from their family of origin. Unfortunately, many teens are so busy and distracted by competing demands and by social media that they do not give their complete and undivided attention to others they are talking with. This tool is designed to help them stop and think about a specific relationship and to help them improve their ability to be mindful in that relationship.

SKILL BUILDING: All types of relationships can benefit from mindfulness. These include the client's relationships with family, loved ones, significant others, friends, co-workers, bosses, employees, teachers, and even pets. Use Handout 17-4 as a guide to help teens examine a relationship of their choice (past, present, or future) and to give them the skills to stay present and use positive relationship skills while they are communicating with others. Tell them to substitute the person they are in relationship with (or an imagined future relationship) for "person" in the steps outlined in the exercise. Some clients will imagine a loved one they have lost. It is okay to leave this choice up to the client, but you may adapt this for the needs of your particular client. For example, this exercise can help a teen who is in conflict with a parent, or who has trouble making friends, or who misses social cues, or who is so absorbed in texting that they don't make good contact with others in person. Be cautious with teens who may have been abused or traumatized to avoid encouraging them to love unconditionally someone who has hurt them.

REFLECTION: Assist clients in reflecting on what came up for them during this exercise. Did they choose a person from the past, future, or present? What did they notice about their emotions while they practiced this process and answered the questions? Some clients will experience sadness as this exercise triggers feelings of loss for a deceased loved one or the absence of a love partner or of a good enough parent or regret about how they handled a relationship. Help them reflect on these emotions. What triggered the emotion? Explore what they learned from doing this mindfulness skill. Were any of the steps difficult for the client? Encourage teens to practice these ten skills with a specific person in their life and process what happened.

MINDFULNESS OF RELATIONSHIPS - TEENS

TEN WAYS TO BE MINDFUL IN YOUR RELATIONSHIPS

All types of relationships can benefit from mindfulness. Substitute any person you are in any type of relationship with (or an imagined future relationship) for "person" in the following steps. For teens this could be a parent, a friend, a girlfriend or boyfriend, a teacher, a sibling, a coach, a boss, a co-worker, etc.

1. **Stop what you are doing and be totally present with your "person" either in person or in your imagination.** Listen to them. Look them in the eye. Smile at them. Give them your undivided attention. Stop texting or using social media. Let them know you think they are terrific. Avoid judgment. Show them your unconditional love and acceptance. Think of all the things you love about them.

2. **Notice what thoughts or feelings arise in you as you think about your "person."** Acknowledge and accept the thoughts or feelings and then let them go.

3. **Ask, "What does my "person" need from me right now?"** Ask yourself how you can give them your unconditional love and acceptance. Tune in to their needs, as well as your own.

4. **Try to see the world from your "person's" point of view.** What stressors do they have? How would you feel if you were your "person?"

5. **Write down your expectations for your relationship.** Are your expectations realistic? Are they in your "person's" best interest? In yours?

6. **Learn to accept your "person" exactly the way they are. Love them unconditionally.** Let them know you love them no matter what. Look past their difficult behavior to the beautiful being underneath. They are already good enough.

7. **Understand what your "person" is feeling.** Let them know you understand how they feel.

8. **Avoid the trap of constantly telling your "person" what to do or how to do it.** Practice being in charge of yourself but not of your "person".

9. **When you need to represent yourself with your "person", do it with kindness.** Use "I" statements to say, "I think, I feel, I want." "I like it when . . . " Be positive, clear, and kind.

10. **Practice compassion and some type of loving kindness mindfulness.** Allow yourself to be still. Be silent. Think about all the things you love, like, and are grateful for about your "person." Focus on the positive.

Chapter 18
Mindfulness of Tasks

Tool 18-1: Mindfulness During Daily Activity

BACKGROUND: One important aspect of mindfulness involves being mindful of doing tasks while doing the tasks. This differs from more formal sitting mindfulness meditations in that it is a skill that kids and teens can incorporate it into their daily routine, while doing tasks or activities, no matter what the task. Practicing mindfulness while engaged in daily activities helps with concentration (and therefore memory), efficiency, and stress. This tool introduces the concept of being mindful while doing any task.

SKILL BUILDING: Explain to clients that mindfulness of tasks simply means paying attention to what they are doing while they are doing it. As soon as they notice that their mind has wandered (that's normal), they should gently return their attention to the task at hand. Describe how they can practice this skill no matter what they are doing during the day. Ask them about what a task is and then what tasks they do. Some examples are brushing their teeth, eating, washing their hands, taking a shower, going for a walk, doing homework or chores, washing the dishes, getting ready for bed.

Ask the client to close their eyes and imagine they are brushing their teeth. Read Handout 18-1 to them. Then help them pick a few tasks they routinely perform during each day and encourage them to use this technique to practice being mindful while doing them.

Tool 23-1- Increase Concentration is another example of this skill.

Another option is to give clients paper and markers and ask them to draw a picture of their family or a favorite pet or toy. Tell them that any time you notice they are not paying attention to their drawing you will draw a dot on their paper. Let them practice and make it fun. See how long they can stay focused on the task of drawing before their mind wanders. See if they can get fewer dots with practice until they can do a whole drawing without getting any dots. Reassure them that it is normal for their mind to wander and its okay if they get a few dots. Help them avoid self-judgment.

REFLECTION: Help clients reflect on what it was like to pay such close attention to every detail of a task such as brushing their teeth or drawing. Did their mind wander? Tell them that with 60,000 thoughts a day it's perfectly normal for their mind to wander. Were they able to notice that it wandered and bring their attention back to the task? Ask them what task they practiced being mindful of during the week. What did they notice about their ability to pay attention? Did they do a better job while being mindful? Was it easier to remember what they did? Was their mind calmer as it turned off the busy distracting chatter while they practiced being present? Did they notice any change in their stress level, worry, or ability to stay on task?

MINDFULNESS DURING DAILY ACTIVITY

No matter what task you are doing, you can be more present and aware of the moment by practicing mindfulness of tasks. Simply pay attention to what you are doing. As soon as you notice that your attention has wandered and you are paying attention to something else, gently return it to the task at hand. Repeat this process until the task it done.

Here's an example. Use this process no matter what task you are engaged in.

MINDFULNESS WHILE BRUSHING YOUR TEETH

- Close your eyes and pretend that you are going to brush your teeth.
- Imagine that you are standing in front of the bathroom sink.
- Look at yourself in the mirror and slowly take a deep belly breath and sigh as you exhale.
- Pick up your toothbrush from wherever it lives.
- As you hold the handle of the toothbrush, pay attention to how it feels in your hand. Is it hard, squishy, warm, cold, sticky, smooth, or rough?
- Now put the toothbrush under the faucet and turn on the water.
- As you do so, notice how the faucet handle feels on your fingers. Is it cool, hot, slippery, smooth, or sticky? Is it shiny or dull? Is it covered with drops of water?
- As the water starts to run into the sink, look at it for a moment. What does it look like? Is it a steady stream? Is it bubbly? Is it dripping or rushing out? Is it going quickly down the drain or starting to fill up the sink?
- Place your toothbrush under the water and notice how your hand feels as the water flows over the toothbrush. Did your hand get wet? What sound do you notice with the water running?
- Pick up the toothpaste container. Notice how much it weighs. Pay attention to how it feels in your hand. Is it warm, cold, smooth, rough, sticky? Is it hard, stiff, or flexible?
- Open the toothpaste tube and smell the toothpaste. What do you notice about how it smells? Is it a fresh smell? Is it minty or some other flavor?
- Notice how your hand feels on the toothpaste tube as you put some toothpaste on your brush. Pay attention to the toothpaste as it glides onto the brush. What color is it? Can you smell it?
- Notice how your mouth feels as you put the toothbrush into your mouth and start to brush your teeth. Is there a tingling sensation from the toothpaste? Is your mouth full of froth? How do the bristles feel on your teeth? How about on your gums or your tongue?
- Now notice how your mouth feels as you rinse it out with water. Run your tongue around your teeth. Do they feel clean, smooth, rough, jagged, bumpy, or slippery?
- Pay attention to how the brush looks as you rinse it with water.
- Notice how your hand feels as you put the brush and the toothpaste away.
- Look at yourself in the mirror.
- Take a slow deep breath and give yourself a big smile as you open your eyes.

Tool 18-2: Mindfulness of Tasks - Homework

BACKGROUND: Practicing mindfulness while doing a task or activity is one of the easiest and most basic forms of mindfulness. Mindfulness of tasks simply involves deciding to focus your attention on all aspects of the task at hand, noticing when your mind wanders, and bringing your attention back to the task. It entails noticing every little detail of what you are doing and involves as many of your senses as possible including sight, sound, touch, smell, and if appropriate, taste. This tool is good for school age kids and teens. It is especially helpful for improving concentration for ADHD.

SKILL BUILDING: Review the concept of mindfulness of tasks with kids and teens. Ask school age clients to close their eyes and listen while you read the Mindfulness of Homework meditation in Handout 18-2 to them. Then encourage them to use this skill when they are doing tasks such as homework during the week and to tell you about their experience next session. A recording of this exercise is available on *Meditations for Concentration* CD at www. pesi.com and www.TheBrainLady.com.

REFLECTION: Guide clients to reflect on what it feels like to be mindful while doing tasks. Ask them what happened when they did their homework mindfully. What did they notice about their concentration, emotions, energy? How did they bring their attention back when it wandered? Did they feel more efficient? Did their busy mind calm down?

MINDFULNESS OF TASKS – HOMEWORK

Close your eyes and take deep breath and let it out slowly. Now listen to my voice.

Let's pretend you are doing your homework. Let's just get it done. Imagine going to your backpack or book bag which is exactly where it is supposed to be. Open the top and pull out your notebook and book for the first subject you have homework in.

Take out your planner where you wrote down the assignment in class. Sit where you always do your homework, where it is quiet and easy to concentrate.

When your mind thinks about playing outside or calling a friend, say "not now" and get ready to do your homework. Is it math, science? How about spelling? Do you need to read a chapter in a book? Imagine you are doing what needs to be done.

Any time your brain thinks about something besides what you are doing, tell it "not now" and remind yourself that you are doing your homework.

If your body wants to get up to move, or you find yourself fiddling with your pencil, say "not now" and think about the homework you are doing.

If the phone rings, say "not now" and let it go to voice mail.

If you hear a text message come in say "not now I'll look at it later."

If your brother or sister starts to talk to you, tell them "not now, I'm doing my homework" and focus your attention on your homework.

Every time your mind wanders, notice it, say "not now" and bring it back.

Isn't it amazing how much homework you are getting done, so quickly now that you are so good at saying "not now" and getting back to work?

You are in control of your thoughts. You are in charge of what you think about.

When you do your homework, let your brain know that now is the time to think about homework and nothing else. Say "not now" to any other thoughts until you finish your homework.

Okay, now imagine that your homework is done.

Open your eyes and return your attention to the room.

Note: To avoid using the negative you might change "not now" to "maybe later" but kids and teens seem to really tune in to "not now".

Tool 18-3: Journal About Increasing Mindfulness of Tasks

BACKGROUND: Being mindful while performing tasks may be a new concept for most kids and teens. Encourage them to journal about their experience as they practice this skill using the journal prompts in this tool.

SKILL BUILDING: Ask clients to respond to the journal prompts in Handout 18-3 either in writing or verbally. Explain the goal of this exercise is to help them reflect on their experience with mindfulness of tasks practice and help them make it part of their life as well as refine their skill.

REFLECTION: Review the client's answers to the journal prompts with them. Process their experience with Mindfulness of Tasks. Explore what arose for them during the practice and during the journaling about the practice.

JOURNAL ABOUT INCREASING MINDFULNESS OF TASKS

Journal Prompts:

- Did you practice mindfulness of tasks while doing your homework and, if so, what happened? Were you able to get it done faster? Did your mind wander? What distracted you?

- What other tasks have you done while practicing mindfulness of tasks?

- Were you able to stay focused?

- What distracted you?

- How did you bring your attention back to the task?

- What did you notice inside you when practicing this skill?

- Did it take more or less time than usual to complete the task?

- Did you make mistakes while doing the task?

- Did you feel more or less stressed than usual?

- Did you notice anything new about this task?

- Did this practice help you calm your busy brain?

- Have you ever done something that you can't remember doing afterwards such as putting something someplace, or telling someone something, or leaving food on the counter?

- Do you find it easier to remember when you are being mindful?

- What tasks might be done better if you were being more mindful?

- If you were having surgery, would you like to know that your surgeon was being mindful?

Picture Prompts

- Draw a picture of yourself being mindful while doing a task.

- Draw a picture of yourself not being mindful while doing a task.

Chapter 19
Mindfulness Compassion

Tool 19-1: Loving Kindness for self and others
Tool 19-2: Acts of Kindness

Tool 19-1: Loving Kindness for self and others

BACKGROUND: Negative self-talk starts very young. Unfortunately, children often receive a lot of negative messages about themselves. One 6-year-old boy with hyperactivity associated with ADHD told me he knew his new medicine was working because "no one yelled at me all day." A 15-year-old teen told me he knew the neurofeedback training was helping, because nobody was yelling or upset with him anymore at school or at play rehearsal.

The negative messages may come from parents, teachers, peers, and often the media. This sets up competitiveness and a pattern of self-judgment. Many people experience trauma and core wounds as they journey through life. Studies show that loving kindness exercises foster acceptance and compassion for self and others (Hutcherson, Seppala, & Gross, 2008; Kabat-Zinn, 1990; The Dalai Lama, 2001). The practice of Loving Kindness is routinely included in mindfulness training.

SKILL BUILDING: Explain to kids and teens that the practice of loving kindness feels good and helps them accept and care for themselves and others in their life and in the whole universe. Susan Kaiser Greenland, in her book, *The Mindful Child*, (Kaiser Greenland, 2010, p 68) suggests using the term "friendly wishes" with young kids instead of "loving-kindness" For younger kids, you might explain that this involves sending friendly wishes to themselves and others in their life such as a parent, sibling, friend, teacher, and then to everyone in the whole world. Teach them that the practice of loving kindness always begins with developing a loving acceptance of themselves or sending friendly wishes to themselves. Then they are ready to systematically develop loving kindness toward others.

Use Handout 19-1 for the basic structure of the loving kindness mindfulness exercise. Explain that there are five types of persons to develop loving kindness toward:

- Yourself
- A good friend or family member
- A "neutral" person-someone you know but are not close to
- A difficult person that you don't like or get along with
- All four of the above equally
- And then gradually the entire universe

Guide clients to choose someone in their life from each of these categories. Then ask them to picture them in their mind and send them loving kindness or friendly wishes each in turn as described in the handout.

You may also ask them to write down the details of specific things they might wish for others. Kids are usually very creative and often very tuned in to what others in their lives might need most. Some examples include: May I be safe: May my Mommy feel better; May my best friend be happy; May the teacher who yells at me be well and feel less grumpy; May the whole universe be safe.

Be careful not to ask kids and teens to send loving kindness or friendly wishes to someone who may have hurt them.

REFLECTION: Process what this exercise was like with your clients. Ask them: Were you able to choose people from your life to send loving kindness to? Did you have any trouble sending loving kindness to yourself? Did you feel any different when sending loving kindness to a friend versus someone you don't like very much? What did you notice about how you felt before, during, and after the exercise?

LOVING KINDNESS OR "FRIENDLY WISHES" MEDITATION

How To Do It
- The practice always begins with sending loving kindness or friendly wishes to yourself. Then you are ready to send loving-kindness towards others.

Five Types of Persons to send loving kindness or friendly wishes towards:
- yourself
- a good friend
- a "neutral" person
- a difficult person
- all four of the above equally
- and then gradually the entire universe

Picture yourself and each of these people in your mind and send them loving-kindness or "friendly wishes" each in turn such as:

May I be well,
May I be happy.
May I be safe.
May my good friend be well.
May my good friend be happy.
May my good friend be safe.
May the neutral person I am picturing be well.
May the neutral person I am picturing be happy.
May the neutral person I am picturing be safe.
May this person I find difficult be well.
May this person I find difficult be happy.
May this person I find difficult be safe.
May all of these people including me be well.
May all of these people including me be happy.
May all of these people including me be safe.
May the entire universe be well.
May the entire universe be happy.
May the entire universe be safe.

Or

May I be safe.
May I have happiness (peace or joy).
May I be healthy (or feel good).
May my life be easy.
Repeat with each type of person as above.

Tool 19-2: Acts of Kindness

> **BACKGROUND:** Performing an act of kindness is a great way to help kids and teens practice being mindful of being loving and kind toward others. It provides an activity that kids and teens can choose, plan, and carry out alone or in a group. This tool helps clients perform acts of kindness to others including outside the session.

> **SKILL BUILDING:** Explain to clients that a great way to practice being mindful of being kind and loving to others is to take a mindful action. Ask them as a group or individually to make a list of something they think would be kind, loving, or helpful to someone or something. Write down their ideas. Be prepared to give them some ideas from your community. Some examples might be: bringing the garbage cans in from the street for Mom, planting flowers outside the school, collecting bottles and cans and donating the money to a shelter; writing a thank-you card to their teacher; picking up litter in their playground or outside your office; smiling and saying "hello" to an elderly person. From their list, help them choose one activity that you can help them manage. If in a group, select three activities and ask the group to vote on which one they will do.

> Another way to do this exercise is to ask clients to name an act of kindness they did or could do for someone.

> **REFLECTION:** Help clients process what it felt like to plan and carry out an act of kindness. How did they feel planning it? How did they feel after they actually did the act of kindness? What other acts of kindness have they done lately? Has anyone done something nice for them? How did that make them feel?

Chapter 20
Mindfulness of Intention

Tool 20-1: Explore Your True Intentions
Tool 20-2: Meditation

Tool 20-1: Explore Your True Intentions

BACKGROUND: Setting an intention is a first step in any activity or discipline including mindfulness practice. It is important for kids and teens to learn that in setting an intention they decide what they intend to pay attention to. Doing so helps them stay focused on a specific goal or task. In mindfulness we must set an intention every time we practice. For example in the Basic Relaxation Breathing Tool 6-4, we must first set an intention to pay attention to our breath. In the Mindfulness of Tasks Tools 18-1 – 18-3, we set an intention to pay attention to the task at hand such as doing homework. This tool provides a structured method for helping kids and teens define their intention and clarify why they set that particular intention and what they hope to gain from achieving it.

SKILL BUILDING: Start by talking about what an intention is. Simply put, an intention is something you plan to do. Use some examples from the present moment to illustrate what an intention is. For instance: "I intend to look at your eyes while I speak to you"; "I intend to explain what it means to set an intention"; I intend to pick up this pencil"; I intend to pay attention to doing my homework"; "I intend to pay attention to the sounds in this room".

Ask them to name some intentions they might have for the rest of the day. Do they intend to go home after this? Do they intend to eat dinner? When do they intend to do their homework? Who do they intend to talk to tonight? What time do they intend to go to bed? This can be done with kids as young as 5.

Explain to older kids and teens that the following exercise provides them with a structured way to figure out what their intention is. Ask clients to complete the sentences provided in Handout 20-1 using "mindfulness" to fill in the blanks. Explain that this process will help them clarify their own intention of becoming more mindful. It will help them explore why they want to increase mindfulness in their life and how they hope it will improve their life. Then ask them to replace the word "mindfulness" with something else they are thinking of doing such as "homework." Completing the sentences will help them clarify what their intention is and why it is important to them.

Remind them that they can use this process for any intention or goal.

REFLECTION: Help clients reflect on what this process was like for them. Ask them: What was it like to answer the questions? What thoughts or emotions came up for you? Did this exercise help you know why you set an intention to do something like mindfulness or homework? Were any of the questions hard to answer? How will you remind yourself that you set this intention and get back on track if you get side-tracked? What other intentions might you use this process to clarify? Does setting an intention help you stay on task?

EXPLORE YOUR TRUE INTENTIONS

This sentence-completion exercise will help you tune in and figure out your true intentions. The following example is designed to explore the intentions behind practicing mindfulness. Simply replace the word "mindfulness" with any intention that you wish to explore:

- I want to learn about (mindfulness) because . . .

- I am hoping that (mindfulness) will give me . . .

- (Mindfulness) is . . .

- If I am more (mindful), then I will . . .

- The real reasons that I want to (practice mindfulness) are . . .

- Ultimately, (mindfulness) will allow me to . . .

- When I (practice mindfulness), it makes me feel . . .

Be as honest as possible when completing the sentences.

Now replace "mindfulness" with something else in your life. Here's an example:

- I want to learn about (my schoolwork) because . . .

- I am hoping that (doing my homework) will give me . . .

- (Homework) is . . .

- If I do my (homework), then I will . . .

- The real reasons that I want to (do my homework) are . . .

- Ultimately, (doing my homework) will allow me to . . .

- When I (finish my homework), it makes me feel . . .

Use this process with any part of your life to help you discover your true intentions. Then set your intention, monitor your progress, and repeatedly check in to be mindful of your intention and adjust your thoughts and actions as necessary to stay on course.

Adapted from (Alidina, 2011).

Tool 20-2: Meditation

BACKGROUND: Visualization and imagining are a great way for kids and teens to "practice" anything they want to improve their ability to accomplish. This tool provides a way to practice setting an intention and staying focused on that intention. It helps them visualize what a mindful morning might look like to help them understand how they can incorporate mindfulness into their day.

SKILL BUILDING: Explain to older kids and teens that an important step in becoming more mindful is to practice setting an intention to do so and then to follow through on that intention. In other words, to plan to do something and then do it. Explain that the purpose of the Intention to Be Mindful Meditation in Handout 20-2 is to help them imagine that they have set an intention to be mindful and that they are following through on that intention while they get ready in the morning. It illustrates how to set and follow through on an intention as well as how to incorporate mindfulness into their day. Read the meditation to clients. Encourage them to set their own intention to become more mindful and practice doing so during their day.

For younger kids, just ask them to imagine they are getting ready in the morning while you read the meditation. Then ask them about their own morning routine and process what it was like for them to listen to the meditation.

Encourage kids and teens to practice paying attention to whatever they are doing during the day. Suggest that they start by setting their intention to pay attention when they get ready tomorrow morning.

REFLECTION: Explore what it was like for kids and teens to imagine they were getting ready in the morning. Explore what their morning routine is actually like. Ask them about what distracts them from getting ready. Do they have trouble getting ready on time? How would setting their intention to pay attention to getting ready change their day? Encourage them to practice being mindful tomorrow morning. Ask them how they did next time you see them.

INTENTION TO BE MINDFUL MEDITATION

GETTING READY IN THE MORNING

Close your eyes and take a nice slow breath in through your nose to the count of four. 1-2-3-4. Now exhale slowly through your mouth like you are blowing a big bubble to the count of eight. 1-2-3-4-5-6-7-8. Now just relax and breathe normally.

Imagine that you have set an intention to be more mindful in the morning when you are getting ready for your day.

Imagine that you just got out of bed. Notice how the floor feels on your bare feet. Is it hot or cold or just right in your bedroom? Lean over and pull the covers up to make the bed. What do the blanket and sheet feel like in your hands? Are they warm, cool, smooth, rough? How does the bed look now that you made it?

Picture yourself getting ready in the morning. Pay attention to each of the tasks you usually do. When you brush your teeth, what does the toothbrush feel like in your hand? What does the toothpaste smell like and taste like? How do your teeth feel when you brush them? How does the water feel when you rinse?

If you take a shower, pay attention to how the water feels as it sprays on your skin. What does the water look like as it comes out of the shower head? Does your soap or shampoo have a nice smell? Is the towel soft when you dry off?

Remind yourself of your intention to be mindful today.

When you get dressed, think about what you are doing today. What clothes are warm or cool enough and just right for what you will do today? Pay attention to how your clothes feel as you put them on. How do your feet feel when you slide them into your shoes?

Every time your mind wanders and starts to think about something other than what you are doing, remember your intention to pay attention, notice the thought, say "not now", let it go, and bring your attention back to what you are doing.

When you eat breakfast pay attention to the color of the food, and the smell and taste of the food as you chew and swallow. Imagine that as you do each task you are paying attention to the task.

If you feel hurried, stressed, or worried, just stop, take a belly breath, bring your awareness to your breath, calm yourself, and then mindfully choose how to pay attention to the next task. Remember your intention.

Imagine you are talking to your mom or dad. Look at their eyes and listen to their voice and their words. Listen carefully to what they say to you. When you notice your mind is wandering, gently pay attention to Mom or Dad.

Now that you are clean, dressed, and fed, you are ready for your day. Open your eyes and bring your attention back to the room.

Chapter 21
Mindfulness of Intuition –
Older Kids and Teens

Tool 21-1: Tuning-in
Tool 21-2: Mindfulness of Intuition Meditation

Tool 21-1: Tuning-in

BACKGROUND: An important aspect of mindfulness is the ability to tune in to our intuition, our inner wisdom. An intuition often shows up as a "gut feeling" about something that you find out later was completely accurate. Kids and teens can be particularly good at connecting with their intuition and often do so without realizing it. This Mindfulness of Intuition Tool for older kids and teens explains intuition and strengthens the ability to tune in and more accurately interpret and trust it.

SKILL BUILDING: Use the handout to discuss the definition of intuition with your clients and explore what they think it is. Give them some examples from your own life or from stories you have heard about. Review with them the process of developing intuition as described in Handout 21-1A. Encourage them to write their own definition. Explore how their intuition shows up for them. Ask them about when they did or did not tune into their intuition or trust or follow it and what happened in each case. Use Handout 21-1B to help them explore how their intuition works. You might ask clients to keep a journal of when they tuned into their intuition and when they got useful information that was accurate.

REFLECTION: Help clients explore what intuition is and how it shows up for them. Discuss what role intuition plays in their life. Explore how they tuned into their intuition. Discuss how their intuition gives them information, for example, via a physical sensation, through a dream, or just a knowing. Explore how trusting their intuition has helped them. Did their intuition ever keep them safe? Did it ever steer them wrong? Examine how they can tap into their intuition more routinely.

TUNING INTO INTUITION

There are many different definitions of intuition:

- Knowing something that is not from knowledge you already have nor from figuring it out.
- The ability to have a quick and accurate insight about something.
- Knowing something about the external world, which can be shown to have come not through the five senses, nor through the contents of our memory (Bernstein, 2005).
- Write your own definition here:

_____

_____

_____

_____

There are various ways intuition can guide us:

- As a "feeling" about someone we just met or about something we are about to do, or about a decision we are trying to make.
- As "information" that we have no way of logically knowing. We just feel it or know it.
- As a warning of danger.
- How has intuition helped you?

_____

_____

_____

Intuition may show up as:

- A physical feeling in our body
- A "gut feeling"
- A knowing
- A hunch
- A dream
- A nudge
- A sudden image, memory or thought
- How does your intuition show up for you?

_____

_____

_____

Intuition happens:

- Instantaneously, in a fraction of a second
- Again and again, until we finally "get it"

INTUITION 101

In order to develop your intuition, you must first decide to focus on it and study how it shows up for you.

You must learn to understand the "language" of how your intuition works and speaks to you. Intuition can come in the form of feelings, emotions, a knowing, and hunches. It may show up in the words you hear from others. It may use symbols to communicate with you. It may come through dreams.

Think about how your intuition works.

Fantasize, visualize, and use your imagination. Find a quiet place, clear your mind, and go inside yourself. Ask for answers to questions or decisions you need help with. Be patient. Feed your intuition the information you have about something you need help with and then let it simmer in your subconscious. Look for signs of the intuitive answers. Keep a daily journal of what you need answers for and what shows up during your day. Make sure to express gratitude when you get your answers. And keep a dream journal to help understand how your dreams are giving you guidance.

Meditate to get more in touch with your intuition.

By meditating, you calm your busy mind and allow your intuition to flow more easily. Meditation helps you and your rational mind get out of the way. Ask for answers or guidance and then be still and quiet and listen for what shows up.

Study your intuitions.

Learn how your intuition works best. Pay attention to which "hunches" were the most accurate. Figure out in what areas your intuition works best for you and trust it when your experience has shown you it's most likely to be accurate. For example, maybe you are always right about people, but not about which line to get in at the store.

Play with it.

Have fun. Your intuition is always operating whether or not you are tuned into it. You will be amazed to discover just how much you use it already.

Tool 21-2: Mindfulness of Intuition Meditation

BACKGROUND: One effective way for older kids and teens to tune into their intuition is to practice a meditation that helps them connect to their inner wisdom or intuition. This tool provides an example of a guided meditation that first helps clients relax and open up to communication with their inner wisdom and then helps them tune in and connect.

SKILL BUILDING: Discuss intuition with your client—what it is, why it is important, how it can be helpful, how it can show up. See Tool 21-1. Explain that the Mindfulness of Intuition Meditation is designed to help them open up the communication channel and tune in to their own intuition. Explore what a communication channel is using examples like the telephone, TV, and computers. Read the meditation in Handout 21-2 to clients. Vary the length of the silent period depending on the age and skill level of clients.

REFLECTION: Discuss what came up for your client during the meditation. Were they able to relax? Did they have a question for the white board? Did they get an answer? Did the white board draw a picture or use words to communicate? What did they do to stay focused? What thoughts, feelings, mental pictures, body sensations, smells, sounds, colors, or memories arose? Did they feel like they got a message from within? Have they heard this message before?

MINDFULNESS OF INTUITION MEDITATION

Find yourself a comfortable position sitting upright in a chair with your feet flat on the floor, legs uncrossed, back resting gently against the back of the chair, arms unfolded resting lightly on your thighs, with palms facing up. Or lie flat on your back with your arms and legs uncrossed.

Take a deep cleansing breath in through your nose to the count of four. Breathe out through your mouth to the count of eight and as you do this relax your mind. Take another deep breath and breathe in healing energy and as you breathe out begin to relax your body. Now allow your breath to be easy and automatic.

Take a moment to continue to relax your body. Start by focusing on your toes, then move up to focus on your legs, your stomach, your back, your chest area, your neck, your shoulder, arms, and hands. Now bring your attention to your face and head. Take a deep breath and fill your whole body with a cushion of warm relaxing air. Now breathe out and let everything go that needs to go.

Now imagine a white light shining down from above into the top of your head, filling your head and body with healing energy, going down your neck and throat and down your spine vertebrae by vertebrae. As it flows down, it shines out in front of you as far as you can see and out behind you and beside you as far as you can see. It flows down through your legs and right through the bottoms of your feet into the earth. As it fills you, it warms, cleanses, clears, opens and heals. It connects you to the universe and to the earth all at the same time.

As your body is enjoying this peaceful, relaxed feeling, imagine that you are walking along a path. You come to a garden gate which has been left open for you. You enter the garden, close the gate behind you and find a comfortable place to sit down amongst the beauty and peace of the garden. You close your eyes, take a slow deep breath and go within.

Set your intention to connect with and listen to your intuition. Focus your awareness on what arises from this calm, quiet place inside you. You might imagine a blank white board in front of you. If you have a question you need answered, write it on the board and wait for an answer. If you don't have a question, just sit quietly. In either case pay attention to any thoughts, feelings, mental pictures, body sensations, smells, sounds, colors, or memories that arise. Allow contact with your inner knowing.

Tune in. Notice if anything gets written on the board for you. Ask for help or guidance if you want it. Ask for signs that help you connect with inner wisdom and intuition. Then relax and wait. Just be. If your mind wanders, just bring it back to your intention to connect with your intuition.

Wait patiently, watch, and listen. Pay attention to what is showing up. And trust that you are receiving exactly what you need to know right now.

Two-Minute Silence (Note: Vary length of this silent period as appropriate to fit the needs of clients.)

Now that you have connected with your intuition and received important messages and guidance, be grateful that you are getting better and better about being mindful of your intuition. Slowly stand up in the garden and walk quietly toward the gate. Open it, walk through, and leave it open as you found it. Walk along the path and return to this room, bringing the peace and wisdom you found in the garden with you. You can open your eyes when you are ready.

Tool 21-3: Journal about Mindfulness of intuition

BACKGROUND: Being able to tap into intuition appears to be an innate skill, but it is often ignored. Journaling about how intuition displays itself and how to tune into it more effectively will help older kids and teens to be increasingly aware of intuitive messages and to learn to trust them.

SKILL BUILDING: Ask clients to answer the journal prompts in Handout 21-3.

REFLECTION: Review client's answers and process what came up for them during their journaling. Explore how intuition plays a role in their life. Examine how their intuition communicates with them. Discuss how the Mindfulness of Intuition tools have increased their ability to tune in to their intuition.

JOURNAL ABOUT MINDFULNESS OF INTUITION

Journal Prompts:

- How has intuition shown up in your life?

- Give some examples of when your intuition was right.

- Is there anything your intuition has been wrong about?

- When did you follow your intuition?

- What happened when you followed it?

- When did you ignore your intuition?

- What happened when you ignored it?

- What helps you tune into your intuition?

- How does your intuition communicate with you?

- Do you trust it?

- What would help you trust it more?

- What does your intuition help you with the most?

- Does your intuition communicate through dreams?

- Have you tried keeping a dream journal and, if so, how did that help you?

- What can you use your intuition to help you with? School, friends, decisions, health?

Picture Prompts:

- Draw a picture of yourself using your intuition.

- Draw a picture of yourself ignoring your intuition.

SECTION IV

TOOLS FOR USING MINDFULNESS FOR SPECIFIC DISORDERS

Chapter 22
Mood Disorders

DEPRESSION

Tool 22-1: Freedom from Depression in the Moment

BACKGROUND: Mindfulness practice consists of paying attention non-judgmentally to something in particular in the present moment (Kabat-Zinn, 2003). When a kid or teen feels depressed, their thoughts tend to be chronically negative and they see everything through a negative filter. This tool provides a technique to increase awareness of the negative thoughts and to shift focus to something that feels better in the present moment. It helps with depression as well as anxiety.

SKILL BUILDING: If your client is depressed, ask them to pay attention to the content of their thoughts to discover if they are chronically negative. Help them decide if a thought is positive or negative. Explain how negative thoughts lead to negative feelings and ask them if this happens for them. Tell them this mindfulness skill will give them a technique they can use anytime they notice they feel down, sad, or depressed to change their pattern of negative thoughts and shift their mood to a more neutral or positive feeling. When repeated over and over again, this process will slowly rewire the brain to automatically think more positive thoughts. Use Handout 22-1 to lead the client through the "Freedom from Depression in the Moment" meditation.

REFLECTION: Guide your client to reflect on what they noticed while doing this meditation. Did they notice thoughts? Were they negative? If so, were they able to inflate and burst them? Did the negative thoughts come back again? Were they able to think of something more pleasant? How did focusing on something in their surroundings feel? What did they notice about their mood? How did it change as they did the meditation? Encourage them to utilize this process any time they feel depressed, sad, or down.

FREEDOM FROM DEPRESSION IN THE MOMENT

Find yourself a comfortable position and take a deep breath in through your nose to the count of four, 1-2-3-4, and blow out slowly through your mouth to the count of eight as if you are blowing a bubble. 1-2-3-4-5-6-7-8.

Now breathe normally and allow your breath to flow in and out of you effortlessly without attempting to change it. Let it flow.

Bring your attention inside to your thoughts. Just notice them. Be aware of each thought as it arises. Then just let it go. Continue this process of noticing and dismissing thoughts for a moment.

If you notice a particularly negative or bad thought, notice how you feel as you pay attention to this thought. Inhale slowly and imagine that you are inflating that negative thought like a balloon until it bursts and disappears. Allow the feeling to vanish with the thought.

Take a deep breath in and, as you breathe out, bring your attention back to the flow of thoughts, allowing them to flow by like leaves in a stream.

If you notice a negative thought that that keeps coming back or doesn't stop when you burst it, just remember something that feels better such as the memory of a beautiful flower, a pretty face, a happy time, a good friend, or a yummy food.

Take a deep breath and look around you and notice something in your surroundings that feels good to look at. Perhaps the sun is shining in the window, or the wall is painted a pretty color, or you are with others who are all on a similar journey, or there is an attractive picture on the wall, or the color of the furniture is pretty, or the air smells good, or the chair is comfortable, or you can hear birds singing.

Find something positive to focus on either inside your imagination or in your surroundings.

Now take a deep breath and notice how you feel as you focus on this positive thing that exists either in your mind or in your surroundings.

How has your down feeling changed since starting this meditation?

Continue this process for a few minutes. Notice the thought, inflate and burst it if it's negative, and, if it recurs, bring your attention to something that feels better either in your memory, your imagination, or in your surroundings.

You can follow this process any time you notice negative thoughts.

Silence. (Modify the length of this silence depending on the needs of the client. Start small with 10 seconds and increase with practice up to 5 or 10 minutes.)

Tool 22-2: Find a Thought That Feels Better

BACKGROUND: Depression is characterized by chronic automatic negative thoughts, which Daniel Amen calls ANTs (Amen, 1998). Often, for kids and teens, in addition to negative thinking, depression shows up as irritability and sometimes oppositional defiant behavior. This tool references Tools 14-4 and 14-5, and provides a technique to help kids and teens recognize and exterminate their ANTs by finding a thought that feels better.

SKILL BUILDING: Explain that a hallmark of depression is chronic automatic negative thoughts. When someone is depressed, their mind gets stuck in a rut and produces a steady stream of negative and discouraging thoughts that typically are not realistic. It is as if depression places a filter over everything that only allows through things that feel bad. Discuss what negative thoughts are and help kids and teens identify theirs.

Use Tool 14-5 to help clients learn to recognize their ANTs and find thoughts that feel better. Encourage them to get in the habit of using this tool regularly to notice negative thoughts and quickly shift their mood.

Use the Changing the Channel Tool 14-4 as an excellent way to focus on something that feels better.

CASE EXAMPLE:

One 9-year-old boy was struggling with a combination of ADHD and subsequent depression. He often made negative self-statements such as, "I'm so stupid", "I can't do anything right", "I hate myself". He was often angry and oppositional. By working with him to help him understand why he said such negative things about himself and teaching him to replace these statements with realistic statements that he could believe, he reduced the frequency of the statements and could more easily shift out of a depressed state. He learned to replace "I'm stupid" with "I wish I could understand my math, but my tutor is really helping me learn it now"; "I can't do anything right" with "Sometimes I don't do as well as I would like, but I got a good grade on my last spelling test"; and "I hate myself" with "I wish I could concentrate better, but I like how hard I try at everything I do."

When he became more aware of how often made negative statements he was able to learn to "change the channel" from his "negative, angry" channel to his "feel better" channel. He loved to skateboard and was pretty good at it so he would change the channel from his "angry" channel to his "skateboard" channel. When he did this, his mood and irritability would noticeably improve.

Using these two techniques, he slowly shifted his pattern of depression and negativity. He loved that he was able to rewire his brain. His smile was so delightful.

REFLECTION: Help clients reflect on the process of noticing and changing automatic negative thoughts. Were they able to notice automatic negative thoughts and, if so, what species were they? Were they able to find realistic thoughts that feel better? How often are they using this skill? Did they notice any changes in their depression? Did their parents notice any change in irritability or oppositional behavior? Have they noticed any change in their patterns of negative thinking? Is there any decrease in negative thinking? Is this getting easier with practice?

ANXIETY

Tool 22-3: Lower and Eliminate Anxiety

BACKGROUND: Anxiety is characterized by chronic worry, restlessness, irritability, trouble concentrating, muscle tension, fatigue, and sleep disturbance. When kids or teens experience chronic anxiety it often shows up as fear, stomach aches, headaches, missed school, social withdrawal and sometimes irritability and oppositional behavior. Mindfulness is an excellent modality for improving all of these symptoms. This tool discusses how to apply mindfulness tools described elsewhere in this book to anxiety.

SKILL BUILDING: Help kids and teens describe what their symptoms of anxiety are and how they are showing up in their lives. Explain that these symptoms are typically associated with an over-activated arousal state in the brain or a brain that is "turned up too high". Mindfulness skills routinely calm down the sympathetic nervous system which is so over-aroused in anxiety and therefore turns the brain down. Remind them that the amygdala (Tool 3-13) is involved in anxiety and, for most anxiety, it is like a smoke alarm sounding when there is no smoke.

Mindfulness practice, calming the busy brain, and focusing on inner thoughts and feelings can sometimes (though not always) heighten anxiety in clients with an anxiety disorder or those with a low self-image. This is especially true for teens as increased self-awareness may increase the already heightened self-consciousness that often accompanies adolescence (Schonert-Reichl & Lawlor, 2010). Keep this in mind as you introduce, teach, and reflect on these various mindfulness skills for clients with anxiety.

Start small, teach breathing techniques and awareness of breath to start, and move slowly from outer focus to inner focus. This approach will be less anxiety provoking for an already anxious client. Explore the client's experience as you go and adjust to ensure the client feels comfortable with the practice and knows how to handle what arises.

Use any or all of the following tools to help clients with anxiety.

Mindfulness of Breath	Tools 6-1 – 6-11
Present Moment Awareness	Tools 7-1 – 7- 6
Mindfulness of Physical Body	Tools 16-1 – 16-9
Mindful Listening	Tools 8-1 – 8-7
Mindful Seeing	Tools 9-1 – 9-5
Mindful Tasting	Tools 10-1 – 10-3
Mindful Smelling	Tools 11-2 – 11-3
Mindful Touching	Tools 12-1 – 12-4
Mindfulness of Tasks	Tools 18-1 – 18-3
Mindful Motion	Tools 13-1 – 13-5
Mindfulness of Thoughts	Tools 14-1 – 14-8
Mindfulness of Emotions	Tools 15-1 – 15-6

REFLECTION: Process each skill as described under the specific tool. When helping clients reflect on their experience, be on the lookout for increased anxiety, especially in young teens. If this happens, process it with them, teach them how to handle it using the tools provided here and, if they can't tolerate this increased anxiety, move to more outwardly focused skills and shorten the mediation time. Then gradually increase time and move slowly to inwardly focused skills. Most clients will notice a decrease in anxiety and an increased feeling of self-control.

Tool 22-4: Change the Channel

BACKGROUND: Anxiety can feel overwhelming to those kids and teens who experience it. It often makes them feel out of control and can lead to being anxious about being anxious. This tool explains how to apply the Changing the Channel Tool 14-4 to help clients gain a sense of control over their anxiety.

SKILL BUILDING: Kids and teen clients with anxiety often feel like their anxious, worry thoughts take over their brain and their life. Use the Changing the Channel Tool 14-4 to help them identify something that feels calm and pleasant that they can put on their "calm" channel. Ask them to list up to 5 different things that feel safe, calm, and soothing to them. This gives them a choice of different calm channels they can watch. If needed, help them by making suggestions based on what you know about them. If possible, do this when they are not in the midst of an anxiety attack. Then teach them that when they notice they are feeling anxious, they can change the channel to any of their calm channels they just defined. Explain that by repeatedly changing the channel to calmer thoughts they will gradually rewire their brain to be less anxious.

CASE EXAMPLE

A 7-year-old girl was so intensely anxious about just about everything that the school was considering an out-of-school placement. Her anxiety interfered with her ability to learn, and her peers found her an easy target to bully and tease. The first time I met with her I taught her what anxiety is. Then I told her how it sounded to me like she was watching her anxiety channel all the time. She smiled and said, "yes, I sure am." I asked her if she could choose to watch a channel that made her feel happy, what would she put on that channel. She said, "I love to dance. I would put dance on my happy channel." I told her that next time she noticed she was feeling anxious to imagine that she was taking out her remote control and pressing the button to change the channel from her anxiety channel to her happy channel and watch that instead.

By the next week her anxiety had diminished dramatically. She was doing better in school and some of her old friends were being nice to her. Within 2 weeks her anxiety was GONE! Her brain quickly rewired when she simply practiced changing the channel when she noticed she felt anxious. I am always amazed at how quickly and powerfully this technique can work, even for young kids.

REFLECTION: Ask your client when they used the Changing the Channel tool. What did they put on their "calm" channel? Were they able to change the channel? What did they notice about how they felt before and after they changed the channel? Would it help to have more than one "calm" channel to choose from?

PANIC ATTACKS

Tool 22-5: Abort and Prevent Panic Attacks

BACKGROUND: A panic attack is a discreet event that involves the sudden and intense onset of fear or discomfort and four or more of the following symptoms: (1) palpitations, pounding heart, racing heart; (2) sweating; (3) trembling or shaking; (4) shortness of breath; (5) feeling of choking; (6) chest pain; (7) nausea; (8) dizziness, lightheadedness; (9) feelings of unreality, detachment from self; (10) fear of losing control or going crazy; (11) fear of dying; (12) tingling;

or (13) chills or hot flashes. This can be extremely frightening to a child or teen. Although often confused with a heart attack, a panic attack responds well to mindfulness breathing techniques that help a client calm their mind and body. This gives them a sense of control and often decreases the occurrence of further attacks. This tool teaches how to apply breathing techniques to abort and prevent panic attacks.

SKILL BUILDING: If a kid or teen is in the midst of a panic attack, use a calm soothing voice and ask them to have a seat. Make eye contact with them. Tell them they are having a panic attack. Then tell them to take a slow, deep breath in through their nose while you count to four. Do it with them. Then ask them to blow out gently and even more slowly, to the count of eight, and to purse their lips like they are blowing a bubble. Count to eight as you do it with them. Now lead them through another slow deep breath and an exhale to the count of eight. Ask them if they are starting to feel better. Repeat the deep breaths for up to four breaths and then stop. Ask them how they feel.

Distract them by asking them about something such as: what color are the walls of their bedroom, what they did today, who they sat with at lunchtime, etc. Stay totally present with them. If the breathing isn't calming them fast enough, tell them to imagine that their hands are soaking in really warm water and feel nice and warm. Tell them that their body and mind are gradually relaxing and sending warmth to their hands. Explain that as this happens they will notice their hands begin to feel heavy. Check in with them and ask how they are doing. Typically by now the panic attack has backed off. If it has not, lead them in the Mindfulness of Surroundings Tool 7-1 to help them get grounded in the present. If needed, start over again with the breathing and repeat.

When they are not in the midst of a panic attack, teach them the breathing techniques described in Tools 6-1 through 6-11. Encourage them to practice the breathing until they feel comfortable with it. Also, teach them the Mindfulness of Surroundings Tool 7-1 through 7-6 to help them get their thoughts into the present moment and away from their anxious thoughts. Then, if they feel a panic attack coming on, they can use the breathing and mindfulness of surroundings techniques to head it off or at least decrease its duration and intensity. As they experience being able to prevent or calm a panic attack, they will soon discover they are having fewer of them, and the attacks may stop altogether.

Sometimes kids and teens can identify what triggers repeated panic attacks. Help them explore what was going on just before their most recent attack and see if you can help them find the trigger. For clients who have experienced a traumatic event, any reminder of it could trigger a panic attack. If a trigger can be identified then help the client explore and process the feelings associated with it. Often, there doesn't appear to be any specific trigger or anything the client is aware of. In either case, the Mindful Breathing and Mindfulness of Surroundings can be very effective.

REFLECTION: After the panic attack has subsided, ask the client how they feel. What, if anything, do they think triggered the attack? Has this happened before? How have they handled it before? What was different this time when they used the breathing techniques? Have they noticed a decrease in frequency or intensity of attacks as they practice the breathing techniques when not in the midst of a panic attack?

POSTTRAUMATIC STRESS DISORDER (PTSD)

Tool 22-6: Decrease PTSD Symptoms

BACKGROUND: Many kids and teens have experienced something that was terrifying to them and they may experience symptoms of posttraumatic stress disorder (PTSD). Keep in mind that some young kids may experience an event as traumatic that might not feel traumatic to others. One characteristic of PTSD is that the person experiences thoughts and feelings that happened during a past traumatic event as if they are happening in the present. This tool helps the client be aware of their inner thoughts and feelings, identify if they are from the past or present, and bring themselves back to the present moment. It also gives them a technique they can use to ground themselves.

SKILL BUILDING: Start by teaching the Mindfulness of Breath skills from Chapter 6. Then use the Present Moment Awareness skills from Chapter 7 to help the client stay focused on the present moment instead of past experiences. Help them dismiss thoughts that are not about the present moment, and bring their attention back to the present surroundings or object they have chosen to focus on. These skills will help them stay grounded in the present. Then introduce them to the Mindfulness of Thoughts and Emotions skills from Chapters 14 and 15.

When you help them reflect on their experience using these skills, help them identify whether the thoughts or feelings are from the past or the present (Tool 14-6) and encourage them to focus on those that are from the present.

The mindfulness skills in Chapter 8 – 16 will also help kids and teens who struggle with flashbacks and PTSD-related physiological reactions to internal or external cues that remind them of the traumatic event to stay present.

REFLECTION: Since the thoughts and feelings that arise in PTSD often originate in the unconscious mind, use this tool to teach kids and teens how to observe and reflect on what comes up for them instead of automatically engaging with it. This will help them make the unconscious more conscious. Help them step back and notice which thoughts and emotions are from the now and which are from the past. Then help them choose to pay attention to the components of those that are in this moment.

Tool 22-7: Contact

BACKGROUND: Kids and teens who experience symptoms of PTSD often have trouble being grounded in the present. They may be reacting to internal and often subconscious cues that stem from the traumatic event. This tool provides a very effective technique to quickly and easily help them bring their attention to the present moment which is usually a safe place to be.

SKILL BUILDING: Explain to kids and teens that you are going to show them how to bring their attention and thoughts to the present moment. For younger kids, ask them what the present moment is and engage in a discussion giving them some examples of things in the past, present or future. Use the Past, Present, Future Game Tool 14-6.

Ask them to pay attention to, and point to, where their feet are touching the floor. Tell them this is a point of contact, where their feet contact the floor. Ask them to repeat after you: "Contact." Now ask them to pay attention to where their bottom contacts the chair. Again, ask them to say, "Contact." Now ask them to pay attention to where their hands are resting on their legs, lap, or arm of the chair. Again, repeat "Contact." Now ask them to pay attention to where their back contacts the back of the chair. Repeat, "Contact."

Ask them to stand up and pay attention to where their feet contact the floor. Ask them to say "Contact." Ask them to walk slowly and to say "Contact" each time one of their feet touches the floor.

Ask them to use their finger to touch their other hand, arm, face, and leg, saying "Contact" each time they feel the touch. Another option is to hold a small worry stone in their hand and then to say to themselves "Contact" each time they touch it with their fingers.

Be creative and make this fun. You might pass a small toy or other object from person to person and ask them to shout "Contact" when the object touches their hand. You might ask them to lie on the floor and say "Contact" as they pay attention to each part of their body that touches the floor.

Encourage them to practice this if they feel worried, upset, angry, scared, or tuned out to help them relax and bring their attention back to the present.

REFLECTION: Help clients reflect on what this exercise was like for them. Did they understand what "contact" meant? Were they able to bring their attention to the point of contact? How did they feel after they did it? Did it help them get more present? Were they able to use it when they felt scared, anxious, distressed, or tuned out?

OBSESSIVE COMPULSIVE DISORDER

Tool 22-8: Increase Awareness of Obsessional Thinking

BACKGROUND: Obsessive Compulsive Disorder (OCD) is a type of anxiety disorder. Kids and teens with OCD become preoccupied with whether something could be harmful, dangerous, wrong, or dirty—or with thoughts that bad stuff could happen. They may feel strong urges to do certain things repeatedly—called rituals or compulsions—in order to banish the scary thoughts, ward off something dreaded, or make extra sure that things are safe, clean, or right in some way. They typically experience a steady stream of obsessive thoughts directed at keeping them safe.

Dan Siegel (Siegel, 2010) explains one way to think about obsessive thoughts is to realize they are typically trying to keep us safe. He names the source of these thoughts "the checker," which is always checking to make sure we are safe and that we survive. He discusses how in OCD this checker often goes overboard to alert us to danger. This tool helps kids and teens to re-frame their obsessional thinking and to begin to be able to recognize their "checker" at work.

SKILL BUILDING: Discuss what an obsessional thought is. Explain how sometimes our thoughts get stuck and we have the same thought over and over and over. Give some examples, perhaps from what you've observed in this particular kid or teen. Explain that each time your client has an obsessional thought, they can simply notice that their "checker" is trying to help them out, or keep them safe—even when this help is not rational, effective, or needed. Explain how sometimes the "checker" works overtime almost like a smoke alarm that keeps sounding when there is no smoke or fire. Use Mindfulness of Breath (Tools 6-1 through 6-11), Thoughts

(Tools 14-1 through 14-8), and Emotions (Tools 15-1 through 15-6) to help kids and teens gradually learn to identify and observe their obsessional thinking without engaging in it or responding with compulsive actions.

Help your client to notice the checker at work and then to begin to understand when their checker is helpful and when it is overreacting.

Use these sample scenarios (and make up your own) to help kids and teens identify a helpful "checker" versus an obsessional thought.

Helpful "Checker"

Every time you cross the street you think about looking both ways first.
Before you leave for school you think to make sure your homework is in your backpack.
You make sure to turn off the water in the sink.
You jump out of the way of a car that almost runs into you.
You check to make sure that you have enough money for lunch.
You remember to wash your hands after you use the restroom.

Obsessional Thoughts – Unhelpful "Checker"

You ask your parent if the front door is locked 25 times every night.
You constantly worry that no one will like you.
You worry that you will be infected with germs every day.
You take everything out of your backpack to double check that you have everything you need for school the next day 5 times before you go to bed. (Obsessive thought leads to compulsive behavior.)
You worry every day that you are going to die.
You always think about a specific fantasy character. (Asperger's)
You worry a lot that your sister will get hurt when she is perfectly safe.
You worry you won't find your classroom on the first day of school for 3 weeks before school starts.
You wash your hands so often they turn red and get chapped.
You have to put every toy or book or belonging in a certain order.

REFLECTION: Were clients able to understand and identify obsessional thoughts? Ask your client what they notice about their obsessional thinking as they do the mindfulness exercises. Explore when they have been able to identify their "checker" at work. Discuss how they can tell when the "checker" is being helpful and when the "checker" is overreacting. How has their obsessional thinking changed through the process of mindfulness practice? Have their obsessional thoughts decreased in intensity?

Tool 22-9: Decrease Obsessional Thinking and Compulsions

BACKGROUND: Obsessional thinking leads to compulsions in kid and teens with OCD. These typically show up as rituals and repetitive behaviors such as hand-washing, checking things over and over again, counting, arranging things a certain way, cleaning, etc. Dan Siegel describes a process for talking back to the internal "checker" and thereby reducing obsessional thinking and the ensuing compulsions, which he playfully calls "thanks for sharing" (Siegel, 2010). It involves identifying recurrent thoughts that are typically irrational and simply don't go away as being generated by their "checker" in an effort to keep them safe—see Tool 22-8. This tool provides the next step for kids and teens to talk to the "checker" in a way that acknowledges its efforts to keep them safe, thank it for its help, and then tell it they don't need quite that much help right now.

SKILL BUILDING: Explain to kids and teens that their "checker" is trying to keep them safe, but typically goes way overboard with concern. Now that your client is getting better at recognizing their "checker" at work (see Tool 22-8), help them establish an inner conversation with their "checker" that acknowledges the "checker's" effort to keep them safe, thanks it, soothes it, and lets it know they are safe.

An example might be if a client has an obsession based on irrational fear of germs (which may be one of many such obsessions). This may lead to compulsions such as repeated hand-washing, cleaning, and avoiding contact with others. Their "checker" might constantly say, "Uh, oh! Don't touch that toy/door knob/pencil. You better wash your hands, quick." Encourage clients to respond inside their head with, "Thanks for sharing, 'checker.'" Thanks for your protection and love. I know you want to keep me safe. I want to be safe. But you are being too protective now, and it's not necessary. My body has plenty of protection against germs built into it. It is safe for me now, and I don't need to wash my hands." Encourage your client to keep an inner dialogue with their "checker" to keep their "checker" "in check," so to speak.

Help clients use this technique with their specific obsessions and compulsions.

REFLECTION: Help clients reflect on when they noticed that their "checker" was over-reacting. Review how they talked with their checker and how it changed their obsessional thinking. Explore how it feels to address their obsessions in this manner. Did using this tool reduce compulsions?

Chapter 23
ADHD

Tool 23-1: Increase Concentration
Tool 23-2: Reduce Hyperactivity

Tool 23-1: Increase Concentration

BACKGROUND: A number of studies have found that mindfulness improves concentration, mindful awareness, and overall global executive control. Refer to Handout 3-21, Summary of Mindfulness Research for Kids and Teens for more detail. (Semple, et al., 2010), (Napoli, 2005), (van de Oord, et al., 2012), (Flook, et al., 2010). Most of the tools in this workbook can be used to improve concentration. This tool describes a technique that helps kids and teens use their imagination to pretend they are doing an activity while continually bringing their attention back to the task at hand. This practice, when done repeatedly, gradually improves their ability to stay focused when they are doing that (or another) task.

SKILL BUILDING: The two brief mindfulness exercises provided in Handouts 14-7A and 20-2 can be used for kids and teens depending on their developmental level. Read either of the meditations to your client and ask them to reflect on what came up for them during the exercise. It will increase the effectiveness of this exercise if you can repeat it a number of times over the course of a few weeks. Recommend that they remember the exercise when they are actually getting ready in the morning or doing their homework to remind themselves to notice when they are distracted and to bring their attention back to what they need to be paying attention to. Help them find a system for reminding themselves. Similar audio meditations are available on the Meditations for Concentration CD available at www.PESI.com or www.TheBrainLady.com.

The basic mindfulness process of setting an intention of what to pay attention to and returning attention to this over and over again, as soon as you notice your mind has wandered, gradually strengthens the brain's ability to stay focused, much as exercising a muscle increases its strength. Therefore, regular practice of the majority of mindfulness skills in this workbook will improve concentration over time.

Use the skills described in Tool 18-1: Mindfulness During Daily Activity to help kids improve their ability to stay on task. Young kids love playing the "dots" drawing game.

REFLECTION: Ask clients what it was like for them to listen to the guided imagery meditation for concentration. Use the reflection guidelines provided in Tool 14-7, 18-1 and 20-2. Ask clients to tune in to how well they are paying attention in school, while doing homework, or while having a conversation. Do they notice any improvements now that they have been practicing mindfulness skills?

Tool 23-2: Reduce Hyperactivity

BACKGROUND: People with the hyperactive/impulsive type or the combined type of ADHD often have difficulty sitting still. Children may get out of their seat, run around, climb, jump up and down, and otherwise constantly move. Teens may fidget, tap their fingers or feet, swing their foot, or perhaps just experience a feeling of restlessness. This tool describes two fun games called "Balancing Chips" and "Freeze Dust" that can be played with clients to help them become more aware of their body and its constant motion. Often, with practice, this awareness increases, they gain more control over their body motion, and they become more able to stay still.

SKILL BUILDING:
Balancing Chips Game

Explain to hyperactive kids and teens that you are going to play a Balancing Chips game with them to see how long they can stay completely still. Follow the guidelines provided in Tool and Handout 16-7. Make it fun and challenge them to see how long they can keep the chips from falling off. Do it over and over and observe if they can balance them longer and longer with practice.

Freeze Dust Game

Tell younger kids that you are going to pretend that you are sprinkling them with freeze dust. Explain that the freeze dust makes them like a statue and they can't move any part of their body, except they can breathe. You might ask them to move or dance and then see what silly positions they end up in when you sprinkle the freeze dust on them. Use a timer to see how long they can stay still. Make it fun. Ask them what kind of a statue they are. Ask them to look at a book or listen to music and see how long they can keep being a statue. Even 4-year-olds love this and can often sit still for 20 seconds or longer. Play this periodically and write down their time so you can let them know when they are getting better at sitting still. Remind them to freeze like a statue when they need to sit still.

Exercise

Studies have shown that exercise may reduce hyperactivity as well as improve executive function in kids and teens with ADHD. (Rommel et al., 2013) Recommend that clients get regular aerobic exercise. Make sure their teacher is not keeping them inside at recess to catch up on work.

REFLECTION: Tell clients what you observed about their ability to stay completely still. Ask them what it felt like to keep the chips from falling off. Did they have trouble lying still while they balanced the chips? Were they able to lie still? If so, how did they keep still? Were they able to freeze like a statue? What did it feel like to stay so still? Did they have fun? Were they able to stay still longer as they practiced? Ask them to notice when they are having trouble staying still and to remember how it felt to stay completely still.

Chapter 24
Chronic Pain, Medical Illness and Sleep Disorders

CHRONIC PAIN

Tool 24-1: Pain Management

BACKGROUND: Mindfulness meditation has been shown to be helpful with chronic pain (Kabat-Zinn et al., 1986). There is a natural tendency to tighten or clench the muscles around the painful area, which tends to increase pain. It is also common to want to escape or distract oneself from pain or ignore it until it becomes unbearable. If only we had paid attention to that little voice inside when it said, "I'm uncomfortable. Please rest or take a short break." Mindfulness skills can help kids and teens to accept their pain, relax their bodies, and distract themselves from pain. This tool provides several options to help kids and teens increase awareness of pain, accepting and, if possible, releasing body tension, staying present, and dealing with the underlying thoughts and emotions that accompany pain.

SKILL BUILDING: The first step in managing pain with mindfulness is to increase awareness of body pain and tension while accepting it or, at a minimum, letting it be. This can be done by first using the Basic Relaxation Breathing Tool 6-4 and then using the Body Scan for Kids and Teens Tool 16-3, which guides clients to check in with each area of the body, notice what's there, acknowledge it, and if possible release any tension or discomfort. The Progressive Relaxation Tool 16-1 can be used to release and relax muscle tension, which will assist in reducing pain. The Remembered Wellness for Kids and Teens Tool 16-8 can be used to help clients remember a time when they were pain-free and imagine feeling better. Remember, the imagination is a powerful tool.

Guide kids and teens to check in with their body at regular intervals, perhaps even setting an alarm to remind them to do so. Ask them to ask themselves, "How is my body?" and to notice what's there without resistance or judgment. Teach them to tune in to their pain as an observer and to resist tightening up the muscles around the pain. Encourage them to rest and take short breaks on a regular basis.

The second step in managing pain with mindfulness is to help clients deal with the uncomfortable emotions that often accompany physical pain such as fear, anxiety and sadness. Use the Mindfulness of Emotions Tools 15-1 through 15-6 to help them observe and be aware of emotions, without engaging with them and to help them allow the ebb and flow of emotions that will occur with pain without judging the experience. Use the Mindfulness of Thoughts Tools 14-1 through 14-8 to help them allow thoughts to come and go without engaging and to find thoughts that feel better.

The third step in managing pain for kids and teens, after they have learned to "be" with it, is distraction from the pain. Use Present Moment Awareness - Chapter 7, Mindful Listening - Chapter 8, Mindful Seeing - Chapter 9, Mindful Tasting - Chapter 10, Mindful Smelling - Chapter 11, Mindful Touching - Chapter 12 and Tool 14-4 - Changing the Channel, Mindfulness of Tasks - Chapter 18 to help kids and teens stay present and direct their attention away from their pain.

REFLECTION: Explore with clients how they typically deal with their pain. Do they try to ignore it? Does it overwhelm them and take all their attention? Does it interfere with their functioning? Ask clients to reflect on what they notice about their pain when they do a body scan. Do they find body tension and muscle tightness around the pain? Are they able to release the tension even a little bit? Are they afraid that if they pay attention to their pain it will get worse? How does the Progressive Relaxation exercise change their pain? Are they getting better at checking in with their body and perhaps taking a short rest when they need to? If so, how does this change their pain? What is their story behind the pain? Explore what their expectations are about the future of the pain. What emotions accompany their pain? What is their relationship to their pain? How does staying present in the moment change their experience?

Tool 24-2: Heal the Pain

BACKGROUND: The imagination is very powerful. Studies show that often the brain doesn't know the difference between something actually happening and imagining it happening. This tool uses the power of imagination to visualize pain and allow it to clear and heal.

SKILL BUILDING: Explain to kids and teens who have chronic pain that this exercise will give them a way to manage and perhaps lower their pain perception. Read the script on Handout 24-2. Suggest that they use their own imagery to "suck up the pain." Encourage them to practice this exercise a couple of times every day.

REFLECTION: Were clients able to visualize their pain? What did they picture when you read the handout? Did they come up with other imagery that worked better for them? What did their body feel like when they did this practice? Did they report any change in their pain? Were they able to manage the pain better when they did this exercise? Did they identify anything they would miss about their pain? If so, is this a secondary gain that they obtain from pain?

HEAL THE PAIN

Close your eyes and take a deep breath in through your nose to the count of 4 and blow out slowly through your mouth to the count of 8. Do it again and relax your mind and body when you blow out.

Now think about your pain for just a moment. Repeat after me:
   "Even though I have this pain I completely accept myself."
   "Even though I have this pain I am letting it be."
   "Even though I have this pain I am ready to let it go."

Now use your imagination to pretend you can see your pain.

What does it look like? Does it have a color? Is it hot or cold? Is it bright or dark?

Now imagine that you are sending tiny ice cream cones and ice cubes to the pain. Watch them surround the pain and cool it off. Let the ice cream and ice cubes soak up the pain and carry it away from you. As you watch this, notice how warm your hands are getting. Allow them to warm up as your pain cools.

Pause.

Now check in and see if the pain level has gone down a bit.

Now imagine a tiny, tiny vacuum cleaner coming along and sucking up all the rest of your pain. Just let the pain go. You don't need it. Again, notice how warm your hands are feeling.

Pause.

Imagine that the area of pain is now being filled with a bright white light. The light is sending healing to whatever needs to be healed. Watch as any area that is dark lights up brightly as it is healed. Allow the light to dissolve any pain that is left.

Pause.

Whenever you need to, allow yourself to take a vacation from pain. Imagine a wonderful place where you can go without your pain. Is there anything you will miss about your pain while you are gone?

Pause.

Now think about something you love to do or whatever makes you feel happy. Imagine you are doing that now.

*Note: At this point you might continue with a Body Scan for Kids and Teens Tool 16-3 and skip the rest of this script.

Now pay attention to your fingers and hands which are still warming. (Note: Use any part of the body that is pain-free for this part.) Move them back and forth a little and just notice how they feel."

Now pay attention to your feet and your legs. Imagine the light is flowing down through your legs and feet right onto the floor. As it flows let it heal and clear and warm you.

Now pay attention to your stomach, your chest, and your back. Imagine the light is flowing down through your chest, your back, and stomach, your legs and through the ends of your feet and onto the floor.

Now pay attention to your shoulders, arms and hands. Watch the light as it flows down through your shoulders, arms and hands.

Now imagine the light is filling your head with healing. Allow it to light up any dark places. Let it bring healing and comfort to your head, your brain, and your whole body.

Take a deep breath in through your nose and blow it out slowly through your mouth.

Open your eyes and come back to the room.

CHRONIC MEDICAL ILLNESS

Tool 24-3: Remembered Wellness for Kids and Teens

BACKGROUND: Studies show that mindfulness practices can improve many types of physical illness (Tool 3-22). Herbert Benson teaches the concept of remembered wellness (Benson, 1996). Remembered wellness is based on the idea that our brains don't know the difference between actually feeling well or remembering a time when we felt well. Therefore, by remembering a time we felt well, we help our brain recreate the internal conditions that were present at that time. This tool references the Remembered Wellness Meditation for Kids and Teens Tool 16-8 for those that are dealing with medical illness or pain. It is designed to tap into the power of healing by remembering a time when they felt well and imaging that they feel well in the present moment.

SKILL BUILDING: Explain the concept of remembered wellness to clients. Tell them that by remembering a time that they felt well, they set up the conditions in their brain to recreate that wellness in the present. See the Remembered Wellness for Kids and Teens Tool 16-8 and read the Remembered Wellness meditation that's included on Handout 16-8 to them. Afterwards, ask them if they were able to find a time that they felt well. Encourage them to repeat this meditation on a regular basis. Be aware that this meditation can initially provoke sadness and feelings of loss for some people as they remember how good they used to feel as they get in touch with losses they may have suffered due to poor health.

REFLECTION: Ask clients if they were able to remember a time that they felt well. Explore their memory of feeling well. Were they able to remember how it felt when they felt well? What did they notice about how they felt in the present as they did the meditation? Did they notice any change in their body or their emotions? Did they experience a sense of loss or sadness? If so, process these feelings, validate them, and normalize them. Give them a realistic sense of how practicing remembered wellness works to shift them into a healthier state.

SLEEP DISORDERS

Tool 24-4: Fall Asleep Tonight

BACKGROUND: In the 1970s Harvard cardiologist Herbert Benson coined the term "relaxation response" as described in his book of the same name (Benson, 2000). The relaxation response elicits a state of deep relaxation in which our breathing, pulse rate, blood pressure, and metabolism are decreased. This tool provides a Meditation for Sleep that provides a progressive relaxation combined with guided imagery designed to invoke the relaxation response to lower the arousal system and help kids and teens fall asleep.

SKILL BUILDING: This sleep meditation can be used for kids even as young as 2 years old. Explain the basics of the relaxation response to older kids and teens being mindful of their age and developmental and cognitive levels, including how doing a relaxing mindfulness meditation can counter the effects of the fight, flight, or freeze stress response. Handout 24-4 contains the text of a Meditation for Sleep. You or your client or their parent can read it aloud and record it so it can be listened to at night when going to sleep. Explain that they will gradually notice their mind and body relaxing as they listen. They will be more able to turn off the busy chatter of their brain and enter into a drowsy state conducive to falling asleep. Encourage your client to listen to the Meditation for Sleep in bed every night at bedtime. Have them make sure that whatever they use to play the recording will turn off by itself and not need their attention, which would interfere with sleep. An mp3 of a similar meditation for sleep is available at www. TheBrainLady.com.

CASE EXAMPLES:

1. A hyperactive 4-year-old boy with ADHD had trouble falling asleep when he was at his dad's house. He experienced anxiety that he would lose his mom while he was at Dad's. He listened to this sleep meditation while at dad's house and within 4 days he was able to go right to sleep without the anxiety or hyperactivity that was keeping him awake. He felt so proud of himself!

2. A 9-year-old boy with autism had extreme anxiety at night and often would not fall asleep all night. When listening to this sleep meditation he was able to fall asleep within 20 minutes on a regular basis. His mother stated they often used it while in their camper and the whole family fell asleep promptly while listening to it.

REFLECTION: After assigning this exercise, ask your client if they have been using the Meditation for Sleep. If not, explore why not, talk to their parent, and brainstorm with them about how to incorporate it into their bedtime routine. If they have used it, explore what they experienced. Did it help them relax? Did it help them fall asleep? What did they notice about their sleep and their ability to stay asleep when they used it? What did they notice about their body tension, comfort, discomfort? Did they experience any emotions as they listened? Were they distracted and, if so, by what? How did they bring their attention back to the meditation? What might they need to change in their bedroom to encourage sleep, such as removing the TV, computer, and other distractions, making sure the bed is comfortable, the room is dark and quiet, and that they get to bed at the same time every night?

MEDITATION FOR SLEEP

Let's begin by doing a few deep cleansing breaths. Breathe in through your nose to the count of four and breathe out through your mouth to the count of eight. Purse your lips as you blow out, like gently blowing a bubble.

Do it with me. Breathe in through your nose and then, as you exhale, relax your mind. Do it again. Breathe in relaxation and, as you breathe out, relax your body. One more time. Breathe in comfort and, as you breathe out, let go of anything that needs to go.

Now breathe normally.

Pay attention to your toes. Notice how they feel. Notice if there is any tightness or discomfort there and let it flow right out through the ends of your toes and onto the floor.

Now focus on your feet: the balls of your feet, your arches, your heels, the tops of your feet. Just pay attention to what's there and let anything that needs to go flow right out through the ends of your toes and onto the floor.

Now concentrate on your ankles. Just notice what they feel like. Send them loving thoughts. Allow any discomfort or tension stored there to flow down through your feet and right through the ends of your toes and onto the floor.

Now pay attention to your calves and shins. Again, just notice what's there. Let anything that needs to go flow right down through your ankles, your feet, and right through the ends of your toes and onto the floor.

Now bring your attention to your knees. Notice what they feel like. Let go of anything that doesn't belong. Let it flow down through your calves and shins, through your ankles, your feet, and right through the ends of your toes and onto the floor.

Now pay attention to your thighs. Notice what's there and allow anything that needs to go to flow down through your knees, your calves and shins, your feet, and right through the ends of your toes and onto the floor.

Now focus on your bottom. Pay attention to what you notice there. Just let go of anything that needs to go and let it flow down through your thighs, through your knees, your calves and shins, your feet, and right through the ends of your toes and onto the floor.

Now bring your attention to your lower belly or abdomen. Spend a moment to notice what you are carrying there. Allow anything that doesn't belong to flow down through your thighs, through your knees, your calves and shins, your feet, and right through the ends of your toes and onto the floor.

Now notice how your lower back feels. Lots of tension gets stored here, and you just don't need any of it. Let it flow down through your bottom, your thighs, through your knees, your calves and shins, your feet, and right through the ends of your toes and onto the floor.

Now concentrate on your stomach. Imagine that you are looking at a rope that is twisted, coiled, and tied up tightly. But as you watch the rope it unwinds, uncoils, and unties until it is hanging limply. Image that your stomach and the area around your stomach have done the same and are now relaxed and comfortable.

Pay attention to your chest and heart area. Take a nice deep breath in through your nose and fill your lungs with a cushion of healing energy. As you breathe out, allow everything that needs to go to flow out.

Now pay attention to your middle and upper back. Lots of stuff gets carried here and you don't need any of it. Allow it to flow down through your lower back, your bottom, through your thighs, through your knees, your calves and shins, your feet, and right through the ends of your toes and onto the floor.

Now focus on your neck and shoulders. Again, lots of tightness gets stored here and you don't need it. Allow it to flow down your back, through your bottom, through your thighs, through your knees, your calves and shins, your feet, and right through the ends of your toes and onto the floor.

Now pay attention to your hands including your fingers, thumbs, palms, and the backs of your hands. Notice what you carry here and let go of anything you don't need. Let it flow through the ends of your fingers and onto the floor.

Now pay attention to your arms including your forearms, elbows, upper arms right on up to your shoulders. Let anything you don't need flow down through your arms, your wrists, your hands, and right through the ends of your fingers and onto the floor.

Now focus on your face including your jaw, cheeks, eyes, and forehead. Drop your jaw and just let it hang totally limp. Let any tension stored in your face flow down through your neck, shoulders, arms, hands, and right through the ends of your fingers and onto the floor.

Now pay attention to your brain. As thoughts arise, imagine they are written on a blank white board. As soon as you see them there, erase them and imagine the board empty again.

Now that your body is completely relaxed and starting to doze, imagine that you are walking along a path in the forest. Take a slow deep breath. The air smells so good here, so clean and natural. You feel connected to the earth. You can hear the birds singing. You notice how the sun is shining down through the leaves and creating beautiful patterns of sunlight and shadow on the forest floor. The forest floor is lush and green. You feel so happy, alive, and content.

As you walk along, you gradually reach the edge of the forest and walk into a beautiful meadow. The air is clear, the sun is shining, the sky is blue, and the temperature is just perfect. You can see pretty butterflies and beautiful flowers all around you. You notice the path here is worn smooth from many feet so you sit down and take off your shoes and socks. You walk along the path barefoot and you feel the smooth, warm earth on the bottoms of your feet. You feel connected to the earth and nature and infinite intelligence.

The path starts to get sandy, and you realize you are walking toward a beautiful lake. You can smell the freshness of the water and the wet sand. The water on the lake is so calm it looks like a mirror. You can see the trees perfectly reflected in the lake about the edges. The sky is blue and the air feels fresh and clean. You can see some flowers blooming at the edge of the beach and some lilies growing off the shore. Listen carefully. You can hear the water as it gently laps up against the shore. Mmm . . . it feels good here, so peaceful, so safe. If you feel like it, walk along the edge of the water and feel the cool, clear water on your feet.

As you walk, you look ahead on the beach and see a chaise lounge sitting on the sand. You walk over to it and lie down on it. It has soft cushions and it feels so comfortable when you lie down. You notice a blanket under the chaise and you reach down to get the blanket and cover yourself with it. You snuggle down.

As you lie on the chaise, you let your mind slow down some more. You let go and any busy thoughts disappear as you tell your busy monkey brain to calm down and relax. You feel warm and cozy. As you take some slow deep breaths, you begin to feel warm and heavy all over your body. Your eyelids get so heavy you can't keep them open anymore.

Allow them to close. Listen to my voice as you let go of your day and begin to drift and allow sleep to come to you.

You realize you are in your own comfortable bed. You are safe. You feel so comfortable and relaxed. You fall into a deep restful sleep. You sleep soundly all night. You will awake in the morning exactly when you need to be awake to start your day and you will feel completely rested, energized, and wide awake. You will have the right amount of energy and you feel happy. You will look forward to your day. You will notice you are completely focused and you can concentrate effortlessly. You will know what you need to do and you will get everything done that you need to do. You will be on time. You will get along with everyone and your friends and family will be happy to see you.

You will stay focused, calm, relaxed, and happy all day. You know you will sleep well again at night.

Sleeping is easy now. Allow your brain to let go. Allow sleep to arrive. Sleep is here now.

Sleep, sleep, sleep.

Goodnight.

Chapter 25
Stress, Anger

STRESS
> Tool 25-1: Reduce Stress Response

ANGER
> Tool 25-2: Blow Away Anger
> Tool 25-3: Don't Flip Your Lid

STRESS

Tool 25-1: Reduce Stress Response

BACKGROUND: The stress response is the physiological reaction to anything that is perceived as stressful, dangerous, or threatening. This is often called the flight, fight, or freeze response. This can include increased heart rate, blood pressure, stress hormones such as cortisol, and anything that makes a person fast and strong in order to survive danger. This helped our ancestors survive when they were confronted with a wild animal and they needed to run away to escape or fight to the death. Kids and teens today are often chronically stressed and their stress response remains too high much of the time. This may result in the onset of a variety of stress-related illness and missed school. A variety of types of mindfulness exercises effectively lowers the stress response. This tool provides guidance on how to use mindfulness tools to lower the stress response.

SKILL BUILDING: Explain what the stress response is and how it helps us survive. Compare it to the relaxation response, which counters the stress response. Many of the mindfulness exercises in this workbook will help to lower the stress response. Teach the Basic Relaxation Breathing technique (Tool 5-1), which works to calm down the physiology by activating the parasympathetic nervous system. Then use the Mindfulness of Physical Body (Tools 9-1 through 9-5) to help reduce body tension and induce relaxation. Use Tool 3-16 to teach kids and teens how to take their pulse to help them monitor how their heart rate responds to stress. Encourage them to use a deep relaxation breath to calm the stress response anytime they notice they feel stressed. Urge them to incorporate a variety of mindfulness exercises on a regular basis that calm their stress response.

REFLECTION: Ask clients to notice how their body feels. As they practice the various mindfulness exercises, help them reflect on what they notice in their body as well as in their mind. Explore what changes they notice in how stressed they feel as they practice mindfulness. Encourage them to remember how they feel at the end of a mindfulness exercise and then when they feel stressed, to take a few deep cleansing breaths while remembering that feeling to calm down their stress response.

ANGER

Tool 25-2: Blow Away Anger

BACKGROUND: Some kids and teens experience intense anger. This tool provides a simple technique they can use in the moment to lessen their anger related physiology and head off intense outbursts of angry behavior.

SKILL BUILDING: Ask kids and teens what makes them angry. Identify their triggers. Help them explore how they know they are getting angry. Often they will get a feeling in their body: heart pounding, chest feels like it's going to explode, face hot, etc. Mindfulness of Physical Body Tools 16-1 – 16-9 can be helpful with increasing this awareness. A key to success in managing anger is the ability to recognize they are getting angry and stop for a moment before reacting to whatever triggered the anger. Use the Basic Relaxation Breathing Tool 6-4 to teach kids how to calm down their anger by breathing. Do it with them and watch them do it to make sure they are breathing in slowly and not take a sharp, quick in-breath which defeats the purpose of this technique. Tell them that when they are blowing out slowly they are "blowing away their anger". Encourage them to remember to "blow away their anger" next time they start to feel angry.

CASE EXAMPLE:

A 10-year-old boy with autism experienced severe and sometimes physically violent angry meltdowns. After he learned Basic Relaxation Breathing Tool 6-4 he was often able to head off the intense meltdowns by taking three or four deep breaths in through his nose and blowing out slowly through his mouth. This would calm down his anger and help him with self-regulation.

REFLECTION: Process with clients as described in Tool 6-4. Were they able to master the basic relaxation breath? Did they use the "blow away anger" technique and, if so, how did it work for them? Did they remember to use it and, if not, what will help them remember next time?

Tool 25-3: Don't Flip Your Lid

BACKGROUND: Dan Siegel uses the hand to illustrate where the prefrontal cortex (PFC) and the amygdala and the limbic system are located within the brain. (Seigel, 2010) See the illustration on Handout 25-3. This tool gives kids and teens a tangible way to help them avoid "flipping their lid" and losing control of their anger.

SKILL BUILDING: Use the illustration in Handout 25-3 and your own hand to show kids and teens a way to visualize where their PFC, amygdala and limbic system are in their brain. Explain that when they are calm the PFC is in control of the amygdala in the limbic system and the fingers (PFC) are curled over the thumb (limbic system and amygdala). When they get angry the PFC loses control, their fingers straighten and they "flip their lid". Help them put their hands in the configuration shown on the handout and ask them to practice "flipping their lid" by raising their fingers. Now explain that when the PFC stays in control it's like giving their amygdala and limbic system a hug. Show them how their PFC (fingers) hugs the amygdala and limbic system (thumb). Encourage them to hug their thumb with their fingers when they start to feel angry to calm themselves down and to imagine that they are giving their amygdala a "hug" to calm it and keep the PFC in charge. This will provide a way to ground themselves physically.

REFLECTION: Help clients reflect on what it is like to imagine that they are "hugging" their amygdala in this exercise. Did they remember to try it when they felt angry? Did it help to calm them down?

Don't Flip Your Lid

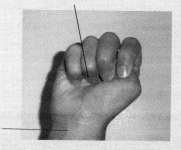

PreFrontal Cortex

Brain Stem

Give Your Limbic System a Hug

PFC in Control

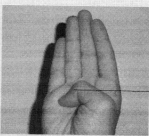

Limbic System

Flipped Your Lid

PFC not in control

Chapter 26
Autism

Tool 26-1: Decreasing Aggression
Tool 26-2: Sensory Overload

Tool 26-1: Decreasing Aggression

BACKGROUND: Some kids and teens with autism act physically aggressive—hitting, kicking, biting, or being verbally aggressive. A study done with aggressive adolescents with autism showed significantly reduced aggression after the subjects practiced a mindfulness exercise called The Soles of Your Feet. (Singh et al., 2011) They practiced shifting their attention from the target of their anger and aggression to a neutral part of their body. This tool provides a similar exercise to help older kids and teens use mindfulness to reduce episodes of aggression.

SKILL BUILDING: Explain to older kids and teens that this exercise will help them handle their anger and avoid becoming physically or verbally aggressive. Read the script on Handout 26-1 to them a number of times and ask them to practice it at home until they understand the basics of the process. The goal is for them to learn to shift their attention from their intense emotions such as anger, frustration, or overwhelm, to a neutral place on their body and thereby avoid becoming aggressive. Encourage them to use this skill whenever their anger, frustration, or other intense emotions are triggered.

REFLECTION: Help clients process what this exercise was like for them. Were they able to recall a time when they got angry? Did they have any trouble shifting their attention to their feet? Were they able to stay focused on their feet? Did this help their emotions calm down? When did they or could they have used this in their day? Are they experiencing fewer episodes of aggression now that they use this skill?

MEDITATION ON THE SOLES OF THE FEET PROCEDURE

1. If you are standing, stand in a relaxed position with the soles of your feet flat on the floor.

2. If you are sitting, sit comfortably with the soles of your feet flat on the floor.

3. Breathe naturally, and do nothing.

4. Remember something that made you very angry. Stay with the anger.

5. You are feeling angry, and angry thoughts are flowing through your mind. Let them flow naturally, without restriction. Stay with the anger. Your body may show signs of anger (e.g., rapid breathing).

6. Now, shift all your attention fully to the soles or bottoms of your feet.

7. Slowly, move your toes, feel your shoes covering your feet, feel the texture of your socks, the curve of your arch, and the heels of your feet against the back of your shoes. If you do not have shoes on, feel the floor or carpet with the soles of your feet.

8. Keep breathing naturally and focus on the soles of your feet until you feel calm.

9. Practice this mindfulness exercise until you can use it wherever you are and whenever something occurs that may otherwise lead to you being verbally or physically aggressive.

10. Remember that once you are calm, you can walk away from the incident or situation with a smile on your face because you controlled your anger. Alternatively, if you need to, you can respond to the incident or situation with a calm and clear mind without verbal threats or physical aggression.

Adapted from (Singh et al., 2011)

Tool 26-2: Sensory Overload

BACKGROUND: Sensory overload is a common experience for many kids and teens with autism. In order to cope with this, some will act out, scream, rock back and forth, engage in repetitive movements and more. This tool provides a way for kids and teens to calm their brain when they feel this sensory overload coming on.

SKILL BUILDING: With each particular client with autism, find out as much as you can about how they experience the world. Many kids and teens with autism have been able to describe feeling overwhelmed with sensory input and they feel unable to cope with it. Others are not able to communicate this issue to others. They often react by making noise, repetitive movements, acting out, screaming, etc. Use a variety of tools from this workbook to help them calm their physiology and to increase their ability to focus on something in particular while filtering out the sensory chaos.

Use with the Mindfulness Bells Tool 3-6, Basic Relaxation Breathing Tool 6-4, Mindfulness of Surroundings Tool 7-1, Water Glass Game Tool 7-4, Mindfulness of Physical Body Tools Chapter 16, and Mindful Listening Chapter 8, Mindful Seeing Chapter 9, Mindful Tasting Chapter 10, Mindful Smelling Chapter 11, Mindful Touching Chapter 12, and Mindful Motion Chapter 13.

Then, when they are better able to filter out the sensory chaos and have a sense of self-control, add the rest of the tools to help with social skills and task completion.

REFLECTION: Follow the reflection guidelines associated with each of the tools used.

SECTION V

TOOLS FOR TRACKING PROGRESS

Chapter 27
Tracking Progress

Tool 27-1: Define Treatment Goals
Tool 27-2: Symptom Tracking

Tool 27-1: Define Treatment Goals

BACKGROUND: Defining treatment goals is important for several reasons. First, by defining treatment goals, the client is setting an intention to focus on meeting these goals. Second, the treatment goals clarify and provide structure for the work to be done with the client. Third, best practice methods and most managed-care insurance companies require them.

It is important to involve the parents as well as the kids or teens in defining treatment goals. This process will ensure that the child or teen client understands why their parents brought them in for treatment. It will also provide a way to monitor progress during the treatment episode. Although some mindfulness gurus nix the idea of setting specific goals for mindfulness practice it is appropriate to set treatment goals when using mindfulness in a clinical setting. This tool discusses the process of defining treatment goals related to mindfulness practice.

SKILL BUILDING: Ask the client how they will know if working with you has helped them. This directly addresses what their treatment goals are. Some kids and teens are extremely tuned in to what they need help with while others will need help with this task. Ask them for 5 to 10 goals that they would like to achieve or symptoms they would like to improve. Involve the parents in this step whenever possible. Refer to Handout 27-1 for examples of treatment goals that research indicates may be improved with mindfulness practice.

REFLECTION: Assist the client and their parent in mindfully defining their treatment goals. Ask them to reflect on what the process was like for them. How was it helpful to clarify what they hope to improve/achieve? Encourage them to update these goals periodically.

SAMPLE TREATMENT GOALS

Studies show that the following symptoms have improved with mindfulness practice. See Tool 3-22.

Client will learn and practice Mindfulness skills to:

- Improve concentration

- Increase emotion regulation

- Improve mood

- Decrease anxiety

- Stabilize mood swings

- Improve sleep

- Increase sense of well-being

- Improve relationships

- Improve health

- Improve stress management skills

- Reduce hyperactivity

- Decrease anger

- Improve memory

- Increase task completion

- Identify and explore feelings

- Decrease rumination

- Improve self-awareness

- Increase ability to repair negative mood states

- Decrease binge eating

- Improve self-esteem

- Improve compassion for self and others

- Improve ability to deal with chronic illness

- Manage chronic pain

- Quit smoking (teens)

- Reduce alcohol use (teens)

Tool 27-2: Symptom Tracking

BACKGROUND: Tracking client progress is helpful for several reasons. First, it keeps the treatment focused on meeting treatment goals. Second, it provides a way for therapist and client to track improvement and monitor symptoms/goals as work progresses. Third, it provides a way to assess the effectiveness of treatment. Kids and teens are typically more invested in the treatment when they can see their progress. And they often enjoy watching their ratings improve. This tool describes one technique for tracking symptoms or monitoring treatment goals.

SKILL BUILDING: After defining treatment goals using Tool 27-1, ask parents and older kids and teens to rate each symptom/goal on a scale of zero to 10 where 10 is worst and zero is no problem. Depending on developmental level and maturity kids as young as 6 or 7 may be able to attach a valid number to their symptom. Some kids and teens with poor self-awareness will need their parents to rate the symptoms. Occasionally, it may prove useful to ask older kids and teens to rate their symptoms and then ask the parents to do so on a separate sheet.

List the goals/symptoms in the left-hand column of Handout 27-2B. Then place the date at the top of the next column and fill in their rating of each goal/symptom. Tally the total at the bottom. This handout was created using a simple Excel spreadsheet. The goal will be to lower the rating on each symptom and the overall total as treatment progresses. Ask clients to rate their symptoms/goals periodically as treatment progress. Show them how their ratings are improving. See Handout 27-2A for an example of a partially completed symptom rating form.

Some clients and their parents may have trouble rating a symptom with a number. They may find it easier to describe changes they are noticing. That's okay. If possible, use this information to rate symptoms yourself. Or, skip the numeric rating and keep a log of changes they report.

REFLECTION: Some clients and their parents find this process easy while a few do not. The goal of this tool is to provide a way to notice change and document symptom improvement. Encourage clients to rate symptoms. Most will provide a consistently accurate rating over time. Showing them their progress inspires hope and motivation for continuing their mindful practice.

SYMPTOM	11/7/13	11/14/13	11/21/13	12/2/13						DATE
Concentration	10	9.5	9	8						
Depression	8	8	7.5	7						
Anxiety	5	4	4	3						
Sleep	6	5	4	4						
Self-esteem	8	7	6	5						
Anger	9	8	7	3						
TOTAL Score	46	41.5	37.5	30	0	0	0	0	0	0

CLIENT SYMPTOM/GOAL RATING CHART

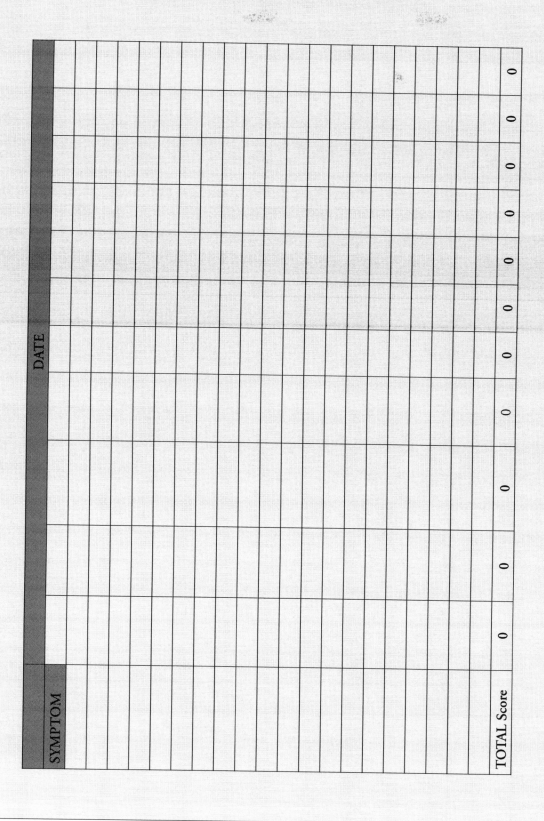

SYMPTOM	DATE																					
																							0
																							0
																							0
																							0
																							0
																							0
																							0
																							0
																							0
																							0
																							0
																							0
																							0
TOTAL Score																							0

References

For your convenience, you may download a PDF version of the Handouts in this book from our dedicated website: go.pesi.com/MindfulnessSkillsKidsandTeens

Alidina, S. (2011). *Mindfulness for dummies.* West Sussex, England: John Wiley & Sons, Ltd.

Amen, D., (1998). *Change your brain change your life.* New York: Random House.

Benson, H., & Friedman, R. (1996) Harnessing the power of the placebo effect and renaming it "remembered wellness." *Annual Review of Medicine, 47,* 193-199.

Benson, H. (2000). *The relaxation response.* (Updated). New York: William Morrow Paperbacks.

Bernstein, P. (2005). Intuitions: What science says (so far) about how and why intuition works. In *Endophysics, Time, Quantum and the Subjective.* Singapore: World Scientific Publishing.

Biegel, G., Brown, K., Shapiro, S., Schubert, C. (2009). Mindfulness-based stress reduction for the treatment of adolescent psychiatric outpatients: A randomized clinical trial. *Journal of Consulting and Clinical Psychology, 77,* 5, 855–866.

Burke, C. (2009). Mindfulness-based approaches with children and adolescents: A preliminary review of current research in an emergent field. *Journal of Child and Family Studies.* Online DOI 10.1007/s10826-009-9282-x.

Childre, D., & Marti, H. (1999). *The heartmath solution.* New York: HarperCollins,1999. www.HeartMath.com.

Dyer, W. (2002). *Getting in the gap: Making conscious contact with God through meditation.* Carlsbad, CA: Hay House, 2002.

Fehmi, L. *Open Focus.* The Princeton Biofeedback Centre, LLC. Retrieved November 7, 2012, from www.openfocus.com/resources/complimentary-programs.

Fehmi, L. (2010). *Dissolving pain: Simple brain training exercises for overcoming pain.* Boston: Trumpeter Books.

Fehmi, L. (2007). *The open focus brain.* Boston: Trumpeter Books.

Flook, L., Smalley, S.L., Kitil, M.J., Galla, B.M., Kaiser-Greenland, S., Locke, J., et al. (2010). Effects of mindful awareness practices on executive functions in elementary school children. *Journal of Applied School Psychology, 26,* 1, 70-95.

Hauss, R. B. (2011). The placebo effect: The amazing power of the mind to heal the body. Hill Rag, June, 2011, pp. 102-103

Hawn Foundation, (2011). *The MINDUP Curriculum, Grades Pre-K – 2.* New York: Scholastic Inc.

Hebb, D. *The organization of behavior.* (2009). Mahwah, NJ; Lawrence Erlbaum Associates, Inc.

Hölzel, B.K., Ott, U., Gard, T., Hempel, H., Weygandt, M., Morgen, K., et al. (2007). Investigation of mindfulness meditation practitioners with voxel-based morphometry. *Social Cognitive and Affective Neuroscience, 3,* 55–61.

Hölzel, B., Carmody, J., Evans, K., Hoge, E., Duse, J., Morgan, L., et al. (2010). Stress reduction correlates with structural changes in the amygdala. *Social Cognitive Affective Neuroscience, 5,* 11–17.

Hutcherson, C. A., Seppala, E. M., & Gross, J.J. I don't know you but I like you: Loving kindness meditation increases positivity toward others; Paper presented at the 6th annual conference Integrating Mindfulness-Based Interventions into Medicine; Worcester, MA: *Health Care & Society;* 2008.

Jacobson, Edmund. "The Progressive Muscle Relaxation of Dr. Edmund Jacobson." *HypnoGenesis.* Retrieved November 8, 2012, from http:///www.hypnos.co.uk/hypnomag/jacobson.htm.

Jha, A.P. (2005). *Garrison Institute report: Contemplation and education: Scientific research issues relevant to school-based contemplative programs: A supplement.* New York: Garrison Institute.

Kabat-Zinn, J., Lipworth, L., Burney, R., & Sellers, W. (1986). Four-year follow-up of a meditation–based program for the self-regulation of chronic pain: Treatment outcomes and compliance. *Clinical Journal of Pain, 2,* 3, 159–173.

Kabat-Zinn J. (1990). Full catastrophe living: Using the wisdom of your body and mind to face stress, pain, and illness. New York: Delacorte Press.

Kabat-Zinn J. (2003) Mindfulness-based interventions in context: Past, present, and future. *Clinical Psychology: Science and Practice, 10,* 144–156.

Kaiser-Greenland, S. (2011). Mindfulness for Children: Q & A with Susan Kaiser Greenland. Retrieved from: http://www.tricycle.com/blog/mindfulness-children-q-susan-kaiser-greenland

Kaiser-Greenland, S. (2006). Information from Inner Kids Organizational Website. www.innerkids.com

Kaiser-Greenland, S. (2010). *The mindful child.* New York, NY: Free Press.

Kaplan, J. (2008). *Mindfulness of emotions.* Retrieved October 9, 2010 from http://urbanmindfulness.org/storage/UM%20Mindfulness%20of%20Emotions.pdf

Kaslow, N. J., & Racusin, G. R. (1994). Family therapy for depression in young people. In W. M. Reynolds & H. F. Johnston (Eds.), *Handbook of depression in children and adolescents: Issues in clinical child psychology* (pp. 345–363). New York: Plenum Press.

Kessler, R., Amminger, G. P., Aguilar-Gaxiola, S., Alonso, J., Lee, S., & Ustun, T. B. (2007). Age of onset of mental disorders: A review of recent literature. *Current Opinion in Psychiatry, 20,* 4, 359–364.

Linden. W. (1973). Practicing of meditation by school children and their levels of field dependence, test, anxiety, and reading achievement. *Journal of Consulting and Clinical Psychology, 41,* 1, 139-143.

Linehan, M. (1993). *Skills training manual for treating borderline personality disorder,* New York: The Guilford Press.

Miller, A.L., Wyman, S.E., Huppert, J.D., Glassman, S.L., & Rathaus, J.H. (2000). Analysis of behavioural skills utilized by suicidal adolescents receiving dialectical behaviour therapy. *Cogntive and Behavioural Practice, 7,* 183–187.

Napoli, M., Krech, P. R., & Holley, L., (2005). Mindfulness training for elementary school students: The Attention Academy. *Journal of Applied School Psychology, 21,* 99-125.

Ott, M.J. (2002). Mindfulness meditation in pediatric clinical practice. *Pediatric Nursing, 28,* 487–491.

Piaget, J. (1962). The stages of the intellectual development of the child. *Bulletin of the Menninger Clinic, 26,* 120–128.

Rommel, A., Halperin, J., Mill, J., Asherson, P., Kuntsi, J. (2013). Protection from genetic diathesis in attention-deficit/hyperactivity disorder: Possible complementary roles of exercise. *Journal of the American Academy of Child & Adolescent Psychiatry, 52,* 9, 900-910.

Saltzman, A. (2011). *Mindfulness: A guide for teachers.* Retrieved from: www.pbs.org/thebuddha/teachers-guide/ 9/6/13

Schonert-Reichl, K., & Lawlor, M., (2010). The Effects of a Mindfulness-Based Education Program on Pre- and Early Adolescents' Well-Being and Social and Emotional Competence. *Mindfulness, 1,* 137-151.

Semple, R.J., Lee, J., Rosa, D., & Miller, L. (2010). A randomized trial of mindfulness-based cognitive therapy for children: Promoting mindful attention to enhance social-emotional resiliency in children. *Journal of Child and Family Studies, 19,* 218–229.

Semple, R. J., Lee, J., & Miller, L.F. (2006). Mindfulness-based cognitive therapy for children. In R.A. Baer (Ed.), *Mindfulness-based treatment approaches: Clinicians guide to evidence base and applications* (pp. 143–166). Oxford, UK: Elsevier.

Semple, R., Lee, J. et al, (2010). A randomized trial of mindfulness-based cognitive therapy for children: Promoting mindful attention to enhance social-emotional resiliency in children. *Journal of Child and Family Studies, 19,* 218–229.

Semple, R., Reid, E., Miller, L. (2005). Treating anxiety with mindfulness: An open trial of mindfulness training for anxious children. *Journal of Cognitive Psychotherapy: An International Quarterly, 19,* 4, 379-391.

Siegel, D. (2010). *Mindsight. The new science of personal transformation.* New York: Bantam Books.

Singh , N., Lancioni, G., Manikam, R., Winton, A., Singh, A., Singh, J., et al. (2011). A mindfulness-based strategy for self-management of aggressive behavior in adolescents with autism. *Research in Autism Spectrum Disorders, 5,* 1153–1158.

Stahl, B., & Goldstein, E. (2010). *A mindfulness-based stress reduction workbook.* Oakland, CA: New Harbinger Publications, Inc.

The Dalai Lama. (2001). *An open heart: Practicing compassion in everyday life.* Boston: Little, Brown and Company.

Thich Nhat Hanh. (2008). *Mindful movements.* Berkeley, CA: Parallax Press.

Van de Oord, S., Bogels, S., & Peijnenburg, D. (2012). The effectiveness of mindfulness training for children with ADHD and mindful parenting for their parents. *Journal of Child and Family Studies, 21,* 1, 139–147.

Verduyn, C. (2000). Cognitive behaviour therapy in childhood depression. *Child Psychology and Psychiatry Review, 5,* 176–180.

Wagner, E.E., Rathus, J.H., & Miller, A.L. (2006). Mindfulness in dialectical behavior therapy (DBT) for adolescents. In R.A. Baer (Ed.), *Mindfulness-based treatment approaches: Clinicians guide to evidence base and applications* (pp. 143–166). Oxford, UK: Elsevier.

Wall, R.B. (2005). Tai chi and mindfulness-based stress reduction in a Boston public middle school. *Journal of Paediatric Health Care, 19,* 230–237.

Wikipedia. Drum. http://en.wikipedia.org/wiki/Drum retrieved 9/30/13

Zylowska, L., Ackerman, D., Yang, M., Futrell, J., Horton, N., Hale, T., et al (2008). Mindfulness meditation training in adults and adolescents with ADHD. A feasibility study. *Journal of Attention Disorders, 11,* 6, 737-746.

FURTHER READING

Boudette, R. (2011). Integrating mindfulness into the therapy hour. Eating disorders. *The Journal of Treatment & Prevention, 19,* 108-115.

Brown, K., & Ryan, R. (2003). The benefits of being present: Mindfulness and its role in psychological well-being of personality and social psychology. *Journal of Personality and Social Psychology, 84,* 4, 822–848.

Davidson, R. J., Kabat-Zinn, J., Schumacher, J., Rosenkrantz, M., Muller, D., & Santorelli, S.F. (2003). Alterations in brain and immune function produced by mindfulness meditation. *Psychosomatic Medicine, 65,* 564–570.

Hooker, K., & Fodor, I. (2008). Teaching mindfulness to children. *Gestalt Review, 12,* 1, 75-91.

Moustafa, B. M. (1999). Multisensory approaches and learning styles theory in the elementary school. *Journal of Consulting and Clinical Psychology, 41,* 139-143.

Newberg, A. B. et al, (2010). Cerebral blood flow differences between long-term meditators and non-meditators. *Consciousness and Cognition, 19,* 899-905.

Pert, C. (1997). *Molecules of emotion: The science behind mind.* New York: Touchstone Books.

Posner, M. I., & Petersen, S. E. (1990). The attention system of the human brain. *Annual Review of Neuroscience, 13,* 25–42.

Siegler, R. S. (1991). *Children's thinking* (2nd ed.). Upper Saddle River, NJ: Prentice-Hall.

Siegel, D. (2007). *The mindful brain: Reflection and attunement in the cultivation of well-being,* New York: W. W. Norton & Company, Inc. p. 291.

Thich Nhat Hanh. (2011). *Planting seeds, practicing mindfulness with children.* Berkeley, CA: Parallax Press.

Thompson, M., & Gauntlett-Gilbert, J. (2008). Mindfulness with children and adolescents: Effective clinical application, *Clinical Child Psychology and Psychiatry, 13,* 395.

Wallace, B.A., (2006). *The attention revolution: Unlocking the power of the focused mind.* Boston: Wisdom Publications.

About the Author

Debra Burdick, LCSW, BCN, also known as "The Brain Lady," is a Licensed Clinical Social Worker and a board certified neurofeedback practitioner. She is a national speaker and author and has been providing outpatient psychotherapy and mindfulness skills to her clients since 1990. She added neurofeedback to her psychotherapy practice in 1999. She is an expert author on SelfGrowth.com.

Debra specializes in ADHD, depression, anxiety, stress, sleep, cognitive function, relationships, mindfulness, and traumatic brain injury. Besides her private practice, Debra worked at the Child Guidance Clinic, Family Services, Child and Family Agency, and Lawrence and Memorial Hospital in New London, CT. She teaches all-day workshops including: *Childhood ADHD: Advanced Non-drug Treatments That Change the Brain, Brain-changing Mindfulness Strategies to Improve Treatment Outcomes for Depression, Anxiety, ADHD, A Holistic Approach to Success with ADHD* and more. Mindfulness training for business leaders and executives is another of her passions.

Debra developed her own mindfulness practice to deal with a chronic illness (now thankfully healed). She found it so helpful in her own life that she started teaching her clients the skills she was using. She went on to develop clinical material on mindfulness skills and created a four-step process for working with clients using mindfulness that she perfected in her private practice and in an intensive outpatient program. Her clients have shown her that mindfulness skills improve the rate and quality of treatment outcomes.

Debra has extensive experience helping children and adults thrive with ADHD. In addition to counseling hundreds of clients over the past 20 years, she parented a daughter who has ADHD, was married to a man with ADHD, and was business partners with someone with ADHD. She combines knowledge gained from her own personal healing journey, her parenting experience, her clients, and her professional study of ADHD and brain dysregulation into her holistic approach.

Her books and CDs include:

- *Mindfulness Skills Workbook for Clinicians and Clients: 111 Tools, Techniques, Activities and Worksheets*
- *IS IT REALLY ADHD? ONLY ADHD? How to Get an Accurate Diagnosis for You or Your Child*
- *ADHD and Sleep—Children and Adults; Sleep Better Tonight*
- *ADHD Treatment Options. How to Choose the Right Treatment for You or Your Child*
- *A Holistic Approach to Successful Children with Attention Deficit/Hyperactivity Disorder—A Home Study System for Parents*
- *Meditations for Concentration CD*
- *Mindfulness Toolkit CD*
- *Mindfulness Toolkit for Kids and Teens CD*

Debra continues to teach numerous presentations, workshops, and teleseminars. She is often interviewed on Internet radio and her work has been featured in *The Day* newspaper, *Self-Improvement* magazine, and Parenting Powers television show.

For more information visit www.TheBrainLady.com. Contact author at Deb@TheBrainLady.com

Made in the USA
Middletown, DE
19 August 2018